.

SUSTAINABLE HEDONISM

A Thriving Life That Does Not Cost the Earth

Orsolya Lelkes

BRISTOL
UNIVERSITY
PRESS

First published in Great Britain in 2021 by

Bristol University Press
University of Bristol
1-9 Old Park Hill
Bristol
BS2 8BB
UK
t: +44 (0)117 954 5940
e: bup-info@bristol.ac.uk

Details of international sales and distribution partners are available at
bristoluniversitypress.co.uk

© Bristol University Press 2021

British Library Cataloguing in Publication Data
A catalogue record for this book is available from the British Library

ISBN 978-1-5292-1797-1 hardcover
ISBN 978-1-5292-1798-8 paperback
ISBN 978-1-5292-1799-5 ePub
ISBN 978-1-5292-1800-8 ePdf

Cover design: blu inc, Bristol
Front cover image: Maxiphoto – istockphoto.com
Bristol University Press uses environmentally responsible
print partners.
Printed in Great Britain by CMP, Poole

Contents

List of Figures, Tables and Boxes

Figures

Tables

Boxes

Acknowledgements

The intellectual seeds of these ideas date back to my time as a PhD candidate at the London School of Economics and Political Science (LSE). This place taught me to reflect critically and to consider various points of view before drawing a conclusion. Earlier, I had been trained to learn facts and to find 'the' single right answer. I am most grateful for the life-changing experience of critical inquiry, freedom and collegial support I experienced at the CASE and STICERD research laboratories at LSE. My supervisor, the late Professor Sir John Hills, was immensely helpful with his support, trust and openness, which allowed me to explore my own interests. A memorable and joyful moment is his long train journey to the south of France when he was reading the final complete draft of my thesis, and made annotations of the locations where he happened to be and of his impressions and feelings. It was the celebration of completing four years of joint work. Exchanges with teachers and researchers including Professor David Piachaud, Professor Howard Glennerster, Professor Lord Richard Layard, Professor Anne Power, Tania Burchardt, Karen Gardiner, Abigail McKnight, Kitty Stewart, Polly Vizard, Sabine Bernabe, Robert MacCulloch, Deborah Mabbett and many others provided precious inspiration and a friendly and welcoming space in general.

My experiences and knowledge of experiential learning embrace a large number of methods which I learnt in depth, including psychodrama, family and couple therapy, constellation work, solution-focused coaching, action-oriented coaching, meditation, mindfulness, yoga, conscious dance practices. They interweave my intellectual quest and urge me to seek more holistic pathways for a good life. I am grateful for my many teachers, fellow group members as well as clients. All of them taught me about myself, about the human soul and mind, about the world, and about the endless possibilities of creating together. I would like to thank to my teachers Gabi Szabó, András Zánkay, Gyula Goda, Júlia Hardy, Kató Barát, Kati Hankovszky-Christiansen,

Roswitha Riepl, Gábor Goda, Silvija Tomcik, Amber Ryan, and many others.

I am deeply grateful to my mentor, Max Clayton (1935–2013), a student of Jacob Levy Moreno – the founder of psychodrama – and Director of the Australian College of Psychodrama, for teaching and showing me a novel way of group leadership and group dynamics; full of life and spirit, at times provocative and surprising, and finely attentive. These experiences taught me that lightness and playfulness was possible for adults and in a group of 'strangers'. I learnt that a facilitator can learn the right tools to support the emergence of these qualities in people and in groups, but first of all she has to become a lover of life herself.

I am extremely grateful for useful feedback and suggestions on this manuscript from the late Professor Sir John Hills and three other anonymous academic referees. Their clarity and supportive tone have motivated and inspired me greatly in the final stages of the writing process. It is a great sadness that John, my PhD supervisor and mentor, passed away in December 2020, and we are not able to celebrate the publication of this book together any more. I feel truly honoured and grateful to have known him and deeply sad to have lost him.

I received very insightful comments and ideas from many generous people, including Bettina Füleki, Balázs Illényi, Barbara Budrich, György Pataki, György Geréby, Móni Göntér, Dani Kovács, Zsombor Cseres-Gergely, Anna Iara, Ágota Scharle, Zsuzsi Kiss, Anikó Kaposvári and Jonathan Dawson.

I greatly appreciate the loving support and presence of my friends and my family during this process, and hope that we will continue to co-create a *flourishing life* together in many forms.

Preface

'Life is hard, so work hard' was the message I received from my parental home. One has to work strenuously and unendingly, essentially resigning one's own wants and desires, and if all goes well, success will come some day. Pleasure can wait till then. I soon realized that this day is likely to arrive only in the afterlife.

This core belief ran in my family for many generations, a script of survival and coping in adverse times. In this world, there was no place for individual pastimes, sport or even for watching the clouds. Joy sneaked in through the presence of children, with whom the adults 'had to' play. The adult world didn't have its own tools for how to be happy, to play or just to 'be', at all.

It resonated with my experiences in public policy. Working at the Budget Department of the Hungarian Ministry of Finance, most of my colleagues had the strong view that the economy needs to grow, to grow a great deal more before we can afford to think of anything 'green' or 'social'.

In the media and everyday talk, Hungarians felt frustrated at lagging behind their rich Austrian neighbour, while being rather indifferent about their own affluence compared to their Ukrainian or Romanian neighbours. There was a collective conviction as to the key to success: we need to strive with gritted teeth to catch up, and finally when this happens, we can finally start enjoying our good life or care about 'higher issues' such as creativity, poorer people or the environment. Actually, most held little hope that this catching up would happen in our own lifetime. The good life was relegated to the future.

The idea of infinite growth, fuelled by individual strenuous work effort, has not yet created a good life for all on the planet. And it has proved to lead to an overuse of natural resources and the overheating of the planet. Yet many of us seem to still hold on to it.

Our individual or collective recipes for success often remain tacit and tend to be taken as if they were laws of nature such as gravity or the change of seasons. It creates a blind spot that limits our ability to live a thriving life and to adapt to the new challenges we face.

Studying economics in Budapest after the collapse of communism and the Marxist idea of planned economy, we simply adopted the neoclassical economic model together with its core assumption that mankind is fundamentally egoist, competitive and pleasure-seeking. We celebrated the tools of 'the West', which were hoped to lead us to its prosperity. Dazed by the novel abundance of consumer choice, we believed that finally we had found the path to the good life.

During my studies of social policy at the London School of Economics we reflected on the common good, the society we wish to see and actively promote. It was a most inspiring experience, but we remained largely at the collective level. We did not deal with our own personal, inner convictions and how they affect our work as scientists or practitioners. Later, in my social science research circles, we did not really address values, strivings and strategies in ourselves: all this was the realm of psychologists, and possibly not meant for 'healthy' and able people like us, who have no need for therapy. My curiosity, as well as dissatisfaction with my ancestors' script of 'life is hard', led me to study happiness economics, positive psychology, as well as psychological counselling.

I found these two realms, the economics of happiness and practical psychology, to be far apart, as if each had its own territory, with a blind wall between them. Working as a researcher, I sought out what of external circumstances could be changed, including the way institutions work. It was exciting: it revealed principles as well as opportunities for intervention. We worked out how money pleases people,and how a fairer distribution of incomes would affect them. This seemed interesting and useful to me, but did not go far enough. After all, external circumstances explain only a fraction of happiness. For one thing, we had not studied a factor more important to the occurrence of happiness: the convictions and beliefs innate in people. We had stopped at the blind wall.

The other realm manages to open the 'black box' of human preferences that economics takes as a given unknown: the inner individual world, where desires are born, satisfied or fade away. This is the realm of psychology, philosophy and of the traditions of spirituality. In contrast to economics, philosophy and spiritual traditions view desires from a greater distance, and do not necessarily approve of them. This realm can help us to become conscious of all that we tend to treat as given: our own motivations, and convictions about the world, about others and about ourselves. Here, there is scope to explore our inner world with its many facets and how these can all be shaped.

The existence of this wall costs us dear. In my view, we cannot afford to keep these two worlds apart, as we need interaction between these two fields to cope with our ecological and social crisis. Not just in little-known scientific disciplines like critical psychology, but on a broader scale, as part of the science of economics, mainstream education and public service media.

The multiple challenges of our time call for multiple and interconnected responses, linking the bits and pieces of the rich knowledge which is already among us, and also a bit more. What else? I would say that it is a curious, exploratory spirit to discover fields in us and among us that we may not have seen before, and not because they are irrelevant and not worthy of our attention, but due to the lenses of our biases, created by our upbringing, culture and convictions. These new fields could be most precious and vital for us.

This inquiry cannot remain intellectual only, as we need ourselves in our whole being: with our physical sensations, intuitions and emotions. We need others, too, as we do not live and grow in a social vacuum. I started to explore this in practice myself.

I named my experiential method the 'Theatre of the Soul'. It is based on my learning of social science, coaching, psychological counselling and group methods, as well as mindfulness. In my work I noticed that many group members had never found out how to fully be themselves, within an accepting environment that creates space for exploration and possible mistakes, or how to devise their own responses to matters of true importance to them. We create a field where childhood curiosity, excitement and playfulness can be felt again. It is a space of freedom, a space for truth and, at the same time, a space for connection.

This way, we become able to resolve our inner conflicting forces, between our pleasure-seeking, instinctive selves and our moral selves striving to live a responsible and meaningful life. We can seek an answer for how to pursue our personal values in a world where many of the mainstream collective rules (of our workplace, our consumer culture, our politics, our social system, our treatment of the natural world) may contradict ours. We can discover our power by becoming an active co-creator of our personal world as well as the larger world. This method is one of the many potential experiential learning methods which can create a powerful learning field about ourselves as persons and as members of the collective, including the whole ecosystem.

It is not just about becoming happier any more. It is high time to challenge what we perceive as progress and success. It is high time to question what we take for granted in us and around us. The challenges of our times urge us to create new strategies for a thriving life that does not cost the Earth.

Introduction: Is There Anyone Who Does Not Want to Thrive?

More and more people find themselves concerned by the dilemma of how to live a life that brings growth and fulfilment, yet that is at the same time considerate of the finite resources of our Earth; a life that is joyful but that can also contribute to our finding a way out of the ecological and climate crisis. A growing number of economists, social researchers and business leaders are critically examining the responsibilities of their own fields and looking for ways in which they could be part of the solution. Many responsible, sensitive people doubt that they are doing enough, and wonder just how they can enjoy life before the arrival of 'the end of the world'.

These gigantic, systemic crisis phenomena dwarf the possibilities of any single person. What can one individual do in the face of global climate politics, trade treaties, international monopolies, national economic and social policies or a global pandemic? We may feel that whatever we do, we cannot have an impact on these things: with or without us, the world goes on as it otherwise would. At the same time, we are already responding to the crisis, just as we are. Our very existence and our current habits have an impact, so we cannot opt out of responding, and our response, whether conscious or not, expresses our connection to these issues.

We probably want to feel that what we are doing (including our work and our consumer habits) is good and is enough – not to let the magnitude of the challenge overwhelm us. One can interpret it as a search for an integration of our pleasure-seeking selves and our moral selves. How can we feel well and do well?

The purpose of this book is to outline an approach to a thriving life that does not cost the Earth, as well as to inspire the reader to explore and scrutinize their existing beliefs, habits and behaviours about success and good life. The aim is to find a life strategy where we can be connected to our own deepest needs as well as to the interest of others, seeing ourselves as part of an organic relationship in which we create and regenerate the world and at the same time are shaped and sustained by it. I call this symbiosis a '*flourishing life*'.

In this quest, I consider economic and societal issues (in Part I), but I do not attempt to offer structural solutions to the shortcomings of our economic, social and political system that contribute to ecological degradation. Instead, I focus on the role of individual people, although with a collective perspective. I discuss the psychological, social psychological and (some) philosophical aspects of the thriving life, and do not offer specific green life-style guidance. If you have a preference for exploring pathways to the solutions, you may find Parts II and III of particular interest.

The challenge: one planet and a good life for all

Although science and technology has reached Mars as well as sub-atomic particles, and the economy continues to expand relentlessly, we are still not able to achieve the dream of our civilization: a 'good life'. As humanity, we do not live a safe, thriving and sustainable life. There is currently no country on earth that is both socially just and ecologically sustainable.[1] In other words, there is no country where basic social safety has been achieved and where the use of resources remains below the ecological ceiling, if we also take into consideration the activities it has outsourced to other countries. Countries in the developed world fail utterly, especially with regard to the latter criterion. Should the developing world follow the familiar trajectory of progress, the situation will become even more dire.

'Physical needs such as nutrition, sanitation, access to electricity and the elimination of extreme poverty could likely be met for all people without breaching planetary boundaries. However, the universal achievement of more qualitative goals (for example, a high life satisfaction) would require a level of resource use that is two to six times the sustainable level, based on current relationships,' argue Dan O'Neil and his co-authors.[2] In my view, the crucial issue in this warning is 'current relationships'. We need to radically revise these current relationships between resource use and life satisfaction. We need to reconsider our strategies for a happy life.

For our own good, we need a novel approach to success, one in which we create a good life for all while remaining within the limits of our planet's resources. An influential recent practical approach is the *Doughnut Economics* of Kate Raworth, focusing on the desirable reform of economics and the role of policy-makers. This book invites for introspection, exploring the motivations and hindrances of living a good life that is also caring and ecologically responsible.

The COVID-19 pandemic has highlighted the vulnerability of our current worldview and world order. Our routines, life-style choices and all that we have so far taken for granted have suddenly been shattered and questioned. The world around us has shrunk, and existing structures have crumbled. The necessity for a profound transformation is no longer the occupation of a conscious minority, but has instead become a reality for us all. In the wake of a collapse, what do we want to maintain and strengthen, and what are we happy to leave behind? What should grow now, and how? What will be our response to long-standing social and ecological challenges? How should we regenerate our world?

Our focus and priorities, as well as what we regard to be useful and essential, have suddenly changed. Social features like solidarity (for example, public healthcare systems, social safety nets, community-supported agriculture, neighbourhood support and the voluntary exchange of skills and resources), which some may previously have regarded as unreasonable, have now become visible and crucial. Certain personal abilities, like autonomy, creativity, having internal goals and drives in life, and the ability to cohabit and collaborate cordially, have become precious and necessary for coping. Our experiences, either benefiting from these traits or missing them, could provide a basis for our future aspirations. It is an opportunity for us to become more aware – to reflect on our existing beliefs and actions, and on our future vision.

Our desire for growth and its failures

Should we let go of our yearning for growth and a good quality of life, as a sacrifice for the sake of future generations and the ecosystem? Although some people may be open to such a proposition, for many others it seems to be asking for too much. Such a call seems to contradict our basic life instinct: we all want to grow and thrive.

The question is, in what form we want to grow: is it in the area of financial success, appearance, popularity or fame ('extrinsic motivation') or, rather, in the form of close relationships, community, self-expression, personal growth ('intrinsic motivation'). We may also call the former 'materialist motivation'. Behaviours and habits based on materialism are a major cause of overconsumption, exploitation of the resources of the earth. It is not an optimal personal strategy either, as it tends to result in lower well-being and greater ill-being.

The empirical results of psychology suggest that many of us may not know and do what is good for us, as is illustrated by examples in Chapters 4, 5 and 6. Our ability to act for our own good is impaired. It may be a result of our early development or our recent and current experiences. According to the self-determination theory in psychology, the darker sides of human behaviour, prejudice, aggression, are reactions to the thwarted fulfilment of our basic psychological needs for autonomy, competence and belonging.[3] We may add overconsumption, ruthless competition, the exploitation and humiliation of co-workers, greed and addiction to this list of harmful human behaviours. If our environment cannot provide for these core needs (and we do not see ourselves as competent, lovable persons and cannot act in truly autonomous ways), we are likely to seek alternative, non-optimal strategies which will actually not be able to meet these needs. Our ability to contribute to these needs of others will be also limited. It is unlikely that we can appreciate and support the autonomy, competence and belonging of others if we do not really know these ourselves.

Our personal strategies for growth may be dysfunctional, as they do not bring us happiness and are harmful to others.

These materialist life strategies are reinforced by our current capitalist economy, with its suggestive and overflowing marketing messages on television, in newspapers, billboards and social media. We see them in public spaces as well as on our private mobile phone screens. Children may also be exposed at an early age. If consumption is a precondition of economic growth, and economic growth is essential, a responsible citizen must consume abundantly.

The 'success story' we are telling ourselves

Our convictions concerning the nature of humankind and the 'rules of the game' in the world strongly affect what we see as the path to thriving in life. These convictions govern our actions and even our experiences. So our choice of stories to tell ourselves, each other and our children is crucial.

My life story, shared in the Preface, is just one of many potential stories. Not because it is not true; it is true – but it is incomplete. This is not the story I would have told about myself a few years ago. It is probably not the story I will tell in a few years' time. Even now, I could choose a number of different themes and guiding threads with which to talk about myself. The story is no mere fiction, however. Through my story, I also construct myself, my identity and my motivation.

Our families, our local communities and our peers also have their own stories. In some families, they are shared at the dinner table; in others, they are more of a latent guidebook about the world, about other people and about 'fate', written in invisible but potent ink. Thus, while they are often about the past, they latently create the future as well.

Our lives are strongly shaped by the stories we tell ourselves, both individually and collectively. We are all storytellers of the world, and through our stories we create our world.

Stories provide understanding in a complex world, and offer a guide and order among the many forces of chaos. However, it is often these very stories that stop us from living life to our full potential as individuals, or socially prevent us from creating a just and ecologically sustainable model for human progress. We are often hardly aware of the origins of these stories, or of our potential to transform them.

The world as a marketplace

A dominant collective narrative is the supremacy of the neoliberal market economy, claiming that it is the best possible mechanism for our progress and prosperity. Markets can be efficient indeed, and economic and technological progress is immense. For some reason, the indisputable achievements of this system overshadow any discussion of its drawbacks and of viable alternatives. It seems to have established an intellectual monopoly, conquering not just economics but ever more domains of the world.

Rather than being seen as part of society, and as part of the natural world, economics now seems to dominate society and ecology. Economic interests repeatedly override ecological considerations, seeing wildlife, thousand-year-old forests, nature reserves harbouring fossil fuels, oceans, fresh water and the Earth as a whole simply as 'natural capital', where items have a price tag and are potential ingredients for production. A forest, with its ecosystem, soil and water retention, fresh air and beauty, has no monetary value in a country's gross domestic product (GDP), and thus has no intrinsic value as such; this is often a death penalty, as we have witnessed with the destruction of large swathes of the Amazon rain forest. The whole world seems to have been turned into a 'marketplace' with interlinked markets: we have a financial market, a housing market, a labour market, an organ market, a market for arts and creative industries, a market for land and water, to name but a few.

It has not been always so. Karl Polányi, in his influential 1944 book *The Great Transformation*, provides a historical perspective.[4] While pre-modern economies were based on tradition, redistribution and reciprocity, with a minor role for markets, industrialism expanded the market principle, and even factors of production like land and labour are now being traded on the market. This has profoundly transformed not only our institutions but also our mentality. Polányi argues that the 'market society' is unsustainable, because it is destructive to human nature, to relationships and the natural environment. By now, this destruction has become more evident.

Nowadays, we can say that the logic of the market can devalue those activities which are not sold but which are vital for sustaining and savouring life, such as child rearing, care work, growing and preparing our own food, voluntary work, or creative pastimes and activities with family and friends. Seeing our lives centred on selling our time, skills and effort for a good price may distort the way we look at ourselves and at each other, and can turn out to be damaging for our human potential and the opportunity to live a meaningful life. Many speak of 'work–life balance', as if work was not part of life, but alien to it. And in many cases, it is so.

These are structural phenomena of capitalism, which affect our life chances, and also how we act and how we optimize our behaviour. In addition, our actions are also shaped by our worldview and our subjective perceptions.

(Unintended) consequences of economics and capitalism today

A key step in finding answers to the complex challenges of our age is to reflect on all that we regard to be self-evident in the functioning of our world today, starting with the image of the human in economic thinking, and the consequences of that image. The notion of the so-called '*economic man*' (rational, egoistic and competitive pleasure-seeker), originally just a set of assumptions for mathematical modelling, despite its deficient assumptions regarding human nature, appears to be impactful far beyond university walls. The notion of the pleasure-seeking human has become a worldview of its own.

Economics today is monopolized by the approach of neoclassical economics. It deals with the external world at the individual and the collective level. It looks at behaviour – for example, what people are spending their money on – and observes personal characteristics. It examines how companies optimize their market strategy, both relative to their competitors and in terms of their own internal resources.

Mainstream economics as it is practised today tends to regard itself as value free, maintaining that ethical questions belong to philosophers or politicians, not economists. Although many prominent economists have already challenged this view, including Anthony Atkinson, Kenneth Boulding and the signatories of the '33 Theses for an Economics of Reformation' nailed to the doors of the London School of Economics in 2017, it appears still to be the dominant concept.

Economics does not examine individual and collective inner worlds, even if these are organically linked to the external world it creates. It does not investigate the specifics of motivations and life strategies, such as how desires are born and changed, and how people seek to satisfy them. It also leaves aside the role of our culture, our common beliefs about what we need to do in order to succeed.

One could say that this is rightly so. Economics has to define a clear domain to be able to operate as a scientific field of study (often interpreted as being mathematical). This might hold, were economics not to breach the bounds of pure science. It proves problematic, however, if its approach is used to address complex problems such as the climate crisis.

Due to the way economics is taught in most places, the relationship between inner and external worlds tends to remain unexamined by many students, scholars and business leaders: how assumptions in economics affect the real world. Empirical research presented in Chapter 1 suggests that the study of mainstream neoclassical economics, with its image of the human as a selfish, competitive figure, may function as a self-fulfilling prophecy, making students more selfish and business decisions more profit oriented. People may adapt to a norm, and do what they regard necessary for success. There seems to be far too little open exchange on what 'success' is, and what the future is that they want to see and contribute to.

It is now evident that prioritizing GDP growth over other objectives does not create a happy or thriving life. Consumer society has had a number of unintended consequences, as illustrated in Chapter 2. It promises abundance, which is appealing to many who have experienced shortages of basic goods (or whose ancestors did so), but it also brings with it systemic shortfalls, including global injustice due to 'imperial life-styles', and the prevalence of food waste and obesity. It promises the opportunity to live like an 'aristocrat' by consuming status goods and services, but, due to the 'hedonic treadmill', is unlikely to succeed, while it also fails the poorest in society. The illusion that our boundless desires can be fulfilled comes at the cost of new forms of addiction.

Exploring and experiencing a thriving life

Some may define thriving life as a happy life. What is happiness? Is it pleasure, joy, satisfaction, a meaningful life, well-being or something else? What are we pursuing, and how? Our choices and strategies affect our physical and mental health, as well as that of others.

The recent 'happiness revolution' in quantitative science has opened up a new perspective on personal development and social progress and thus can help us find alternatives that enable us both to thrive and to survive.

Quest for happiness

There seems to be a paradox: while happiness seems to be 'good', bringing as it does a wealth of positive benefits, the search for happiness falls short of being an optimal life strategy (Chapter 3). Why is this so? Our approach to our own well-being fundamentally influences our pathways and our experiences. The question is what exactly we seek and how we do it. Scientific evidence suggests that it is not helpful for us to try to maximize happiness or to follow a general 'maximizer' strategy. Well-being is not a state of continuous euphoria; it requires the experience of 'mixed emotions', with shorter spells of negative feelings. (Longer spells of such feelings and extreme suffering may well require external support.) 'Forced positivity' and being 'happiness-greedy' are therefore both strategies that we can refute.

Ancient hedonism is fundamentally different from its current simplified incarnation. Both Aristippus and Epicurus enjoyed all that the present moment offered, but warned of becoming slaves of one's desires (Chapter 4). A number of intriguing stories from the lives of these philosophers illustrate what they actually meant by this. Aristotle argues for aspiring for a mean state of pleasures, between asceticism and indulgence. He also calls for differentiating between necessary and optional things, and focusing on the former in our aspirations. The Greek philosophers could teach us how to master hedonism in its pure sense without harming others or ourselves. In the 21st century, it might be called 'sustainable hedonism'.

Happiness, according to Aristotle, is not the gift of the Gods, not a matter of luck, but, rather, the result of virtue-based actions within the community (Chapter 5). He held that there was a perfect order in the heavenly spheres (cosmos) and that the goal of human effort is to align to this by creating this order in one's own inner world. Virtues play a key role in this, as well as '*friendship*', and community. His term for happiness, '*eudaimonia*', is most often translated as a '*flourishing life*'. It has inspired contemporary psychology as well, which has interpreted and enlarged the original ideas.

Science, philosophy and human experience have accumulated a wealth of knowledge on what the *flourishing life* could be for us as individuals and as a community. We seem to understand ever better how to get closer to our 'true preferences', our innermost needs, in contrast to 'revealed preferences', our observed behaviour, which may be based on misinformation.

Flourishing life, based on Aristotle and on recent empirical psychology can be interpreted in the following ways:

- it gives joy as well as ensuring mental and physical health;
- it is aligned to our values and our aspiration to live a meaningful life;
- it is based on conscious action, the persistent practice and development of virtues;
- it has universal features, but its actualization varies from person to person;
- it does not harm others and does not endanger the planet's future; and
- because friends, relationships and the community are vital elements of it.

In positive psychology as in happiness economics, the epicentre is the individual and their quest for happiness. They provide useful guidance for this, but it is, in my view, a limited approach. A key component is often missing: the consequences of our actions on others. We cannot live a truly flourishing and happy life at the expense of others, so we need to be aware of the consequences of our individual actions on others – a case powerfully made by Aristotle.

Academic studies suggest that purposeful activities bring more joy and greater life satisfaction than does '*radical hedonism*' (Chapter 5). This is already true on the following day, but even more the case in the long run. A meaningful life promotes physical health and longevity. People living a *flourishing life* are more likely to care about others and to be generous and attentive. All in all, if you had a choice, you would probably want to live with someone who lives a *flourishing life*. And if you wanted to be happy and healthy, you would do better to choose the *flourishing life* as a life strategy – and your 'only' task would be to find your unique way to pursue this. Viktor Frankl, the Austrian psychotherapist who survived the Nazi concentration camps, argued that we can choose and create a meaningful life under any circumstances.

A relatively less known important strand of research shows that there is no contradiction between a happy life and environmentally conscious life-style, including voluntary simplicity, reduction of meat eating or other green adjustments, and explains the pathways for increasing both (Chapter 5). *Sustainable hedonism* appears to be a realistic strategy.

Values for a thriving life

Many have called for a greater reliance on ethics in economics, or on moral values in the actions we take to tackle climate change. What are the values we want to rely on?

Happiness? Liberty, equality, fraternity? God, family, country? Community, identity, stability? Serve the people? Peace, rain, prosperity? Be fast, bold, open and build social value? Respect resource limits, create resilience, freely share ideas and power? Protect people and the environment? Passion for excellence, growth and learning?[5]

We may appreciate some of these values, but some others could make us feel ambivalent, given our history and present. Facebook is certainly bold, but many question that it is building social value in its current form. The last two mottos belong to two multinational energy corporations, the American Chevron and the Russian Gazprom. Both of these companies were named among the top 20 companies behind a third of all carbon emissions.[6]

Even though we all have our own values which guide us, many find any reference to values unappealing. Stated values may contradict actions. Values are often associated with a bias, in the worst case even fanaticism: a complete surrender to absolutist ideologies or to extremism, one which may even override loyalty to closest family members or common sense.

For all these recurring dangers, I believe the values of our civilization to be constantly evolving. We live in an age where we have a great opportunity to combine the experience and knowledge of previous eras. It is now ever more possible to belong to a community without denying our freedom. We can honour our traditions without denying progress. We can enjoy life while make it also meaningful and ethical. This requires a value synthesis in which we are able to transcend the ideology of earlier ages – ideologies that often sought exclusivity – by unifying their merits without denying or trying to destroy them.

Such a synthesis is not achieved overnight. It requires openness, friendliness toward ourselves and toward others and the ability to accept that one does not always know the 'right' answer in all situations. This is a dynamic synthesis. There is no single, static, ultimate solution, as external challenges may require new solutions. To venture on the journey to create such inner synthesis requires courage, as well as inspiration from others. The benefits of it are manifold, however, in terms of our individual mental and physical health, as well as of our collective ability to survive and thrive.

Humanity could also create institutions which reflect and implement its universal values. According to the global survey of values by Shalom Schwartz, the three most widely acclaimed values are *benevolence* (friendship, love), *universalism* (tolerance, peace, love of nature) and *self-direction* (freedom, creativity), as shown in Chapter 6. These findings hold across diverse cultures and continents, implying that humanity has a majority consensus on our core values. This shows that the presumptions of the worldview of the *economic man* do not hold: people are not primarily egoistic pleasure-seekers. At least, this is not what they aspire to nowadays. I am inclined to interpret these values as aspirations: this is how we (want to) see ourselves. If the aforementioned three universal values guided our actions, we would live in a different world from the present one. The question is how we can live up to our own aspirations and how can we integrate these in our daily lives, in our institutions.

Pathways to a thriving life: experiential learning

Anthropologist Jane Briggs travelled to investigate the Inuit in the 1960s and witnessed with wonder how they teach their children to manage their anger and hard feelings by the use of role play. Role play and theatre belong to our human history as a way of creative storytelling, and 'ordinary people' can also become the artists and creators of their own lives and our collective culture, as Jacob Levy Moreno argues. I present the Theatre of the Soul, the method I use, as developed by Moreno and his followers.

I explain why, in the context of the *flourishing life*, I regard it as an efficient and useful method (Chapter 7). For example, it creates opportunities to enact the '*flourishing self*', to explore and experience personal strengths, to visualize values and future visions for individuals and groups, or to create celebrations and rituals. With these tools, *flourishing life* at a communal level (be it the *flourishing life* of the group itself or their vision of the *flourishing life* at the societal level) can be visualized and strengthened.

The Theatre of the Soul offers a creative and playful form of self-expression for all, with a safe space for exploration, guided by the core values of openness, acceptance and curiosity. A group experience can powerfully change norms and behaviour. Group work and specific tools (such as role reversal) can boost empathy and social competence, and can increase one's ability to cooperate with and trust others. Therefore, in my view, positive community experiences can be one of the keys to finding solutions to the global crisis.

Egoism and extreme pleasure-seeking, and indeed a *flourishing life*, are not simply external phenomena in the world, but are also the products of inner motivations and conflicting forces within the individual psyche, as explained in Chapter 8. Meeting our inner '*progressive*' and '*saboteur roles*' helps us to gain greater freedom to take action for our own good and to the benefit of others. Role training can provide effective support for this. I propose archetypal roles which may promote and hinder the *flourishing life* in a person, including for example the Overachiever, the Orphan, the Tyrant, the Fool, the Rebel, the Friend, the Explorer, the Artist and the Sage.

Role theory is a bridge between the person and the community, as it encompasses phenomena in the personal psyche as well as interactions among people. Moreno's vision is that the dramatic tools can transform human culture to make it more creative, spontaneous and healing.

Our life as a living field

To understand a thriving life and to transform our own mentality and ultimately our culture, we need both knowledge and a great deal of creative energy.

To do this, we do well to draw on our intellectual insight and critical thinking. But, beyond that, we also need to get in touch with our instinctive impulses. In this discovery we can be helped by our playful, curious self, which is ready to become acquainted with our desires, impulses and the many different parts that represent them. We do not need to deny anything in ourselves: neither our fears and our pains, nor our strengths and our uniqueness. This makes it possible for all this not merely to remain theoretical knowledge, but to turn into transformative experience.

The 'flourishing' inherent to a *flourishing life* is itself a living, natural quality. It expresses the realization of a potential, just as a bud becomes blossom and reveals itself in its fullness. It evokes the image of a flourishing field, too, with myriad forms of blossom that create a rich and colourful field together. I wish this book not to remain one of theory, but instead to come alive.

PART I

The Challenge

1

Unintended Consequences
of Economics as a Science

Who was never born, never lived, yet overran the world? The answer is *homo economicus, economic man*: a selfish contender and something like a supercomputer; fully informed and perfectly rational. His main aim is to 'maximise his utility' – to be as happy as can be. Such traits allow him to act effectively for his own good while also producing an optimum on a social scale. He is the protagonist of mainstream economic models and the main figure in the university teaching of economics; in fact, he is a gender-neutral human who is called a 'man' only due to historic convention. Beyond the university walls, *economic man* has now become a belief system that promises to offer a pathway to prosperity, both individually and socially.

It seems a mystery why *economic man* has become so popular, because we know very well that this is not what human beings are like.

Not rational and not egoistic

Many have challenged the suppositions behind *economic man*.[1] These days, criticizing the assumption of rational decision making is by no means an exotic notion or indeed one beyond the range of the economics profession. Both Daniel Kahneman in 2002 and Amor Tversky in 2017 received the Nobel Prize in Economics for doing just that.

People do not necessarily do what is good for them. According to János Harsányi, a Nobel Prize-winning Hungarian-American economist, a person's behaviour does not necessarily reflect their deeper interests and *true preferences*, which may be due to ignorance or to incorrect information.[2] He gives the example of someone with a sore throat who has a choice between two drugs; of the two, according to the current scientific knowledge, A is the best medicine. If he nevertheless chooses medicine B, out of ignorance, then his action is not in his true interest. His *true preference* was actually for medicine A.

The human is not perfectly rational, but rather 'predictably irrational', as explained by behavioural economists.[3] We are indeed irrational: the human mind is far from being a perfectly rational supercomputer. Yet we remain predictable: our irrationality has its abiding patterns, so our minds are not simply full of chaos. In Kahneman's view, for example, we are inclined to overrate the chances of unlikely events, or we tend overly to cling to things we already possess.[4]

The basic presumption that one is inherently selfish is also widely disputed, as is the Darwinian worldview of the survival of the fittest. Many scholars argue that it was, rather, our ability to cooperate that secured our survival and our evolutionary success.[5] It is unlikely that one will be happy, successful and reach a peaceful state of mind at the expense of all others, as argued by major religions and spiritual traditions. The so-called 'Golden Rule', treating others as you wish to be treated, is a general ethical principle.

While some continue to attach importance to the clarity of these basic assumptions for the sake of mathematical modelling,[6] more and more people believe that the hegemony of this assumption within economics prevents the discipline from providing an effective answer to the challenges of the 21st century.[7]

If we have so many arguments against the accuracy of the features of the human being depicted by *economic man*, how is it possible that he can still form the basis of a popular recipe for success? What explains its success beyond university campuses? It may be that we can recognize ourselves in *economic man* in some fundamental way, that our gut instincts crave to satisfy our needs and to find pleasure. Who would want to live without pleasure?

Self-fulfilling prophecy

Economists may become (more) selfish

Meeting the idea of *economic man* can change personal character, behaviours and ultimately institutions. According to surveys, economics students are, on average, more selfish and more competitive than other students.[8] In experiments they were found to be more inclined to pursue free-rider behaviour or to refuse to cooperate. Economics students seem to be more likely to prefer profit-maximizing decisions, even when such decisions are in conflict with other values.

Ariel Rubinstein compared the behaviour of students from various faculties at Tel Aviv University: economics, mathematics, philosophy, law and business economics. Each student was given the challenge of imagining that they were a deputy director of a company who had to choose between maximizing the company's profits by firing half their workforce or making less profit and dismissing fewer people. Economics students were more likely to prefer a profit-maximization strategy over other strategies; their behaviour was markedly different from that of other students. This was confirmed by a follow-up study at Harvard University and among readers of the Israeli business daily *Globe*. A similar pattern was observed among students at the University of Verona with respect to profit maximization.[9]

There are observable differences within economics as well, according to a major study of 93,000 students in Zurich: while business economists are typically more frugal, political economists are not.[10]

Two prominent British economists, Nicholas Stern and Andrew Oswald, criticize their colleagues for neglecting the climate issue: 'We suggest that economists are failing the world – and their own grandchildren.'[11] The *Quarterly Journal of Economics*, which is currently the most cited journal in the field of economics, has never published a paper on climate change. According to a Dutch survey, both economics students and practising economists care less about the environment, tradition and rules than others do.[12]

Not all economists are alike, however. These studies typically describe average patterns; there may of course be significant variation across individuals. But such studies do highlight overall phenomena that are worth paying attention to in our quest for solutions.

Today's university education seems at least partly responsible for the increasing tendency of economics students to display such behaviour.[13] Why do their studies have such an effect? It may be due to beliefs regarding human nature: if humankind is inherently selfish, then personal selfishness is a natural response as a strategy for coping and success. Thus, it seems students are exposed to a belief system that claims that competition and self-interest are the best way to success in the world. In addition, competitive behaviour may appear to be clear, transparent and fair: let the most able win. If competition is clean, the system will be optimal and balanced, and will produce the best outcome for everyone. What could be wrong with that?

The economist is not a value-free outsider

Mainstream economics tends to regard itself as a value-free science, dealing with 'ascertainable facts', a science that explains human behaviour – that is, 'what is', and not 'what ought to be': this was the claim of Lionel Robbins, a prominent British economist at the London School of Economics, in the 1930s.[14] This still seems to be the case today.

Practitioners of economics may therefore tend to see themselves as serving an objective, scientific truth, and be unaware of the possible impact of their personal values on their professional choices and beliefs. Yet such scientific objectivity does not exist: 'there is no view without a viewpoint', warned Gunnar Myrdal, the Nobel Prize-winning Swedish economist and sociologist.[15]

Science does not merely describe the world; it also creates the world it explores. The researcher, in this case the economist, is not an outsider, not an objective observer; rather, his presence and activities shape the world. This and its implications were discussed by economist and philosopher Kenneth Boulding in his 1968 speech in Chicago as the chairman of the American Economic Association. As science advances, it moves from descriptive knowledge toward control and creation. What kind of world does science create? A world that is considered to be a good world by contemporary society and its scientific subculture: they wish to realize their common values. So this is an ethical decision as well – a decision about values.[16]

Economics is thus inseparable from ethics. Economics is essentially a moral science.[17] This position is reinforced by the '33 Theses for an Economics Reformation',[18] nailed to the doors of the London School of Economics in December 2017, the 500th anniversary of Martin Luther's 95 theses that led to the Reformation of the Catholic Church. The 33 theses plead for a break with the monopolistic belief system of neoclassical economics, and propose a new way forward in the teaching and practice of economics.

In my view, we have the choice as to whether we consciously reflect on this narrative and the underlying values within us and our communities, or whether we let these values shape our attitudes and actions in only a latent fashion. If someone believes that their values and worldview do not affect their hypotheses, assumptions, decisions and actions, they are effectively ignoring a blind spot. This holds for those researchers, business leaders, politicians and indeed all who tend to believe that their actions are based on clear facts and the objective truth.

Recent pioneering research by Hendrik P. Van Dalen from Tilburg University has explored the relationship between personal values and academic endeavour. He found that economists who are self-centred and who value performance highly are more likely to support mainstream economic ideas.[19]

In sum, the teaching of mainstream economics is more than likely to have an impact that, as a self-fulfilling prophecy, enhances behaviour patterns akin to those of *economic man*. This simplistic approach to human nature could help to instil in a student a personal life strategy based on selfishness, competition and pleasure-seeking.

This is a crucial question to be discussed, observed, explored and critically reflected upon, both within university campuses and beyond. What kind of world does our work create? Is this the world we wish to create and reinforce with our joint efforts? What is the alternative?

The responsibility of economists

We have seen that the personal values of economists permeate not just the discipline itself but also the institutional system it creates. The question is how they do this.

I believe that a reflection on core values must be an integral part of the education of economists as well as part of their subsequent professional activities. This includes (1) the values conveyed by economics and economic decisions, and (2) personal motives and values.

An example for (1): What does it really mean when we use only the principle of profit maximization? What other aspects could be considered? How would this affect the outcome?

And for (2): Who is behind the numbers? How do they feel about the world, about others and about themselves? Do they consider the world a good place in which collaboration is desirable? Are they driven by trust? Or is the world a threatening place of scarcity, uncertainty and conflict? Are they fundamentally driven by a sense of insecurity and mistrust?

The fundamental question, I think, is whether one recognizes that all this is not a given, not an 'objective' attribute of the world, but is also shaped by their perspective and by their actions. Can they recognize their potential to transform these core beliefs?

These are existential questions, and not just for one's personal fate. Economists have an enormous responsibility, as they influence the design and operation of institutions. The nature of their beliefs does not remain a private matter. Today, this belief system pervades our everyday world as well as our public affairs.

The idea that *economic man* is in fact a worldview is not a novel one. It is a worldview that already attracted strong criticism in the early 20th century.

Not the recipe for success

In 1939 Peter Drucker, the Austrian-born American management consultant and educator, predicted the end of an era in his book *The End of Economic Man*.[20] The First World War and then the Great Depression of 1929–33 brought misery, unemployment and, in turn, fear. The prevailing system was fundamentally shaken: the masses lost their faith in the existing economic order and turned away from the ideal of the individualistic *economic man*. They no longer believed that hard work and competition were the way to improve one's lot. They no longer believed that the world was in order.

In their fear, they chose fascism, which gave the promise of belonging to a community, and offered security. According to Drucker, the serum against fascism and other oppressive systems is that one's basic need to belong to a community must be met.

Even Winston Churchill wrote an appreciative review of Drucker's book.[21] Churchill added that the failure was the way capitalism tried to establish *economic man* as a social ideal. Freedom and equality are key European ideas, but people no longer believe they can be achieved through competition. This is the cause of ongoing social bankruptcy, Churchill claimed.

In our current age, another aspect of this ideal has become of pressing concern. More and more people are criticizing greed, together with the endless economic growth that it triggers.

We may regard the fulfilment of desires to be a good thing, but we are at once aware of its drawbacks and excesses. This knowledge is part of our cultural history, tales, art and religions. And, for the most part, there is nothing attractive about it, plus there is a moral stigma. Our culture exposes a caveat: there is a limit to everything.

Greed in arts and tales

The Grande Bouffe (a 1973 French-Italian film directed by Marco Ferreri) starts off promisingly: four successful middle-aged friends retire to a country mansion finally to give way to their desires. After a breakfast fit for a king, prostitutes are called in while the men are constantly stuffing themselves. There is no stopping them. At some point, even the prostitutes cannot stand it, and they leave. The men devour themselves to death. The last of the four gorges a pink, soft, breast-shaped cake with his last effort, and then breathes his last breath into the big bosom of his female companion. At the film's premiere at the Cannes Film Festival the audience watched in silence during the first half, but this turned into constant whistling. Many could not stand it; a good number walked out of the screening. According to critics, it is a very good movie, but unpalatable and disgusting. What makes the film interesting is that the four main actors appear with their real first names, including Marcello Mastroianni as Marcello, so fantasy and life coincide. Are we so greedy and so disgusting? And is this really so deadly?

One well-known story of insatiable greed is a German fairy tale collected by the Brothers Grimm, *The Fisherman and his Wife*. One day the poor fisherman hauls a strange talking pike out of the sea: it turns out to be a cursed prince. At the pike's request, the fisherman throws him back into the sea. However, at the urging of his wife, he returns to the pike with a wish: he asks for a small house instead of their current hovel. The pike grants this to him, together with a soft bed, a full larder, livestock and an orchard. But desire turns out to be stronger than the pleasure of sudden abundance. The next morning, the woman comes up with another wish: she wants a castle instead of the house. This wish is also granted. But the story is not over. Now she wants a kingdom instead of the castle, then a papacy instead of the kingdom, and, finally, instead of a papacy, she wants to become the Lord God herself. This time, the sea greets the reappearing husband with a hurricane and black water. The pike says, "Well, just go home. You'll find your wife sitting in the shed again."

In the Purgatory of Dante Alighieri's *Divine Comedy* of 1320, the souls of the avaricious and prodigal lie on their stomachs, motionless, their hands and feet connected, their eyes, as earlier in their lives, clinging to earthly things. Those driven by gluttony are starving and thirsty. In the fourth circle of Hell we find the 'money addicts', the hoarders and wasters who spend eternity rolling giant boulders up a high hill only for them always to roll back down. All their efforts are futile. In the medieval worldview of the poet, suffering from excess desires and actions was associated with external divine justice, but today we have ever more knowledge of how man suffers in his own inner world. Life can be hell, too.

Beyond the model: our yearning for pleasure and freedom

The pleasure-seeking nature of humankind was not invented by economics, any more than it was invented by Sigmund Freud, the father of psychoanalysis. It has been a recurring theme of our intellectual history for thousands of years, in a myriad incarnations and approaches.

Hedonism: pleasure as the ultimate value

What is notable in economics and in the philosophy of 18th- and 19th-century utilitarianism that underpins it is the centrality of the notion of pleasure. They made pleasure the overall guiding principle of life and spread this idea throughout the modern world. The English philosopher Jeremy Bentham, the founder of utilitarianism, writes:

> Nature has placed mankind under the governance of two sovereign masters, pain and pleasure. It is for them alone to point out what we ought to do, as well as to determine what we shall do. On the one hand the standard of right and wrong, on the other the chain of causes and effects, are fastened to their throne. They govern us in all we do, in all we say, in all we think.[22]

In this view, the driving force behind human action is the search for pleasure and the avoidance of pain, and the ultimate goal of life is to achieve the most pleasure attainable. The root of this approach is the philosophy of ancient hedonism.

'Hedonism' comes from the Greek ἡδονή (hēdonē), meaning 'pleasure'. The ancient Greek philosophy of hedonism holds that pleasure is the ultimate good and that it has intrinsic value – that is, it is not merely a means of achieving something else, and there is nothing more valuable. By contrast, pain has no value. Here the definition of pleasure and suffering is quite broad, and can be physical as well as emotional. Pleasure can come from good food, but also from rejoicing over good news. Pain can be a wound on the sole of the foot as well as emotional disappointment.

In its simplest form, hedonism holds that the components of our world – our relationships, actions, achievements – matter only in as much as they contribute to our enjoyment (Figure 1.1). All are just a tool for the attainment of more pleasure. There is no independent value, say, to friendship or integrity.

The concept is rooted in ancient hedonism, but it is based on a considerable simplification and misunderstanding of it. Evoking the original view of the ancient Greeks can be very helpful in learning to enjoy life to the fullest without harming others and the planet, as explained later in Chapter 5.

Figure 1.1: Pleasure as an ultimate value

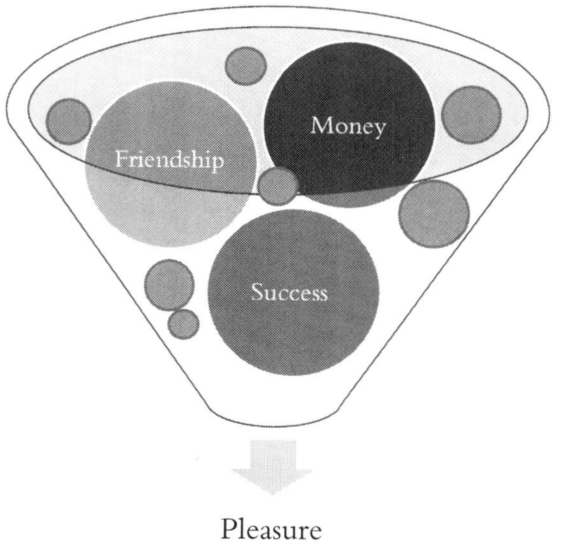

Pleasure

Source: Author's own.

Do desires drive the world?

Desires drive the world, say economists, without pausing to think what desires are. *De gustibus non est disputandum* ('tastes are not to be disputed') recalled the Nobel Prize-winning economists George J. Stigler and Gary S. Becker in a 1977 article on the subject of 'preferences'.[23] Consumers know what they want and that will suffice, they argue; due respect can then be given to human liberty. Let people wish freely for what they want and decide for themselves how to enjoy it. This will make them happiest, and will ensure the greatest bliss for the most people, both individually and socially (technically speaking, it will maximise utility). It becomes ever clearer that this logic does not hold, and for several reasons. The explanations for this will be discussed in more depth later on – this is one of the main topics of this book.

Many academic economists fail to ask what the nature of desires is. We hang out the banner of freedom, leaving humankind to flounder amid the greatest undertaking in human life. In so doing we take the two cornerstones of the system - desires and the pleasure of fulfilling them - as a given, without delving into them thoroughly. We have chosen cornerstones made of a material whose composition is unknown to us. Does this not mean that the house of civilization is in fact built on blind faith?

Celebrating freedom

I met *economic man* as an economics student in Hungary. I gradually came to realize that these were not merely sterile assumptions but an entire worldview. *Economic man* was a mythical hero of individual freedom, no longer bound by a distorted political and economic system. The ideal was Western neoclassical economics – as a replacement for the Marxist planned economy that had failed badly on many fronts.

Finally, nothing and no one would hold back individual initiative! There would no longer be a narrow elite governing by its own rules. Now the phenomenon of shortage would disappear. At long last, we could travel freely to the West. We could say what we thought. There was no need to stand to attention during school celebrations, to salute the flag adorned with the hammer and sickle, or enthusiastically to sing the 'Internationale'. We could finally be open about who we were. We could explore who we were able to be, because there was no longer any barrier to our progress.[24]

In this vision of the world, free market competition was interwoven with political freedom, democracy and personal freedom. Although this optimism mixed with naivety has since been dashed for many, the figure of *economic man* still lives and dominates university education, not only in Eastern Europe, but also in Western Europe and the global North.

Why is this so? On the one hand, these simple assumptions facilitate modelling. They help economics to become more and more of a pure science, which, in the aspirations of theoreticians, means that it can be more closely related to mathematics. But that cannot explain the comprehensive and sustained popularity of the idea. A narrow scientific circle could not have such a widespread effect. Modellers rarely dictate the rules of the game. It is more likely to be related to the fact that the image of *economic man* is intertwined with both an individual and a communal vision of a good life.

What drives this vision? It may be the desire for freedom. In a free market economy, it may also be the desire to fulfil one's deepest longings. That is why this idea often evokes intense emotions.

The manifesto of the pleasure-seeking person: the worldview

A key to the worldwide success of *economic man* is that he promises an enjoyable and free world. It is attractive because it offers the promise of success and satisfaction. Who would not want to have a successful and satisfied life? Who would not want their desires fulfilled?

The pursuit of enjoyment has become the cornerstone of our world – especially in societies where personal freedom seems self-evident. Freedom here means first and foremost the freedom to satisfy desires. This general ideal could be called the 'pleasure-seeking person'.

The urge to satisfy our desires is with us from birth. It drives us. We also see growth as the realization of our potential, which goes beyond simply ensuring our survival. That is why the pleasure-seeking person's beliefs – or the main elements of those beliefs – could possibly affect us so powerfully. And in today's world we are developing ever more advanced technologies and institutions to fulfil our desires and to prosper further.

The everyday manifesto of the 'pleasure-seeking person' can be put like this:

- 'I enjoy, therefore I am.'
- Enjoyment is the ultimate good, and the more of it, the better – it is the benchmark of our success and the ultimate purpose of our life.
- Greed is a sign of life force, while satisfied greed is a sign of success.
- All pain is bad and to be avoided; if there is no other way to do this, it must simply be denied.
- People know what they need, and what pleases them.
- So receiving all of this is the only means to attaining bliss.
- Enjoyment is holy and inviolable; there can be no questioning of it.
- Everyone is a good promoter of their own enjoyment, and all can achieve it plentifully if they act effectively in their own interest.

Some people may not, for some reason, like to think or speak of pleasure, but are more likely to use words like 'contentment' or 'achievement' in their personal dictionaries to describe the end state where their needs and aspirations are met. It may well be that for many people the 'seeking' element is more obvious than the 'pleasure' one. These people may be stuck in the state of seeking per se, rather than enjoying the results of their efforts.

At the social level, this ideal of the pleasure-seeker is intertwined with a rather one-dimensional economic notion that consumption is good, to be encouraged, and that the main measure is its quantity and the resulting profit. In this view, economic growth is indispensable, its scope is infinite and it will resolve all the world's problems almost automatically – through the growth of resources and thanks to technological innovation – and so it needs to be our central concern.

The primary task of natural resources is to assist economic growth; all else is secondary. The economy is our main treasure, compared to which society, culture, nature and all else are subordinate - of concern only in as far as they promote or impede the economy, and otherwise devoid of intrinsic value.

At the same time, these priorities retain promise: a world that is enjoyable, and in which the possibilities are endless. This is the utopia of joyful freedom.

The Narrative of Success in Capitalism, and Its Failures

The hope that material progress will make us happy and free

John Maynard Keynes, one of the greatest economists of the 20th century, who, as one of the greatest critics of the free market fundamentally reworked macroeconomics and economic policy, had a dream. In 1930 he dreamed of a future for the generation of grandchildren with 15 hours of work that would provide enough for everyone. He had dreamed of this just at the beginning of the world economic crisis, which he considered to be only a temporary disturbance. He was optimistic, believed in economic development and believed that this would make life better. He predicted that the age of abundance would come, and that since the beginning of creation this would be the first moment in history when man would encounter his only real problem: how to use his freedom, how he can live wisely and well.

According to Keynes, skilful money makers can bring an age of abundance to humanity, but in this new era they will no longer be important. Rather, the important will be those who enjoy life itself and are able to make fruitful use of it. They do not confuse the ultimate goal with the means that leads there, economic prosperity.

And when the accumulation of wealth will no longer have social significance, there will be a fundamental change in morals as well. Many distortions that result from loving money for itself, not as a means to live well, will disappear. Keynes puts it radically:

> The love of money as a possession – as distinguished from the love of money as a means to the enjoyments and realities of life – will be recognised for what it is, a somewhat disgusting morbidity, one of those semi-criminal, semi-pathological propensities which one hands over with a shudder to the specialists in mental disease.[1]

Keynes's utopia did not come true. Material prosperity did occur, but it did not ensure the well-being of everyone. It signals as if we did not share Keynes's vision of the good life: we did not cut working time dramatically to finally be able to focus on 'living wisely and well'. Nor has his prediction on the love of money been fulfilled: we still do not consider it pathological.

Many people are still inclined to identify well-being with material welfare, and believe that material abundance will automatically bring a good life. So much so, that often material abundance becomes the absolute priority, the end goal of our strivings.

GDP growth does not bring happiness

Economic growth does not bring happiness, argued Richard Easterlin, a professor of economics at the University of Southern California in his 1974 article, triggering an intense debate. He found that, despite many decades of income growth in the US, average happiness has not increased at all. Later he expanded his analysis for a large number of other countries, using data covering half a century, and concluded that national income growth does not lead to an increase in happiness here either.[2]

Easterlin's work produced a big wave of response: it was extensively tested and debated by many others whether GDP growth increases happiness or not, and what is the right methodology to test this. Currently there seems to be stronger evidence finding that it does not, in support of the Easterlin thesis. Is this the right question, however? Why would GDP growth be the main (or only) driver of average happiness? Actually it is not, thus the analysis had to be extended. Other important factors were found to have an impact on well-being (which are also partly related to GDP), such as the level of inequality, life expectancy, inflation, unemployment or the quality of institutions (government efficiency and stability, curbing corruption, the rule of law, accountability) or the degree of social trust.[3] In sum, an increase in national income makes it possible to expand the provision of essential goods and services, which actually have a larger positive impact on overall happiness than an increase in national income itself. The key issue is thus *how* a country spends its growing national income, rather than the extent of growth as such.

Inequality in the distribution of resources is crucial. As indicated by Thomas Piketty, Emmanuel Saez and Gabriel Zucman, in the US, over a generation, the poor and the rich have experienced a completely different reality, as if they had lived in two separate countries. While the poorer half of the population did not benefit at all from economic growth between 1980 and 2014, the income of the rich skyrocketed.[4] The gap is as large as the average income gap between the US and one of the poorest countries in the world, such as the Central African Republic or Burundi.

A further and ever more acute question is: what is the price of this growth, in terms of negative ecological and social consequences? Are we paying for our 'progress' with our happiness, our health and irreversible environmental degradation?

Alternative indicators, such as the Genuine Progress Indicator (GPI) question whether we can speak of progress at all in recent decades in richer countries. While global GDP has increased more than three-fold since 1950, GPI has actually declined since 1978. It was also calculated that, globally, GPI/capita does not increase beyond a GDP/capita of around $7,000/capita, suggesting that material wealth above a certain level does not contribute to well-being.[5]

In contrast to GDP, GPI accounts for income inequality, negative activities like crime and pollution, as well as the benefits of volunteering and household work, considering altogether 24 different components. It is not a perfect measure, but it clearly highlights the problem of the traditional growth perspective and shows one potential alternative, among an ever-growing number of alternative indicators.

The weak relationship between GDP growth and average happiness is not surprising. GDP was not meant to be the main indicator of progress, not even according to its creator, Simon Kuznets. It is as the consequence of simplistic thinking that GDP has become so prominent. So the main 'fault' of GDP may not be its nature and its deficiencies but, rather, its use. GDP is not suitable as a key indicator of progress or well-being, as argued by countless prominent economists, including Joseph E. Stiglitz, Amartya Sen, Alan B. Krueger, Thomas Piketty, Tim Jackson, Richard Layard and others.[6]

Box 2.1: Why GDP cannot be a main and sole measure of welfare and well-being

GDP expresses the total income of a nation in a given year, that is, the sum of goods and services produced in a given year. The level of GDP (national GDP or even per capita GDP) does not show the distribution of incomes (who benefits from rising incomes or who loses during a recession), nor what the state is spending money on and, ultimately, the quality of public services.

GDP includes all public spending, including 'bads' such as prisons, military spending or the elimination of an environmental disaster as value-generating activities.

Due to the nature of GDP, it measures income flow (flow variable), which does not examine assets (stock), the accumulated wealth, and it does not say anything about the condition or change of environmental goods. It does not show, for example, if a country pollutes its drinking water. And if all the trees are cut down, that will even increase GDP in a given year. GDP does not include voluntary work, childcare at home or working without pay – all activities that do not involve a market transaction and have no price.

The '*Beyond GDP*' initiative of the European Commission has proposed a number of alternative ways to reconsider our measure for progress: GDP can be adjusted with important factors such as environmental damage, it can be expanded with social indicators (life expectancy, poverty, unemployment, education), environmental indicators (natural resources, pollution, waste management) and well-being indicators (for example, life satisfaction).[7]

Individual-level studies have also challenged that money making is a path to happiness. As shown, money increases life satisfaction when basic needs are being satisfied, beyond which money has little or no impact.[8] There are numerous other, more important determinants of our happiness than money, such as nurturing our relationships and our mental health.[9]

Focusing on material goals is like taking a poisonous pill that brings unhappiness: it is likely to make a person insecure and anxious, to damage their relationships, and also to reduce their sense of freedom, as shown by the extended research of Tim Kasser, an American social psychologist.[10] In a meta-analysis of 175 studies using 258 distinct samples, it was found that materialism was associated with more compulsive consumption, engaging more frequently in risky health-related behaviours (like smoking cigarettes and drinking alcohol), a more negative self-image, less positive feelings, more depression, more anxiety, worse physical health and lower life satisfaction.[11]

The promise of consumer society, namely that everything can be bought and all we have to do is earn the money for it, can displace natural forms of human interaction, such as helping each other, sharing skills and goods with each other for free, voluntarily, without expecting compensation. It can displace simple forms of joy that are independent of consumption, including activities we choose to do just because we enjoy them or that are dear to us because we hold them to be meaningful and important.

In sum, confusing the *end goal* (of good life, may it be happiness, freedom or a wise life) with the *material means* leading to it (money) is damaging to us. If we prioritize financial objectives as a precondition of a good and healthy society and world, we may end up neglecting the latter.

Three unfulfilled promises

The idea of economic progress appeals to us for other reasons as well. We have high hopes about the improvement of our personal situations. These hopes are often created or reinforced by the mainstream culture. I call them promises of a good life. I would like to highlight three of these, reflecting on the nature of these promises and how they typically fail us in their realization. It is not a complete assessment of the economic system as such. Rather, it aims to illustrate that our culture and our personal convictions as to success and a good life may not always benefit us and can even be harmful.

The promise of abundance: the richly set table

Even in the Global North, the experience of abundance is new. The majority of the older generation has, through war or deprivation, experienced a shortage of basic goods. Our parents' or our grandparents' generation experienced starvation or struggle for survival. There is a good chance that they have passed this experience on to us, perhaps subconsciously, as a key lesson for life. Our collective memory holds many struggles.

Seen on the broader historical scale, there is now an abundance accessible to many in the North that was previously unimaginable. And we enjoy this abundance. At the same time, the visceral fears and lessons of our ancestors about scarcity, survival and security may live on in us. Our physical bodies and instincts are also optimized for survival, formed in an evolutionary time dimension. All these urge us to eat abundantly, if possible. But what happens if it is always possible?

The darker side of abundance

We can easily turn a blind eye to the devastating effects of this abundance: the harm done to others elsewhere, the injustice of this system at the global level. Why? Because we easily can. Many of us believe, in good faith, that if we have paid the price of a product, then we have properly compensated others for the costs it involved. What is more, we have done good to the producers, because we have enabled them to go on making a living. This would be true if the price reflected the product's true value, fairly and without distortion; if the price included all costs and negative impacts, including fair wages, social security costs, health risks and environmental damage. Unfortunately, this is usually not the case.

There is a glaring inequality in the use of the Earth's resources, as well as in the distribution of the profits reaped from them. The natural life-style of the North is an 'imperialist life-style', one that is still exploiting the cheaper South rich in raw materials.[12] This system is kept in place by a sense of entitlement and by current consumption habits, as well as by the existing structures of the world economy.

Our plates hold exotic goods from the far ends of the world, goods that used to be a rare delicacy on the plates of aristocrats. Fish, mussels, spices, exotic fruits and other specialities. One can finally eat tomatoes, strawberries or even avocados all year round! One can finally eat plenty of meat – several times a day, if one so wishes. Efficient, large-scale industrial agriculture is able to feed us at affordable prices.

The vulnerabilities of industrial agriculture and large-scale international trade have been particularly exposed during COVID-19 lockdowns. Food shortage has become a real threat in some places. Although the devastating impact of vast agricultural monocultures and large-scale animal production on soils, drinking water and the ecosystem has been highlighted by countless critics for many years, these still seem to be the favoured option, often supported by state subsidies or EU agricultural subvention in Europe. Cheap food, however, may cost us dear in the end.

We waste food: no less than one third of the food produced globally is discarded.[13] According to Food and Agriculture Organization (FAO) data, the average person in Europe and in North America throws away about 100 kg of food in a year. Even more is thrown away during production and distribution. Around the world, 1.4 billion hectares of land are used to produce food that is ultimately wasted – an area greater than China. The volume of water that is used to produce wasted food is equivalent to three times the volume of Lake Geneva. Food loss and waste is responsible for about 8 per cent of global greenhouse gas emissions. Safe and nutritious food that is lost, discarded and wasted could feed some two billion people – more than double the number of the undernourished in the world.

Our food and our life-style may not nourish us but, rather, strain us, making us sick or overweight. More than one in two adults and nearly one in six children are overweight or obese in high-income, OECD countries (Organisation for Economic Co-operation and Development).[14] In the US, overweight, including obesity, affects seven in ten adults. In the UK, the rate is six in ten. Obesity rates are highest in the US, Mexico and New Zealand, affecting three to four in ten adults.

This weight problem could be seen as the loss of a healthy balance. It affects not just physical health but also mental health, self-image, relationships and many other areas of life.

The physical strain is exacerbated by additional mental strain caused by the beauty industry, marketing and sales branches that spread an unrealistic body image, so that body-image disorders and consequent low self-esteem are widespread.

It seems that many of us no longer feel instinctively what is good for us, what nourishes us. We may become alienated from our own bodies, our most intimate companions. This is not the abundance we were longing for.

The promise of high status: 'we can all be aristocrats'

There is no need to be born into nobility today. The promise of today's consumer society is that we can all be high and mighty in the social hierarchy. All we have to do is to consume accordingly. If we have the right status goods (luxury brand of watch and clothes, gemstone jewellery, fashion items, a sports car and so on) and habits we can belong to the elite. Status goods and services are meant to be the signals of our talent, hard work and success. It is especially so in places with a strong collective myth of meritocracy, where wealth and its external signs are seen as signals of talent and hard work, a well-deserved success.

Success is often seen as the possession of goods, a display of life-style, intertwined with power and influence, all externally visible criteria of rising above others. According to the belief that 'everyone can make it', everything is possible for all and personal growth has no limits.

Elite status promises the external confirmation that we are valuable and are doing well. People will respect us, love us and pay attention to us, we rise to significance. We will have an easy path to the perfect partner and no limits to meeting our need for intimacy and belonging. We will no longer suffer from the deep existential fears of human existence: that we are living for nothing (meaninglessness) and that there is an insurmountable separation between us and others (isolation).[15] Our status is hoped to secure us and liberate us by providing identity, control, a sense of competence and belonging.

It is just a seductive mirage

The consumption of status goods and services is not new. As early as 1899, American sociologist Thorstein Veblen sharply criticized 'conspicuous consumption' intended merely to indicate social status; in addition to not serving social development, it was wasting resources.[16] Veblen condemned the ruling class who did not work themselves but, rather, made others work for them. By now, the phenomenon of conspicuous consumption is widespread, not just limited to the elite. Buying status goods can be seen as a sign of longing for status.

Longing for status can be understood for the psychological reasons mentioned earlier. It is, however, not an optimal strategy for meeting the deep longing for a meaningful life and for belonging.

The psychological downside to a status-seeking life strategy is that it calls for continuous competition and effort, and also for constant benchmarking and comparison. Our life, our being is not treasured as such; it has no value in itself. We have to be worthy, on an ongoing basis. We have to deserve acceptance or appreciation in a continuous strenuous effort. Our judges are outside of us, with an immense power over us. Therefore, this strategy brings with it existential uncertainty and vulnerability. As the benchmark is external, based on fashions, trends, cultural expectations, it impedes the free exploration of who one really is and what ones wants to become, and what the meaning is that one could personally give to his/her life.

Some may regard status seeking as a natural biological trait with evolutionary roots, as a fight for mates and resources ensuring our personal survival and reproduction. This view, however, ignores a vital element of our human species: collaboration and community, which have actually ensured our survival and evolution as a species.[17]

Status-and power-seeking as an *ultimate* life strategy is self-centred, as it focuses on individual advantage. Others are seen and judged according to whether or not they are useful for this objective. People, animals and other living beings of the Earth, as well as its resources are seen as means only, subordinate to our own person and our own success. It is thus damaging on a collective level.

There is a clear relationship between affluence and environmental destruction. From 1990 to 2015, carbon dioxide emissions rose by roughly 60 per cent, and nearly half of this growth was caused by the richest 10 per cent (those with incomes above about $35,000 (£27,000) a year).[18] The emissions linked to the top 1 per cent alone grew by more than three times as much as those linked to the bottom 50 per cent globally. A major cause is high-carbon transport, especially overseas flights or private jets – key elements of the high life. It seems that rising incomes tend to escalate self-centred and resource-intensive consumption, where individual pleasure or convenience overrides considerations about others. If this trait of our elites and its supporting culture remain unchanged, rising incomes globally are likely to further escalate the problems of excessive carbon emissions and climate change.

In addition, the status-seeking strategy offers a false recipe for success, as it is unattainable for many. By definition, the majority cannot be part of a privileged elite, as this would no longer be an elite. Therefore this promise implicitly abandons the vast majority of society from the outset.

In the collective myth of *meritocracy*, 'unlimited opportunities' where 'anyone can make it if they want to', the better-off may easily stigmatize all those who are destitute as 'lazy' or 'undeserving', failing to see their suffering as a potential social injustice, a sign of unequal opportunities.

Even for the 'lucky' minority whose income or status continues to grow over time, belonging to the elite can be an ongoing struggle. The change of status usually changes the so-called *reference group*, the circle of people with whom we compare ourselves. Our benchmark may turn out to be not our former peers but, rather, some global elite. In a world of immense capital concentration, this is an almost impossible undertaking. This may explain the paradox that some people find themselves frustrated rather than satisfied when they prosper financially.[19]

Empirical research has found that, while people crave material growth, its presence does not make them feel rich or satisfied in an enduring way.[20] As people's income grows, they usually get used to their new situation rather quickly, and will not settle for it. Instead, their financial aspirations also increase, and thus they need more and more money to maintain their life-style.[21] They are trapped in a '*hedonic treadmill*', where, for all their intensified efforts, the material abundance they desire will always float a few steps ahead of them, forever moving away from them as they approach it.[22] The underlying mechanism is similar to other types of adaptation, and serves to maintain and enhance perception and to redirect motivation. A sensory example is that we get used to the dark, and it helps us to cope with the new situation, maintaining and enhancing our perception. We are likely to lose our sensitivity to what we have and what we know (desensitization), unless we deliberately refine our senses by noticing and appreciating the 'obvious' in our everyday life, in our habits, in our belongings. This is the objective of mindfulness for example.

Some researchers tested the existence of the *hedonic treadmill* by analysing lottery winners, whether they have become happier as a result. I will not review their findings here as, in my view, this research question and the outcomes reveal little about the core issue of the *hedonic treadmill*: materialism, financial aspirations and their endless pursuit, which is personal but embedded in a culture which reinforces it. The analysis of lottery winners is an interesting exploration of how people react to an external shock, be it that they get what they dreamt about, but it has little relevance with regard to the issue of our endless search for success. (In regard to lottery winners, in my view, they are not a homogeneous group. Whether somebody finds a good use for their unexpected fortune or will be absorbed in self-destructive indulgence or explosive conflicts, ending up in a worse situation than before, is likely to be determined by their values, goals and their mental ability to handle external shocks, even if positive ones.)

Rising average incomes and rising material aspirations affect all, including the poorest in society. It takes ever more resources to stay out of poverty, according to the currently widespread *relative poverty* approach. Escaping poverty is not just about having enough to eat for one's survival or having shelter – that is, being able to meet basic physical needs; it is also about the psychological need to belong to a community, to be able to participate in its life. Money may be the metric used (to define poverty level of income), but the ultimate concern includes both physical and psychological needs. The approach of *social inclusion* makes this even more explicit, moves beyond the simple money metric and includes other indicators of the good life such as supportive relationships and social and political participation.[23]

The common-sense list of '*necessary*' things keeps being upgraded. For example, the average floor space of apartments is growing: what used to be enough is now too little, especially if we think back one or two generations. At the same time, many societies still do not manage to provide basic shelter for all their members. Air conditioning is regarded as a 'must' in ever more homes, overriding traditional solutions for cooling or coping with heat. Taking regular overseas holidays has become standard practice for many, while others may not be able to afford a holiday away from home at all. The number of cars is skyrocketing, as well as their power. Some poorer households opt for purchasing a car on credit, while underestimating the cost of instalments and maintenance, including petrol.

Previously we knew little about the riches of the elites, as they lived in secluded ways and interacted with their own circles; now we are confronted in numerous ways with their exuberance in the media and on social media. It takes more and more for someone to keep up, if they use a materialist metric as an indicator of a good life.

Our perception of the world and our own 'basic needs' is biased, as it is steered by the powerful advertising industry. Not just our own desires are triggered by the refined psychological and visual tools applied. We may start craving for things that we did not miss before. In addition, we witness and may slowly accept a 'normality' which is artificially created, and is far from being real. We may start to believe that an attractive woman needs a new set of clothes and shoes every season, that a sensible car owner purchases a sports utility vehicle for their city drive, that a decent middle-class couple needs regular weekend getaways hundreds of miles away to unwind, and that an open-minded, healthy, spiritual person has to fly to East-Asia for a proper yoga and wellness retreat. Naturally, we will be most affected by the stories about the life-styles of our own existing reference group, or the group of people we want to belong to.

We are likely to find it painful if we lag behind in the race for status and status goods, unless we choose a very different yardstick for measuring the success of our lives and deliberately opt for living a radically alternative way of life, based on non-materialist values. Then, voluntary simplicity is not a loss, but rather a source of joy.

The promise of plenty: 'all desires can be fulfilled'

The promise of today's neoliberal market economy is that we can satisfy all our desires – moreover, instantly. The choice is overwhelming, and it suits the most delicate tastes as well. No need to wait until we get bored with our clothes or until our gadgets break: we can replace them any time. There is no need to go to the shop or wait for opening hours, as we can shop online. How much time and money we can 'save'! We do not have to wait until we have the money, as we can buy it on credit. The time between the birth of a wish and its potential fulfilment is getting ever shorter, and any delay in gratification seems to be an unnecessary self-restraint, a futile masochism.

Countless forms of pleasures can be bought. Even our desire for recognition, acceptance and love is promised to be fulfilled through social media and the internet, or the consumption of certain goods or services. All this is not an innovation of the 21st century, as, for example, noble titles were also bought in the past and prostitution is as old as civilization, but the expansion of supply and the simplification of access is new. What variety and what freedom of choice!

New forms of addiction

Entire industries try to lure us into consumption and even overconsumption. Today *addiction* is no longer limited to alcohol, drugs or gambling, but can be applied to shopping, spending, porn, gaming, online relationships, the internet and much else occurring in an obsessive and compulsive way. We also have specific words for some of these: shopaholism, compulsive shopping or compulsive spending. We can regard it addiction when desire takes control and the person loses their freedom. Addiction is when one pays for a transient pleasure with longer-term suffering or loss, and continues with the behaviour despite the (ever increasing) negative consequences and even when the activity itself is no longer pleasurable. It has features such as compulsivity and withdrawal symptoms. A *behavioural addiction* activates the brain reward system with effects similar to those of drugs of abuse.[24]

In Silicon Valley an entire industry is centred on reinforcing and nourishing people's dependence on a neurobiological basis: the 'likes', the jingling of each alert, all give us instant gratification, and the hormone dopamine grants us a sense of reward, such that we want to repeat it and still we want more of it. The extensive use of social media and social networking sites is so pervasive that it has become almost 'normal'. One potential driver is the 'fear of missing out'.[25]

More than 4.5 billion people now use the internet, while active social media users have passed the 3.8 billion mark, according to a 2020 global survey.[26] The average internet user now spends 6 hours and 43 minutes online each day and uses social media more than one third of this time. Mobile phones account for over half of the time spent online. We are now using apps for all aspects of our lives, including entertainment, news, finances, work, sports and even meditation. The

COVID-19 epidemic has further boosted this trend with a surge of online meetings, work organization and shopping.

While the internet is now an inevitable element of our lives, with many advantages, it could become like a boundless river, flooding everywhere. Inapt use of the web can lead to constant distraction, loss of ability to concentrate, distortions of self-image, anxiety, depression or dependence. It can also damage sleep, our most elementary way of regeneration. A good number of people sleep with their phone, go to bed and wake up with it, as if it were their intimate partner. A 2016 UK survey of 2,750 11- to 18-year-olds showed that 10 per cent of teens checked for notifications more than ten times a night, and almost half kept their phone by their bed at night.[27] A 2019 US survey of parents and their children found that over one quarter of parents and one third of teens check their phone within five minutes of going to bed and within five minutes of waking up: it is the close of the day and the very start of it.[28] For many, their sleep is interrupted by notifications. For some reason, they opt to receive notifications non-stop. The survey results showed that some people sleep with their phones in their hands.

Our economic system has a significant interest in making our desires as materialistic as possible. It suggests that we can buy happiness. Our habits, relationships, even how we make love and what we think of our own bodies, have all been transformed, and mostly not for the better. Without our awareness and careful attention, our human relationships can also become objectified, impersonalized. In an era of endless choice, someone who is content with what is 'good enough' appears to be a fool.

So, it is no wonder that so many people spend much of their free time searching for the 'real thing' or 'the one', whether in the physical world or virtually, from shop to shop, from profile to profile. They do what they can, to the best of their ability, for their own good. Yet something is wrong; the anticipated feeling of fulfilment is often absent; they may experience 'buyer's let-down'. This is especially true in the case of impulsive shopping and for those who are highly materialistic.[29] The items we purchase are gradually overflowing from our cupboards and rooms, so that we need ever larger houses in which to store them.

For most people, eating, shopping or using social media tend to bring pleasure; that is why we do these things. Our relationship with them can be varied, ranging from a refined enjoyment based on inner freedom (such as Epicurean hedonism, as presented in Chapter 4), through casual but not particularly conscious enjoyment, to obsessive addiction. It is a continuous scale. Do we know where we stand? Our dependency may be disguised for us as simple everyday habit.

There is a strong counter-movement for regaining control over our money, time and attention. Ever more people relate critically to the seduction of consumption and seek ways out. They are reluctant to buy new items, and opt to prolong the life cycle of things they already have, or share their items with others or repurpose old objects by creative upcycling. Now about half of internet users apply ad blockers to block online advertising.[30] The popularity of screen-time trackers is growing, to increase awareness of time use, as a result of which some decide to decrease their online engagement. Over one third of social media users in the US and UK say that they have decreased their time on social media, and one in five users deactivated a social media account in 2019.[31]

Losing control: the story of the Golem

I am reminded of the Prague Jewish story of the strong Golem. The Rabbi modelled the Golem from clay from the banks of the River Vltava and magically breathed life into it through a tube of magic paper with God's name pencilled on it. For a time, the Golem served him and the community faithfully and truthfully. The Rabbi had power over him: he could turn him back into a lump of clay by just removing the paper. One day the Golem rebelled, turned into a monster and menaced the whole city, trampling all that came in his path. Only the Rabbi who made him could eventually regain control over him. The worldview of capitalism resembles a maddened Golem. He wants to be a lord, not a servant. He looks at the world as if in a trance. The hills and dales become mere sources of raw material; forests and their myriad inhabitants are no more than potential farmland. Corporations, free trade and global money markets create seismic movements with outcomes that have direct effects on whole peoples and countries. It has all become too big to be 'amoral', to be guided just by a desire for gain, disregarding all other aspects of the common good. The damage wrought by the Golem can be felt but not averted, as if the redeeming sacred paper and the Golem's original creator have been lost.

Capitalism has become a belief system that claims to be a recipe for progress, for how we can all do best, individually and socially. In this it has suffered total defeat. Its beliefs in selfishness and rivalry not only fail to bring the freedom and equality Churchill cites, but only add to the ecological catastrophe that threatens us all. The other living creatures on Earth have long suffered under mankind's dominion; many have even died out under its tyranny. Now the ramifications of human activity do not spare humans, either: pandemics, heatwaves, forest fires, droughts, water shortages and rising sea levels threaten the lives of millions.

Who is the master who can stop this Golem? While the roles of decision makers, superpowers and giant corporations are the most prominent, it may be that there will not be a breakthrough unless a sizeable number of individuals and self-organizing groups demand and reinforce one. Transformation can occur at many levels, and the processes that bring about positive change can be mutually reinforcing.

What world do we want for ourselves?

The COVID-19 pandemic brought an abrupt and radical disruption to the world as we knew it. Many people seek to return to what feels familiar to them. For many others, who are open to change and less bound by their old habits and the norms of the pre-COVID-19 world, this may become a turning point. They are inclined to reflect on the alternatives and on the desired transformation of their own lives and efforts.

While individual freedom is an essential and vital achievement of our liberal democracies today, it is often simplified as the 'right to do whatever one happens to want' – the behaviour of a selfish, social moron. This is very far from true freedom. This sense of personal entitlement is hostile to self-transcendent values or collective solutions, and often denies the existence of major global problems. It hampers us in creating a world with a good life for everyone, based on our real preferences and our deepest longings.

Therefore we need to devise new mechanisms to increase our ability to live in line with our real preferences, while also being able to consider the interests of others. This will help to reconcile our freedom with our aspiration to live a good life both individually and socially.

We may wonder whether *economic man*'s assumptions about human nature are true or not (whether we are fundamentally selfish or cooperative, whether competition is coded into our genes or is a learnt trait, and whether we put our own pleasure first and foremost). These questions are more profound on a personal level, scrutinizing ourselves. Who are we to each other: rivals or partners, opponents or friends? What is life all about? What are we looking for? How do we handle our impulses, desires and quest for pleasure?

This vital question is, on a personal and collective level: what is our goal? What is our vision of the good life we are striving for? What are the values we want to pursue with our limited lifetime and available resources? What is real growth for us?

PART II

What Is a Good Life?

3

Pleasure, Joy, Satisfaction, Purpose: Refining Our Quest for Happiness

Happiness is both cultural and personal. Our culture penetrates our concepts, our language and ultimately even our experiences. Our upbringing, our education, the values of our religion or our community, our current economic system, our beliefs about human nature and the pathways to progress and prosperity, the advertising industry and the media tell us stories about 'how to make it', how to enjoy life and how not to. 'Work hard'; 'bring home the bacon'; 'a bird in the hand is worth two in the bush'; 'all work and no play makes Jack a dull boy'; 'eat, drink and be merry'; 'lunch is for losers'; 'keep smiling'; 'finish everything on your plate'; 'you should not finish everything on your plate'; 'you can buy happiness'; 'you cannot buy happiness, but you can buy a hair appointment and that's kind of the same thing'.

We learn how we are supposed to relate to joy and happiness: some forms are more acceptable and we are rewarded for them. For other forms, we pay with a sense of guilt or shame, or just numb ourselves to them. Some others are simply beyond the scope of our attention, as if we were blind to them.

Happiness is also personal, not simply in the sense that it is we who feel it, but in the sense of each of us has a subjective attitude to happiness, that we develop through our experiences and our aspirations. We make decisions about what kind of joy and happiness (or whatever we call the 'good feeling' we strive for) we pursue, and how.

These are existential decisions, very close to the core of our existence. Despite the gravity of these decisions, they are often not conscious, and this may not be to our benefit. It may be our strategy for striving for a good life which hinders us from becoming as happy, healthy and wise as we could potentially be.

As much as we have learnt how to seek pleasure, joy and happiness, we can also unlearn it gradually. Although our desires and strivings may feel hard wired into our gut feelings, they can actually be transformed. We can also learn to be more aware of our senses, feelings and thoughts.

Updating our emotional strategies from the Stone Age

Happiness, from a biological point of view, occurs as a 'by-product', rewarding and reinforcing actions that help survival. The human being today is essentially still very similar to the prehistoric human with respect to emotions.[1] No matter how much we have evolved, we are still biologically adapted for Stone Age existence, because the time elapsed since then is not long at all in evolutionary time. Human emotions are basically related to survival, and support it.

Biologically, the state of satisfaction is natural, and primarily it is our optimal basic state: this is the time when the body can rest, regenerate, recharge. This condition occurs when basic needs are met and there is no physical pain. At the same time, the feelings that trigger flight or attack, such as fear, anger, pain, are activated quite easily, as immediate reaction was important during the Stone Age. We are therefore more prone to unpleasant feelings 'by design'. Such feelings become problematic when we give an automatic and quick response to them in today's circumstances, or when these feelings 'burn into us' and become persistent, for example in the form of stress, anxiety, depression or chronic pain. This is more likely to occur if we are not aware of the early warning signs.

'How are you?' We have probably answered this question countless times. It seems so simple. But do we really know our own answer to ourselves? Strangely, many of us are not aware of the full spectrum of our experiences. It is not one of the skills we tend to learn at school or that appear to be useful in many segments of society. Family and cultural norms may shame or supress certain experiences, or may regard them as a sign of weakness. Yet, this skill largely affects our ability to take care of our own needs, our physical and mental health, as well as our emotional intelligence in relationships. Many of us decide to learn this as adults, although few start with it before experiencing a crisis or a major problem.

Mindfulness exercises, for example, provide detailed guidance on how to become more aware of momentary physical sensations, pleasant and unpleasant emotions, as well as thoughts and mental states. Jon Kabat-Zinn, an American professor of medicine and Zen Buddhist student, developed the method of mindfulness-based stress reduction, which has now entered the mainstream of medicine and society.[2]

His approach emphasizes a friendly and accepting attitude where we do not judge ourselves for anything that arises. We also learn how not to be overwhelmed by what arises. Nevertheless, it may take time and practice to develop this attitude and ability for self-awareness and self-care.

Although we still carry our Stone Age selves, our brains are docile, and we can use for our own benefit and for the benefit of our companions. Our brain can be taught to deal with unpleasant and pleasant impulses and feelings.[3] This ability is the key to our development. Thus, we need to actively 'update' our Stone Age selves on how we handle our emotions, how we seek pleasure and happiness, in order to be able to live a creative and meaningful life.

The science of happiness: new perspective on progress

The recipe of a good life can be inspired by science, according to the rules and worldview of the scientific world. It does not take the place of ancient teachers such as Buddha, Confucius, Jesus, Plato, Aristotle and many others, as it does not say anything about what true happiness or a complete life should be. Rather, it observes, describes and measures what it can.

The inquiry of happiness took a new turn in the 20th century: well-being became measurable thanks to large-scale databases, detailed follow-up studies (longitudinal and panel studies, where data on selected people are collected over time so that changes can be observed and their causes investigated), new laboratory tools and progress in informatics. All of this resulted in a methodological and scientific explosion.

The science of happiness has opened new doors. In addition to exploring more and more about how to live happily, it has inspired reflection on both a community and an individual level on what world we want to live in. At a social level, material indicators of development, such as GDP, are increasingly being questioned and alternatives are being proposed. At an individual level, it explores various approaches to a good life that is worth living.

New scientific branches have also emerged, such as positive psychology and happiness economics. In contrast to the classical psychotherapeutic approach, which starts primarily from an illness or a problem, positive psychology is driven by the intention to promote well-being. Happiness economics, according to its own definition, is a complementary approach to traditional mainstream economics that observes behaviour.[4] More and more scholars claim that observing human behaviour does not provide enough information, and it is important to consider emotions or social relationships, including social status.[5] The alternative, 'subjectivist' approach inquires how people see themselves, how they value their own lives.[6]

Ever more efforts are being made to explore how the individual and social levels are intertwined. In general, happiness economics examines what are the external circumstances, the institutional settings that affect people's life satisfaction or happiness. (Positive) psychology focuses on those individual actions and habits that help to increase happiness, including a person's response to external circumstances as well as inner impulses. There are also specific approaches that emphasize the relationship between social forces and the personal psyche (social psychology, critical and radical psychology, critical psychiatry, critical community psychology, the solution-focused approach to collective transformation), but some branches of economics, psychology, sociology and ecology are also trespassing ever more boldly on traditional borders.[7]

While economics observes what is external, the institutional system, public policy and behaviour, positive psychology focuses on the internal and seeks to change one's attitude. Measurement results show that attitude, deliberate actions, determines the variation of happiness more than do external circumstances. According to Sonja Lyubomirsky and her colleagues, attitude explains 40 per cent, while conditions explain only about 10 per cent on average of self-reported happiness and the remaining 50 per cent is of genetic origin.[8] Income explains no more than 2 per cent of the variance in happiness in any country.[9] More important is the relative income, a person's income compared to the incomes of others, but this is also of rather little importance for explaining the level of happiness. Overall, there is a fine interplay between inner attitudes and the external world (circumstances, institutions, nature or culture), and the latter can also support a person's ability to develop their own optimal attitude for a thriving life.

Pleasure, joy, happiness, meaning: thousand-faced happiness

Happiness may feel celestial, distant and immense, or to the contrary, it may seem extremely mundane, overused in commercials and headlines.

Despite the phrase itself becoming worn out, the longing for something is probably there in most of us. What is it?

Joy, pleasure, purpose, happiness, well-being? What exactly are we looking for? Is there – and, if so – what is the difference between them? In the text so far, sometimes I have talked of happiness, other times of well-being. Do they mean the same thing? And does it matter? This is not a splitting of hairs exclusively for scientists. Our language shapes how we see reality and ourselves in it.

This section is about measuring happiness in a quantitative way. Psychology and social science speak of 'subjective well-being'. It is a collective term that includes dozens of possible metrics, and it is called subjective because the respondent evaluates how he or she feels.

For describing happiness, we can base our assessment on the body, on emotions or on thoughts. The three related questions are: what do I sense? What do I feel? What do I think?

The body is the source of physical and sensory pleasures. These pleasures reach us through our sensors of taste, smell, touch, hearing and sight. We can also experience other physical pleasures, such as a state of ease and deep relaxation, where we feel safe and well and simply enjoy the state of 'being'. Displeasure and pain also originate in the body. Our senses, our physical ability to feel (dis)pleasure, seem to be an 'objective' quality, but actually are also subjective, and subject to learning. We can refine our senses and grow our physical awareness. Interestingly, positive psychology speaks little about physical pleasures, and focuses more on emotions.[10]

Emotional states are typically measured by psychologists with the so-called *'affect indicators'*, and describe the sum of 'positive' and 'negative' feelings. The affect indicator captures a momentary emotional state or mood and is therefore variable over time. The 'affect balance scale' assesses the balance of positive and negative feelings over a period of a few weeks.

When I speak of a 'positive' or 'negative' feeling in this book, I am referring to this scientific language. At the same time, I do not think that 'negative' or unpleasant feelings should or could be excluded from human life. Anger or sadness are natural human feelings, especially when one recognizes their changeable nature. Feelings can be thought of as signals that prompt action in a particular situation, and that can induce progress, transformation to a new stage of life. Prolonged or very challenging negative feelings, such as a depression, suicidal thoughts or post-traumatic symptoms, however, require external help.

Economists are particularly interested in the measurement of happiness because it is seen by many as an indicator of utility, allowing

Table 3.1: Sources and forms of happiness, and related scientific approaches

Where?	Body	Emotions	Thoughts	
What?	Pleasure: physical, sensory pleasures (taste, smell, touch, hearing, sight), sense of relaxation and ease Displeasure: tension, pain	Positive emotions: such as joy, elation, contentment, pride, affection, ecstasy, thrill Negative emotions: such as guilt and shame, sadness, anxiety, anger, stress, depression, envy	A reflective assessment on a person's life: life satisfaction or overall happiness	Sense of meaning or purpose
How to measure?	Experimental psychology: laboratory tests	Psychology: 'affect' measures, such as 'affect balance score'	Happiness economics: 'hedonic measures', measures of 'experienced utility'	Typically (positive) psychology: 'meaning of life'

empirical testing of many theoretical theorems and opening up new areas. They mostly use *cognitive measures* of overall life evaluation. These indicators are sometimes referred to as *'hedonic' indicators*, referring to the theoretical background of economics. Hedonic metrics measure how satisfied or happy a person is in general. Such indicators are also included in many international and national surveys.

- 'All things considered, how satisfied are you with your life as a whole nowadays?'
  - This question is answered on a scale of 0–10, where 0 means extremely dissatisfied and 10 means extremely satisfied.
- 'All things considered, how happy are you?'
  - This question is answered on a scale of 0–10, where 0 means extremely unhappy and 10 means extremely happy.

What people mean when they think about these extremes is left up to them.[11] Interestingly, these completely subjective, individual responses also have regularities.

The reliability of the indicators is confirmed by the fact that they are closely related to a number of other external metrics (the respondent's heartbeat, frequency of smiles, what others say about their well-being, number of positive and negative events recalled and clinical interviews).[12] In addition, there are recurring patterns for social groups, where potential 'measurement noise', individual differences, cancel each other out.[13]

Momentary good feelings differ from lasting happiness, inner peace. The latter is a state where a person's life has a broader, self-transcending perspective and orientation. In this sense, one can be happy even if one's momentary comfort level is low. Raising a child is a good example of this.

The meaning of life is a philosophical and spiritual concept with infinite perspectives, but by now statisticians and data analysts have also entered this field with their own approach. In the UK, a comprehensive social and expert consultation was conducted on what happiness is and how it should be measured. 'Meaning of life' was a priority for many, thus it became one of the four main subjective well-being indicators that the National Office for Statistics regularly measures. The specific question follows:

- 'Overall, to what extent do you feel the things you do in your life are worthwhile?'
  - Responses are given on a 0–10 scale, where 0 is not at all worthwhile and 10 is completely.

What do the specific indicators focus on? Pleasure can be observed from physical sensations and emotions. Affect indicators reflect an emotional state. Evaluative indicators, such as overall life satisfaction or happiness, are cognitive measures, related to our thinking about our lives. Meaningfulness and purpose in life may be based on a reflection from a more distant perspective. It may be that someone feels that their life is fundamentally meaningful while currently they are going through a challenging phase of life and feel sadness or restlessness.

In scientific papers, the term 'happiness' is often used in a broad sense, referring to the philosophical concept or to a whole range of indicators (rather than solely to the above-mentioned happiness measure) applied for testing the robustness of the results. I follow this convention when I speak of happiness or happy people.

In addition to these approaches, there are many advocates for alternatives, for example a 'humanistically informed positive psychology', that would supplement scales with intimate, in-depth portraitures.[14] Aristotle also had a much broader approach to happiness. According to the philosopher, happiness is not a hedonic measure, and it is not simply a momentary feeling, as explained in Chapter 5.

Well-being, therefore, has a thousand faces: it can be a comprehensive evaluation of life, a set of momentary emotions, pleasurable physical sensations, a sense of meaningful life and much more. A feature of the main types of indicators described earlier is that they can be measured in large-scale surveys. This brief overview has aimed to both inspire and to provide a basic guide to better understand the results of happiness research.

The benefits of happiness

Good feelings have value in themselves – what a good thing it is to feel joy – but they do not stop at the inner, psychic world, as they also have a number of positive consequences. A large body of empirical research has concluded that happy people are successful in life: they usually earn more, their marriages are more lasting and they even live longer. Happy people treat themselves and others better. In addition, happiness seems to enhance those mental features and behaviours which are crucial for a just and sustainable society.

The secret to long life is a positive outlook on life, according to a study of nuns.[15] According to an analysis of nuns' life histories, nuns who reported positive feelings in their short resumes at the time of their entry into the convent (on average at the age of 22) lived 7 to 11 years longer, six decades later. Happiness prolongs the lives of healthy people by several years, although it does not protect against serious illnesses. The size of the effect is comparable to that of smoking or not.[16] Hundreds of research projects have concluded that subjective well-being, which is a comprehensive scientific concept of 'happiness' as discussed in the previous section, improves physical health and mortality. These findings are based on longitudinal studies, just like in the case of the nuns, following the people in the sample over a longer period of time and thus allowing the study of causal relationships between well-being and health. Why does happiness have such an effect?

Those who feel well tend also to treat their bodies well, are less likely to become ill and recover faster. A high level of subjective well-being was shown to be associated with health-promoting behaviours such as healthy eating, regular physical exercise and non-smoking.[17] Happier people are less willing to take risks, as shown, for example, by a study using a 300,000-person US sample analysing seat belt use and car accident statistics.[18]

In addition, subjective well-being is closely related to the incidence and rate of recovery from diseases such as cardiovascular disease,

Figure 3.1: Positive impact of happiness

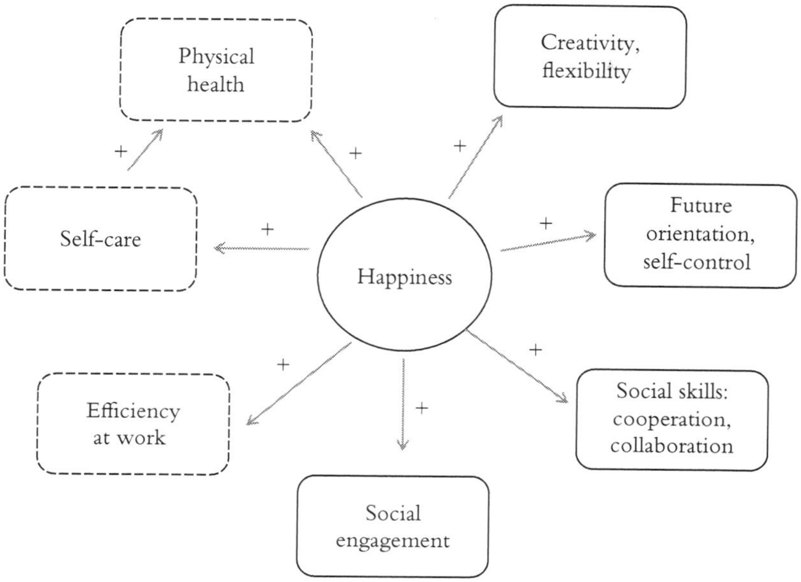

Note: The more relevant impacts for a just and sustainable future are marked with a continuous line.

Source: Author's own.

inflammation, viral disease or stroke.[19] Positive emotions have a physical imprint and in the long run make it easier to manage stress or to cope with difficult situations. In the same way, negative conditions such as depression and anxiety, in addition to causing mental suffering, are also causes of physical maladies such as coronary heart disease. It may well be that (un)happiness had an impact on the incidence of COVID-19 and recovery from it.

From the point of view of our current exploration (how to live an enjoyable life which does not harm others), a number of additional impacts have high relevance: mental abilities like creativity and flexibility, the future orientation of people, social skills and social engagement (see Figure 3.1).

It has been shown that the creativity and cognitive flexibility of happy people are outstanding and that they are characterized by cooperation and collaboration in the workplace, particularly so in situations involving negotiation.[20] These are also powerful arguments as to why a company should pay attention to the well-being of its employees.

Happy people typically live with a longer-term perspective. Experiments have shown that people with positive feelings are better able to sacrifice a certain immediate benefit for a greater future benefit, that is, they are more likely to pursue long-term goals because they have self-control, they are able to wait in order to satisfy their desires.[21] Happier people typically save more and spend less and make more informed decisions, and if their income increases, they spend a smaller portion of it on consumption.[22]

Happy people have been shown to have a more community-oriented behaviour. They are characterized by self-transcendence, caring for others: they are more likely to donate money, donate blood or to volunteer.[23] Happiness increases participation in social interactions, and happiness is also 'contagious' through social networks, reaching even those who are personally unknown.[24] Happiness therefore has significant economic and social benefits that go far beyond an individual's own life.

Thus, individual happiness has a social dimension, and not only in the sense that the happiness (or subjective well-being) of a person positively affects other people: their family, their colleagues, the fabric of society and social institutions as well. In addition, the described positive consequences may be crucial for addressing our current crisis as well.

A crucial issue, however, is whether we think of happiness (or subjective well-being) as a feature of people that can be observed, or whether we think of happiness or pleasure-seeking as a motivation. While being happy (or being well) is a sign of good health and a predictor of many other favourable outcomes, the life strategy centred on the quest for happiness often fails, due to cultural and personal reasons. These reasons were partly described in Chapter 2, in the context of the unfulfilled promises of current capitalism, and will be discussed further in Chapter 4, with respect to pleasure-seeking and hedonism. Actively seeking happiness may backfire.

The right to be unhappy

In *Brave New World*, written by Aldous Huxley in 1932, human society has solved thousand-year-old problems. It has managed to get rid of ageing, illness, pain, love torment and even inconveniences like mosquitoes. The world is a masterpiece of technological advancement, mixed with the pill of happiness available at any time, the 'soma'.

> And if ever, by some unlucky chance, anything unpleasant should somehow happen, why, there's always soma to give you a holiday from the facts. There's always soma to calm

your anger, to reconcile you to your enemies, to make you patient and long-suffering. In the past you could only accomplish these things by making a great effort and after years of hard moral training. Now, you swallow two or three half-gramme tablets, and there you are. Anybody can be virtuous now.[25]

Soma has 'All the advantages of Christianity and alcohol; none of their defects'. [26] It can be taken at any time with an immediate effect. Everything in this world is about the greatest comfort possible. At the same time, however, life loses substance, becomes empty and meaningless. This fills the Savage, who has not yet lost his sense of judgement and independence, with despair.

> 'I don't want comfort. I want God, I want poetry, I want real danger, I want freedom, I want goodness. I want sin.'
> 'In fact', said Mustapha Mond, 'you're claiming the right to be unhappy.'
> 'All right then,' said the Savage defiantly, 'I'm claiming the right to be unhappy. Not to mention the right to grow old and ugly and impotent.' [27]

Brave New World depicts a failed effort at social engineering for creating a happy or, rather, comfortable, future centrally, by coercion. Also doomed is the individual strategy of taking 'soma' or anything alike that is numbing and gives a 'holiday from the facts'. These are likely to create a negative utopia socially or personally.

Even though a government can do a lot for social progress and the reduction of human suffering, it cannot guarantee us happiness.[28] Neither can corporations. Anybody who promises to spare us the effort needed to accomplish a good life is likely to want our freedom or our money, or both.

Negative feelings and positive feelings are not opposites

The economics of happiness fundamentally measures happiness in one dimension: the happy–unhappy scale. Unhappiness is the lower end point of the scale, which then gradually rises all the way to full happiness. This may be a useful measure for modelling, but it might suggest to others that it is enough to add a little happiness, drop by drop, to unhappiness in order to reach total happiness, as if the issue is just a matter of quantity: is there enough happiness?

Back in the late 1960s, in a pioneering survey the American psychologist Norman M. Bradburn explored the detailed patterns of mental health in a normal population, focusing on the relationship between an individual's life situation and his psychological reactions to that situation.[29] In other words, how 'normal' people react to the everyday stress and strains of life. He came to the conclusion that negative feelings and positive feelings are not simply opposites on a linear scale, but have different characteristics and explanations.

Neurophysiology confirms all this with research findings on brain asymmetry. Positive and negative emotions are associated with activation of different brain areas.[30] Using magnetic resonance imaging (functional MRI) technology, it has been shown that the left prefrontal cortex is more active when the subject feels happy. In contrast, the right prefrontal cortex is more active when one is sad. In addition, positive feelings and negative feelings are associated with different neurotransmitters.[31] Dopamine motivates action – for example, eating or mating – and rewards this with pleasure, while the acetylcholine neurotransmitter is responsible for stopping action and depression.

In addition, a range of seemingly contradictory feelings can be present in a person at the same time. Ed Diener, a pioneering psychologist of the study of subjective well-being, and his colleagues found that good feelings do not exclude unpleasant ones.[32] Pleasure and displeasure are two different types of feelings that can be experienced at the same time if one of them is of low intensity. For example, someone can be both restless and optimistic. Exceptions to this are extreme conditions, emotional peaks or ups and downs which may bring overwhelmingly extreme feelings of one sort.

It is thus clear that happiness is not just the lack of unhappiness, but that these are fundamentally different from each other. They are not simply two end points on a continuous scale. Beyond that, we can have a myriad of different feelings in parallel or within a brief period of time. And happiness does not necessarily mean that we are full of good feelings – joy, gratitude, enthusiasm, confidence, optimism – but it can also mean that we are satisfied with our lives beyond our current feelings, or that we can trust that our life has meaning.

Forced positivity

The downside of popular happiness guides can be the denial of and disregard for hardship and suffering. In the worst case, it can even lead to insensitive victim-blaming, stigmatizing the suffering person: 'you could be happy if you really wanted to be!' This simplistic approach seems to ignore that anyone may suffer a great loss, or that simply moving from one stage of life to another is typically accompanied by a smaller or larger crisis (called normative crisis). Not to mention our diverse emotional resources related strongly to our early life experiences.

This simplistic 'positive' approach can also mean that it makes the individual responsible for things that actually stem from harmful external circumstances. It may be that the individual suffers from things like the deficient public health treatment of mental health problems; or inadequate social policy not providing a sense of basic safety; or the corporate culture being based on exploitation and impersonality; or inadequate urban planning causing stress and isolation together with traffic noise and limited access to community spaces or green areas. And while a heroic person can cope with these or even more extreme external situations, others are not able to, and it is not right to label this as a personal failure.

'Positivity' can also be forced, or even toxic because it can nail one to the superficial pattern of 'keep smiling', where one wants to feign happiness as a sign of success in life. Suppression can actually make coping with unpleasant emotions, challenging events and external shocks more difficult. A negative feeling or experience does not disappear simply because we ignore it. If we actively look away from something, our neck will be strained and we will not see one part of the world. Denial may deter necessary healing and psychic development, and move a person away from their authentic existence.

Therefore, it is worth expanding our vision of reality with additional dimensions beyond happiness.

The value of 'mixed feelings'

It is especially helpful for someone to be able to experience 'mixed feelings', with good and bad feelings at the same time. First of all, it has positive impact on health. Among those people who were observed to have intense 'mixed feelings' there was a much smaller rate of deterioration in health over a ten-year period than in others.[33] There is plenty of further research suggesting that these people are more resilient and better able to adapt to a new life situation.

What could it mean to 'experience mixed feelings'? A specific example: gratitude also appears when a widow talks sadly about her deceased spouse. Or someone in a tough situation discovers the opportunity inherent in the situation and this makes them feel hope, respect or kindness. Such was the 'how we enjoy prison' initiative with which Ferenc Mérei (1909–86), the Hungarian psychologist, made his prison years bearable. Mérei was sentenced to ten years in prison in 1958 for 'anti-state conspiracy'. During his imprisonment he taught his fellow prisoners languages, and he and his peers invented the 'enjoy the prison!' action. It was then that he also created his four-volume masterpiece, the *Psychological Diary*, written on toilet paper for lack of anything better, which was then smuggled out of prison in batches. After his release, he chose psychodrama as his field of interest. He remained able to create, play and connect with others, curiously, both during and after prison.

A precondition for this is the ability to find good feelings even in a trying situation, without denying the suffering and its intensity. Herein lies man's inner freedom: in any difficult situation, we have a choice as to what attitude we take. It is this inner freedom that makes us flexible and resilient amid challenging external circumstances.

Less is more: the pitfalls of maximizing

The basic premise of classical microeconomics is that individuals seek to maximize utility. What does this mean? When it comes to spending money, the question is how to spend it in such a way that you get as much utility (pleasure) as possible. In every case, one strives for as much pleasure as possible; this is what guides the person's actions. This may sound right and rational at first, and we may think it is a realistic and good endeavour. What would be the problem with that?

'Maximizers'

There is ever more evidence that this is a problematic strategy. One of the elementary traps in the search for happiness is insatiable greed, as argued in Chapter 2. Based on this, it seems that it is not worth striving for as much happiness as possible – at least not in the 'hedonic' dimension of happiness. It may not be even worth striving for the 'most' in anything, actually. Why not?

On the one hand, it is beyond a person's reach, since their brain is not a perfect supercomputer. Herbert A. Simon (1916–2001), a Nobel Prize-winning American economist and cognitive psychologist, criticized the basic assumption of economics that man strives for as much as possible. In a sterile model a researcher can presume this, but in reality it does not hold because the world is way too complex and human rationality is limited. According to Simon, in the real world, therefore, one does not strive for the maximum but, rather, for satisfaction, for something that suffices. He calls this strategy *'satisficing'*, which comes from the words 'satisfying' and 'sufficing'. This strategy means that a person searches only until an option reaches their threshold of acceptability. That is, instead of the best possible, they strive for something which is 'good enough'.

Why might it not be worth it to strive for the maximum? What could be wrong with someone aspiring for the best possible?

American psychologist Barry Schwartz and his co-authors have conducted numerous experiments on this topic. The 'maximizing' life strategy was identified based on a number of different life situations.[34] For example:

- When I watch TV, I channel surf, often scanning through the available options even while attempting to watch one program.
- I treat relationships like clothing: I expect to try a lot on before I get the perfect fit.
- No matter how satisfied I am with my job, it's only right for me to be on the lookout for better opportunities.
- I often fantasize about living in ways that are quite different from my actual life.
- I'm a big fan of lists that attempt to rank things (the best movies, the best singers, the best athletes, the best novels, etc.).
- When shopping, I have a hard time finding clothing that I really love.
- No matter what I do, I have the highest standards for myself.
- I never settle for second best.
- Whenever I'm faced with a choice, I try to imagine what all the other possibilities are, even ones that aren't present at the moment.

Based on the responses of 1,750 participants, the researchers found that 'maximizing' behaviour was associated with lower happiness, optimism and self-esteem and a higher incidence of depression and remorse. That is, people are much more likely to regret their decision, to fantasize about 'what would have happened' or even to gather information about missed opportunities.

'Maximizers' are very likely to keep comparing themselves to others, which makes them more vulnerable. The researchers looked closely at two different groups of students, the 'maximizers' (those who scored high in the maximization questionnaire survey, the upper third) and those who are 'satisfied' (those who had a low score, the lower third). Students were told this was a 'cognitive performance' survey. Each of them completed tests in a lab, while a putative other participant – who was actually an undercover team member – completed the task spectacularly faster or slower than the student. It was then assessed how this experience affected students.

The two groups reacted completely differently. Those 'maximizers' who experienced that their partner was faster than them started to question their own abilities and felt worse. Students in the 'satisfied' group, on the other hand, barely reacted to their partner's performance. They did not care and they were not particularly affected by it.

Beyond these features, one might think that the 'maximizers' might not simply want the most in life, but could well be disconnected from what they have already and keep seeking joy elsewhere. Would they notice that they already have the 'best' job, the 'best' partner? Would they notice if they are just having the 'best' moment in life? In the tale of the *The Fisherman and his Wife*, gratitude could have made the couple both wealthy and happy.

The attitude of searching a 'best' thing out in the world may easily underestimate our creative power as humans, may forget about our role as co-creators of our experiences. It is through our presence, our dedication and our abilities that a particular film, a job, a partner will show its 'best' and has a chance to become the 'best' for us. In my view, our 'best' world is not independent from us, not an external reward, but originates from the quality of our presence and our ability to relate. These are skills we can learn, practise and over time gradually master.

Aiming for perfection may well be the fulfilment of an older conviction, life plan or pattern, running in the family, in the community or in the society. We may have very fixed ideas about what would make us happy, and these may prevent us from actually becoming happy.[35] It is as if we viewed life as a running race and saw ourselves placed at the starting line, and all we knew is that we have to run the best time in our lane. Are we sure that it is our lane, our race?

Overall, therefore, a 'maximizing' (striving for as much as possible, the best) life strategy has a myriad of adverse psychological consequences.

Not an endless peak experience

Excessive happiness can also be an obstacle in life. Research has shown that intense positive feelings can lead to overconfidence, riskier behaviour, lower cognitive performance and less political participation, and lower the chances of re-employment.[36] People in elated mood tend to perform worse in moral dilemmas, or are more likely to use stereotypes in their person-perceptions than those who are in a neutral emotional state or a sad mood.[37] In experiments, intense bouts of positive feelings were found to have potentially negative health effects.[38]

Adam Grant and Barry Schwartz speak of an 'inverted U-shape': positive traits and states have benefits, but only up to a certain limit, where their effects turn negative.[39] Their approach was inspired by the Aristotelian mean, which will be explained in more detail in the next chapter.

An extremely positive emotional wave is not a permanent condition, so the question is, what is before it and what follows after? It may be that it is preceded or followed by a particularly bad feeling or period, thus it is an experience of a strong emotional contrast.[40] Looking back to this peak state from the perspective of, say, a week or a month, what does one feel about it? Is this positive episode pleasant or unpleasant?

Thus, research shows that extreme happiness does not help people to see clearly, perform well intellectually or even adapt properly to a situation. They are overwhelmed by what they are experiencing – and that makes the world small for them. More successful are those who 'just' feel good, but not terrifically.

We can say that happiness is not a continuous peak experience but, rather, an optimal state in which there can also be unpleasant feelings that we are able to be with, and in which we can experience the variability of feelings. It also includes having bad moods and unpleasant feelings from time to time, provided they are not lasting. Feelings such as anger, shame, sadness, anxiety, guilt, restlessness, disgust, belong to life, are often warning signals and can trigger a necessary change or inspire action. Dissatisfaction, for example, can inspire political activism or social engagement.

Happiness with a thousand faces: aspects for personal investigation

Our brain can be taught vital skills for emotional well-being. We can learn to deal with our negative and positive impulses and feelings, as well as to choose the right actions which benefit us. This ability is the key to our development. To this end, various approaches are available. Mindfulness practice takes the approach of awareness of all emotions and experiences without trying to deny, hide or resist them or immediately aspiring to change them. With an attitude of curiosity, friendliness and attunement to the present moment we can be more aware of our feelings and physical needs, which helps to accept ourselves and our situation as they are. It can largely reduce the negative impact of difficult events and feelings, and, thereby, acute and chronic stress as well. Positive psychology takes an approach based on action: it has developed certain practices that help to increase well-being, for example gratitude, or awareness of character strengths. Somatic and experiential methods integrate somatic and emotional awareness, sensing what 'is' with a playful and curious exploration of what 'could be' (Chapter 7).

As shown, there is no problem with happiness per se; in fact, it is a great indicator of someone's being well. This is why it is good measure of quality of life, and is already applied as one of the new indicators of social progress.

Happiness is not simply an indicator of being well. In addition, happiness has been shown to have a number of consequences on behaviours that are crucial in our response to contemporary challenges, including future orientation, self-restraint, cooperation and social engagement. From this, one might conclude that one should do everything possible to get happier. This, however, may not hold. In this chapter, two possible happiness-seeking strategies have been refuted: 'forced positivity' and 'happiness-greed'. The analyses of large-scale databases show that the search for as much happiness as possible does not lead to a 'good life' (which means mental stability, physical health, supportive relationships, adaptability to new situations, resilience). It may lead to avoiding or ignoring bad feelings, which does not make them disappear or have an impact. Instead, it is more desirable to develop a proper attitude to bad feelings. Naturally, extreme mental suffering requires external support, and also professional help. Currently only one quarter of those who need help receive treatment. Richard Layard argues that mental health issues should be put to the front of the welfare system.[41]

The challenge is how to relate to the negative feelings and suffering in ourselves and in the world without becoming paralysed, helpless or overwhelmed by them. For this, a spacious perspective can help, and absence of exclusive identification with a negative feeling, experience or problem.

Happiness may be a good (but not only and not exclusive) sign of a life well lived, but seeking happiness (or pleasure or joy) directly may not be the best life strategy, as will be argued in the next two chapters.

Exploring the refined and multifaceted nature of our own well-being could help us to take care of ourselves as well as relate to others well. To do this, the reader may want to ponder on the following questions.

- Which aspect of well-being seems to be relatively little cultivated in your life: enjoying the present moment through the senses, ability to relax, feeling content, acting for a meaningful life, avoiding automatic reactions to anger, sadness or other unpleasant feelings? (If you find it useful, you could spend some time with a thought experiment, imagining what would change in your life experience, had you had a transformation in this respect.)

- Are there written or unwritten rules in your family, in your work, about what kind of feeling 'should not be shown'? Can positive feelings, enjoyment and happiness be shown and shared with others? What are these rules? How could they be formulated as brief statements?
- Can you be present with integrity and the fullness of your emotions, sensations and thoughts in your important relationships, in your work, with your colleagues? If yes, how does it affect you and what does it enable? If no, what would it be like if that happened?
- What is your measure for 'good enough'? What helps you to rejoice in what you have?

These are questions that can be answered – but it may well be that there is no ultimate answer to them, just the 'best possible' answer for the current situation and time.

4

Sustainable Hedonism

One may see a conflict between living well and living fair. Two strong opposing forces affect us: the human quest for pleasure and good life and the external call to reduce our resource use, with the adjustment of personal life-styles. The former relates to our pleasure-seeking self, the latter calls upon our moral, value-seeking self.

How could values that might seem distant, such as ecological balance, solidarity and the common good, override what is immediate, personal and enjoyable? Why would people curb their consumption and adjust their habits if it feels like a loss to them? Why would anybody choose voluntary simplicity amid the constant lures of abundance? Why would anyone opt for minimalism in the world of maximizers? Ecologically responsible behaviour is often perceived as a loss of happiness and life quality, evoking resistance or even anger.

If this is so, only a tiny minority will seek an austerely simple life and not mind abstaining from life's normal pleasures. We may call them ecological hermits.

The idea of loss is unlikely to motivate to adjustment. A more viable path is to refine and fine-tune our relationship to joy. We need to find a life strategy that both is joyful and does no harm to others and does not endanger our future on this planet. I call this *sustainable hedonism*.

Resource overuse and the 'global rich'

Our consumption has gradually outgrown the limited resources of our planet. World Overshoot Day fell on 29 July in 2019, a calculated illustrative calendar date on which humanity's resource consumption for the year exceeds the Earth's capacity to regenerate those resources that year.[1] In 2020, the date fell on 22 August, given the economic contraction related to the COVID-19 pandemic. Using another metric, the world's population demands 64 per cent more than what nature can regenerate in one year – through overfishing, over-harvesting our forests and, primarily, emitting more carbon dioxide than our ecosystems can absorb.[2] In the 25 years from 1990 to 2015, annual global carbon emissions grew by 60 per cent, approximately doubling total global cumulative emissions.[3] The impacts include wildlife habitat loss and fragmentation, collapsing fisheries and climate change.

Our global elite, in particular, pose both an environmental problem and a cultural problem if we take them as our standard for comparison. According to an analysis of Oxfam and the Stockholm Environment Institute covering 117 countries, people of higher income levels contribute a growing amount to global carbon emissions. The average per capita consumption emissions linked to the top 1 per cent in 2015 were over 100 times greater than the average per capita consumption emissions of the poorest half of the world's population. The emissions of this top 1 per cent were estimated to originate predominantly from rich people living in North America, the Middle East and North Africa, China, Europe and Russia/Central Asia.[4]

The global rich seem to be addicted to overconsumption, and to carbon-rich travel in particular. A minority of the world's richest citizens have a disproportionate impact. One question is political: how to curb individual rights to pollute, or nudge people toward self-restraint and pro-environmental life-styles. Another question is the social role of the wealthy elite. Do we see them as role models? Do we envy their life-styles? Would we do the same if we had the chance? How would we spend our higher income or an unexpected fortune like a lottery gain? On the other hand, we cannot point our finger at the super-rich, as most of us are already part of the problem as well. The mainstream standard for consumption has become oversized.

Many of us living in the Western world are actually rich in global terms, and our overconsumption is also part of the ecological problem. The top 10 per cent (those with incomes above $38,000 a year) were linked to nearly half of global emissions, similar to the middle 40 per cent, the global middle-class (see Table 4.1). The emissions linked to the top 10 per cent grew by nearly as much as the middle 40 per cent over the previous 25 years. This highlights a clear global injustice, as it leaves practically no scope for the world's poorest households to increase their consumption, given the limited global carbon budget.

Given the crucial role of the global rich, let us explore the geographical distribution of their carbon emissions. A large share of the emissions of the global rich (the top 10 per cent income group of the global population) were estimated to originate from people living

Table 4.1: Carbon emissions associated with the consumption of individuals in different global income groups

Global income groups	Income per capita ($)	2015 emissions		Total cumulative emissions (1990–2015)	
		Share of total carbon emissions (%)	Per capita average carbon emissions (tCO2)	GtCO2	%
Top 0.1%	Above 402,000	4	216.7	32	4
Top 1%	Above 109,000	15	74.0	111	15
Top 10%	Above 38,000	49	23.5	372	52
Middle 40%	6,000–38,000	44	5.3	299	41
Bottom 50%	0–6,000	7	0.7	51	7
Total		100	4.8	722	100

Source: Nathan et al (2020) tables 2 and 3. Adapted by the author with the permission of Oxfam, www.oxfam.org.uk. Oxfam does not necessarily endorse any text or activities that accompany the data, nor has it approved these adapted tables.

in North America and Europe (16 per cent and 8.5 per cent in 2015, respectively – Table 4.2). During the past 25 years, the rapidly growing and industrializing countries gained a larger proportion. The emissions of the global rich residing in China, India and in the Middle East and North Africa have risen considerably.

These are relative shares within global emissions, highlighting the disproportionate share of the rich. In addition, the absolute level of emissions has reached an unsustainable level.

According to carbon footprint calculations, US citizens are demanding four and a half times the resources and waste that our planet can regenerate and absorb in the atmosphere.[5] UK citizens need over two and a half planets. Currently, all EU countries are above this planetary limit, including lower-income countries such as Bulgaria, Romania and Croatia. These figures are national averages, but highlight the magnitude of the problem. Everyone can easily check their own personal footprint or their own Overshoot Day with online tools like the personal footprint calculator.[6] Based on this, it seems rather clear that our economic system as well as our personal behaviour requires a radical adjustment.[7]

Table 4.2: The global rich and their shares of total carbon emissions by region, 1990 and 2015 (%)

	1990	2015
Global rich: top 10% income group	50	49
Of which: people living in North America	21.2	16.0
Europe	14.2	8.5
China	0.2	7.3
Other Asia	5.1	4.7
Middle East and North Africa	1.8	4.5
Russia/Central Asia	4.7	2.6
India	0.1	1.9
Latin America	1.3	1.3
Sub-Saharan Africa	0.6	0.9
Other rich	0.8	0.9
Global middle-class: middle 40% income group	42	44
Global poor: bottom 50% income group	8	7
Total	100	100

Note: Shares of total carbon emissions associated with individuals in different global income groups from different countries and regions. These are income groups of the global population; thus, in a high-income country more than 10 per cent of the population may be part of the global rich.

Source: Nathan et al (2020), table 5.

The urgent call for adjustment of our life-styles is clear, and yet it often evokes resistance and a sense of loss. It presents as a loss of entitlement and a loss of hedonic pleasure, both of which seem unacceptable in a general culture of *radical hedonism*, reinforced by the positive appraisal of material consumption. In this worldview, a personal choice of voluntary simplicity is simply foolish and irrational – so much so that facts and scientific evidence may also be dismissed, which is an easy way to solve the potential inner conflict. Maintaining old habits is regarded as a legitimate defence of personal freedom, rather than a resistance to change. A variant of this is to delegate all responsibility for the solution to others, the 'big players', big corporations or governments, which is partly rational (given the importance of these actors), but fails to address the personal ethical aspect of the issue, which is our personal response based on our belonging to and responsibility for the world.

Beyond the personal psychological elements, cultural aspects play a major role. Any critical adjustment of life-styles is hindered by the general culture of pleasure-seeking, often in its radical form.

Radical hedonists

Our simplified 21st-century version of hedonism encourages *radical hedonism*, unrestrained, egoist pleasure-seeking. Consumer society inflates desires and encourages their unrestricted satisfaction through consumption. This approach implicitly holds that momentary desire equals real need. According to Erich Fromm, *radical hedonism* is when the ultimate aim of life is the maximum pleasure and fulfilment of any desire a person may feel.[8] In *radical hedonism*, enjoyment is the ultimate goal, the only one to which all actions and aspirations are directed. Life is best when there is as much pleasure as possible, while keeping the pain to a minimum.

The *radical hedonist* does not assess how their actions affect others, but seeks pleasure primarily as their own pleasure. They tend to view another person as an object that is more or less useful, depending on whether they are helping or hindering their enjoyment. *Radical hedonism* is often coupled with selfishness, exploitation of others, materialism and excessive consumption.

At the societal level, this leads to a lack of solidarity, wealth hidden in tax havens and the depletion of the planet's resources. The *radical hedonist* is a slave of searching for pleasure, so much so that their perception is dulled: they opaquely see the other person, or the next generation, or perhaps even their future self. So they do not do what is good for themselves or others in the long run.

We may easily spot a radical hedonist in someone else. But who would admit it of oneself? This is especially true when we take our desires, our needs as given. An exploration of the subject, together with a friendly self-examination can be helpful.

The art of enjoying life: ancient hedonism

Classical hedonism is quite different from its simplified, 21st-century version. Aristippus and Epicurus, the ancient hedonists, enjoyed all that the present had to offer, they were masters of pleasure, but they also taught the importance of inner freedom: one should not become a slave to desires.

Abounding pleasures: the ultra-hedonists

A distinct and radical school is Cyrenaic hedonism, founded by Aristippus of Cyrene (435–356 BC). The remnants of the text expressing his views are fragmented, so one can only deduce what the whole worldview might have been like.[9]

Aristippus lived in prodigal luxury, surrounded by an abundance of perfumes, clothes and women.[10] He openly kept a lover, the courtesan Lais, which was considered scandalous at the time. He enjoyed the extravagance of the Elder Dionysius, the Greek tyrant of Syracuse, and that of his son, Dionysius II, in whose courts he spent part of his life.

Many of his contemporaries blamed him for his waste, for how much money he spent on delicacies and feasts. When a young man once challenged him on this, Aristippus answered with a question, "Wouldn't you have bought this if you could have got it for three obols?" The answer being in the affirmative, "Very well, then," said Aristippus, "I am no longer a lover of pleasure, it is you who are a lover of money."[11] Once, when the servant carrying the coins collapsed under their burden, Aristippus encouraged him to throw away most of his load and keep only what he could comfortably carry. His independence from money is also mentioned in a script describing that, while sailing at sea, he threw his money into the sea as pirates approached.[12]

He was a disciple of Socrates, and he seems to have had a deep curiosity about the why and how of life. He was born in Cyrene, in ancient Libya, and came to Greece for the Olympic Games. There he inquired of Socrates, and what he heard captivated him. He definitely wanted to meet Socrates, so he went to Athens to find him and get to know him. Aristippus became a disciple of Socrates and remained with him until his death and execution (399 BC). Unlike his master, however, Aristippus sought payment for his philosophical teachings, as the first of Socrates' disciples. Through his way of life and choices, he also gained the attention, and sometimes anger, of his philosopher contemporaries.

However, according to contemporary writings, Aristippus was not influenced by circumstances; in the face of bad luck and in the midst of adversity, he maintained a deep calmness. He was able to adapt well to an event, its actors and circumstances, playing a role that was just right for the situation. Dionysius liked him more than anyone else because he could always turn the situation around.[13] While in Asia,

Aristippus was taken prisoner by Artaphernes, a Persian satrap. "Can you be cheerful under these circumstances?" some one asked. "Yes, you simpleton," was the reply, "for when should I be more cheerful than now that I am about to converse with Artaphernes [having learnt that from Socrates]?" He enjoyed what was just present and did not bother to seek something that was not at hand.

He could enjoy life infinitely, but at the same time he considered it important not to become addicted to pleasures. He wanted to enjoy the pleasures on offer freely, with inner freedom. When one day he entered the house of a courtesan, one of the young men with him blushed. Then Aristippus remarked: "It is not going in that is dangerous, but being unable to go out."[14] With regard to pleasures, he held that "it is not abstinence from pleasures that is best, but mastery over them without ever being worsted".[15]

The ultra-hedonists (the Cyrenaics) thus considered the enjoyment experienced in the present to be the greatest, especially bodily pleasure. The role of the senses was of critical importance, as bodily pleasure comes to man through these.

Luxury and extravagance were a natural part of life, but were coupled with an inner independence. Aristippus was a philosopher, a devoted disciple of Socrates, who asked for money for his philosophical teaching, but it happened that he threw away money or just threw it into the sea. As for philosophy, it was also an instrument of civilizing and inner independence, ensuring ease in social life and providing a deep serenity in the midst of adversity. The ultra-hedonists enjoyed life abundantly, as it was just present, but did not long for something that was not. Their power over pleasures meant that they enjoyed the present to the fullest, but they were also able to step out of an enjoyable situation. They confessed and lived the possibility of pleasure, without the compulsion of it.

Moderate pleasures: Epicurus

Fifteen years after the death of Aristippus, Epicurus (341–271 BC) was born, who carried on and moderated the earlier hedonist teaching.[16] He began to practise philosophy early on, at the age of 12–14. For him, philosophy, the quest of wisdom, was not just a theoretical subject but a practice, a way of life. This remained the case later in his life, as evidenced by the Epicurean communities he founded.

According to Epicurus, humans instinctively do what gives them pleasure.[17] Epicureans, by examining the behaviour of the infant, came to the conclusion that the infant seeks at every moment what gives him pleasure and avoids pain, so this is the basic law of life. They also studied the behaviour of adults, although they regarded this phenomenon much more ambiguous, as adults are influenced by their own beliefs and social system, which can easily steer them in the 'wrong' direction.

The definition of pleasure by Epicurus is astonishing: according to him, it is a state of rest ('*ataraxia*'), and moderate asceticism leads to it. This recipe is in stark contrast to the Cyrenaics, who enjoyed extravagance and abundance. Epicurus' approach to pleasure is so peculiar that instead of a hedonist, he could be called a 'tranquilist'.[18]

According to Epicurus, the happiest life is where one is free from fear and need. In such a life, a person is not afraid of gods and death and he is master of his own needs. Epicurus, thus, does not profess the principle of 'the more pleasure, the better', nor does he hold that we should obey our impulses or follow our desires. No, not at all. According to him, these are not external endowments, objective things, but we are partly responsible for what we wish for ourselves. Therefore he discouraged people from visiting fairs because these entice.

Desires, he said, should be limited to 'necessary and natural desires', such as for food and lodging, and thus a simple life. There is no need for 'vain and empty desires'. According to Epicurus, we must avoid developing wasteful, luxurious demands that can be difficult to satisfy later. Is not such a life extremely boring, his critics have suggested. It would certainly be boring for most people, Epicurus nodded in agreement, but that would be only because they were 'spoiled', he added. Ingratitude is the cause of the proliferation of desires. If one has cleansed and diminished his desires, he will enjoy their fulfilment, and a simple life will be bliss for him.

Epicureans say that pleasure or pain can be spiritual – in fact, this can be even more intense than a physical experience. Thus, the Cyrenaics' interpretation of pleasure or pain – who thought that these were based on bodily sensations – was broadened. While physical pleasures and pains always occur in the present, spiritual pleasures and pains can come from the present, but also from the past and the future. Recalling a painful past experience, such as being taunted at school, is painful in the present. Remembering a past experience, for example winning a race, is joyful. Anxiety about the future, such as punishment from a god, causes spiritual pain in the present. The thought of future joyful event, such as the birth of a child, can be a source of joy in the moment.

Recalling the sweet experiences of the past was an prominent practice of the Epicureans. Everyone was encouraged to do so, and Epicurus supposedly mastered the practice himself. When he was dying, he was able to bear calmly the immeasurable bodily pain caused by gallstones by thinking back to an old philosophical conversation with a friend.[19]

Researching the nature of pleasure, the Epicureans argued that pleasure may come either from the gratification of desire or from a state of calm free of desires, termed by them as 'moving' and 'static' pleasure. 'Moving pleasure' is the process of satisfying a desire, that is, feeding a hungry person, for example, when he takes pleasure in eating. 'Static pleasure' is a state of calm, that is, when one is already full, when a person is free from desire, not hungry any more. Epicurus considers this pleasure to be of higher value than the former, the pleasure of satisfying desire. Enjoying satiety is therefore, in his view, a nobler pleasure than the enjoyment experienced while eating. According to Epicurus, therefore, a happy life is a state of calm, a state of freedom from desires.

He asserts that it is not achievable alone, and the company of friends and a community are much needed. In this community, through trust, we can practise the abilities that help to bring tranquillity and to curb desires. Such a community is able to protect against external troubles, and it is the support of this community that provides peace of mind. Epicurus not only taught about this, but also sought to accomplish it in his own life.

He established communities first in Mytilene and Lampsacus; then, when he travelled to Athens in 306 BC, he founded the Garden there.[20] The Garden was both a school of philosophy and a community of practice where they sought to live according to the teaching. The Epicurean community was inclusive, ensuring equality for its members, and was open to women and all classes of society, which was extraordinary at the time. Epicurus was famous for his kindness. In his will, he ensured the survival of the Epicurean community both financially and mentally, for example by prescribing certain ritual festivals. These included the birthdays of himself and other important Epicureans. Epicurean communities were popular and widespread throughout the Greek world.

Epicurus also proclaims freedom from fear. You cannot be happy if you are afraid of the possible plagues of the future. Be content with little and trust that you will be able to deal with the difficulties of the future when the time comes. 'Don't fear god, don't worry about death; what's good is easy to get, and what's terrible is easy to endure.'[21]

In sum, Epicurus, encourages us to take pleasure seriously, but also calls for domination over 'vain and empty desires', a simple life that results in tranquillity. It is a path of awareness and self-restraint towards individual happiness, supporting and strengthening each other in community. This approach is close to the contemporary practice of mindfulness, which aims to purposefully bring one's attention to experiences occurring in the present moment through meditation or other training.

The ancient Greek hedonist philosophers Aristippus and Epicurus and their followers enjoyed the present, but one could also argue that they did so because they could not do better. They did not believe in the existence of the 'cosmos', the perfect order of the celestial spheres and of the world. They did not think that their actions could have a significant effect on the course of the world. Therefore, they were not active in politics either.

In contrast, Aristotle saw all human actions in the larger context of the cosmos, community, and political life was an inherent part of this. Aristotle did not think much of the life of enjoyment, regarding it superficial as it is based only on the reception of things and is slavish to tastes. In contrast, he thought the highest good must be something that is ours and not easily taken away from us. His ethic was not centred on pleasures but, rather, on '*flourishing life*' (which will be discussed in detail in the next chapter). He was not a hedonist philosopher, but he engaged with their ideas and developed his own approach to pleasure and pain.

Aristotle: the school of 'good' pleasures

Receiving pleasure and pain is a matter of habit, and it can be trained, learnt. A right kind of education is one that teaches children how to receive pleasure and pain from the 'proper objects', says Aristotle, referring to Plato. Childhood education and the habits we grow up with have a decisive influence on our later lives: what we find joy in and whether we are able to give up a momentary enjoyment for a long-term goal or higher value that is important to us.[22] Childhood education, a greater focus on emotional skills and mental well-being, could largely enhance the ability of future generations to act in a pro-social and pro-environmental way.

In his concept of education, Aristotle includes not only parents and educators but also the state and political life, within which a person acquires experience. In our current approach in this book, the latter includes social norms, referring to an (often tacit) agreement on what we consider to be appropriate and correct. Major important current social issues include direct advertising targeting children, the norms related to meals and snacks at school and at home, as well as the use of mobile phones, the internet and the media, just to name a few examples.

Although childhood education is extremely important, we do not have to give up on learning and the possibility of change later. Aristotle also suggests that as adults we should learn from a wiser man.

The sign of successful learning is a growing inner freedom that enables a person to recognize their real needs, what serves their own good and what serves others, and to gain self-control. This reduces the suffering from desires. At the same time, their inner peace and joy grow.

The intriguing question today is what do we consider necessary and what optional. What is our personal strategy? Are we deviating from what we consider to be the social norm? What do we consider 'necessary', 'optional' and 'neutral' in our own lives? Has there been a change in this respect, and what has changed?

Scrutinizing desires: 'necessary' and 'optional' things

Desires are often signs of real needs, but not always. Aristotle distinguishes between necessary and optional things. Physical needs, such as food, are necessary things, while victory, wealth or honour are not necessary, but are 'worthy of choice' (Figure 4.1). The philosopher thus does not see money, power and glory as avoidable or bad in themselves, and says that they are neither naturally worth choosing nor naturally avoidable. They are neutral in themselves, and it is the way they are used that makes them either a tool for or a barrier to a virtuous life. An important test for this is friendship and human relationships, as discussed later in detail.

Contemporary psychological experiments by Kirk Warren Brown et al found that people with *materialist values* spend more money on purchases of necessities than do those scoring lower in materialism (calculating with the same income level), and that *materialists* make more discretionary purchases, acting upon their sudden impulses.[23] These findings imply that those who seek pleasure in material terms tend to feel that they need more as 'necessity' than do those who are less materialist (with the same income level). If someone tends to assess their success, advancement and good life in the material dimension (implying money, power and reputation or, in the language of Aristotle, victory, wealth and honour), they are also more prone to seek pleasure in this way. It also implies that they have more 'necessities', fewer 'options' and thus ultimately less freedom (Figure 4.2, which presents my own interpretation of these findings).

Figure 4.1: 'Necessary' and 'optional' things, according to Aristotle

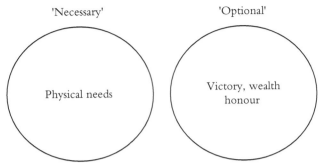

Source: Author's own.

Figure 4.2: The shift between 'necessary' and 'optional' things for materialistic people

Source: Author's own.

Aristotle also thinks that certain material goods are necessary for a good life: 'he is happy who is active in accordance with complete virtue and is sufficiently equipped with external goods, not for some chance period but throughout a complete life'.[24] He argues that many things can be achieved only through certain means, such as friends, wealth or political power. Among the basic things necessary for a happy life, he mentions health and food.

Basic needs in contemporary social science

Recent theorists of *basic needs*, including Manfred A. Max-Neef and Len Doyal and Ian Gough argue that there are a finite number of basic human needs that are universal and satiable.[25] They thus challenges the basic proposition that needs are infinite. We do not need to be stuck in an endless *hedonic treadmill*, always chasing our ever higher financial aspirations. 'Needs' differ from 'wants', and the solution lies in focusing on the 'needs' rather than being enslaved to 'wants'. On the other hand, Max-Neef argues that all of our *basic needs* need to be met, otherwise it generates a pathology for the individual or for the collective. The *basic needs* in his approach include not simply subsistence and protection, but also affection, participation, idleness, creation, identity and freedom. In general, if *basic needs* are finite, sustainable development is possible: we can provide a good life for all without damaging natural ecosystems.[26]

According to prominent social scientists of the past century, John Rawls and Amartya Sen, there are universal principles of justice, and there are also general basic human needs that a just society must care about.[27] Rawls argues that certain *primary goods* (including *natural primary goods* such as health, intelligence and creativity, as well as *social primary goods* with basic liberties and opportunities) enable people to have a sense of self-worth and pursue their goals with self-confidence. Amartya Sen, a Nobel Prize-winning economist, speaks of access to basic life opportunities, so-called *'capabilities'* for all.[28] Sen did not provide a comprehensive list of basic capabilities but, rather, outlined the philosophical framework and provided some examples, including the avoidance of poverty and deprivation.

Sen's concept was applied by Martha Nussbaum: she organized women's groups for jointly formulating the basic needs as well as the desirable dimensions of a good life.[29] Ten *'central human capabilities'* are identified: life; bodily health; bodily integrity; senses, imagination and thought; emotions; practical reason; affiliation; other species; play; and control over one's environment.[30]

This approach goes beyond the level of physical necessities and includes a number of elements which are related to a full life in a non-materialistic sense. I particularly welcome the inclusion of creativity and playful existence, as it resonates with the experiential work presented in Part III of this book. However, we do not all want to play the same way. Nussbaum added that the actualization of these items has to take into consideration local and individual differences. According to these theorists, these basic human needs could be satisfied in a wide variety of ways among individuals in different cultures.

The golden mean of pleasures

Regarding pleasure, Aristotle suggests a mean state, which we could now call a golden mean. Those who taste all kinds of pleasure and abstain from none lose their self-control. The price of excess enjoyment is both moral obscurity and suffering. At the other extreme, according to Aristotle, those who avoid all pleasures become dull and lose their faculty of perception. Modern science also warns of the radical pursuit of hedonic impulses, as it reduces our own well-being and health.

The Buddha, Siddhartha Gautama, who lived probably a few years before Aristotle in ancient India, taught about the '*Middle Way*' between self-indulgence and asceticism. While ordinary people may suffer from the former, monks could be addicted to self-mortification, extreme self-denial in order to liberate themselves from their physical constraints. The Buddha warned against both extremes. He experienced both of them, and neither brought him happiness or spiritual awakening.

Gautama was born as an aristocrat and lived in luxury and abundance until the age of 29, when he was confronted by suffering in the outside world. He resolved then to renounce his wealth and family. He left his palace during the night to become a wandering ascetic. He explored various different teachings and practices, then turned to extreme asceticism, depriving himself of sleep and food and undergoing radical meditation exercises to silence his senses, to control his breath and his mind. It nearly cost him his life, but it did not bring spiritual awakening. So he abandoned this extreme ascetic approach and adjusted his quest.

According to a traditional story, the Buddha recognized the Middle Way as he sat on a river bank. Hearing someone playing a lyre in a passing boat, he realized that the string could be neither too tight nor too slack in order to make a pleasing sound.[31] The term Middle Way was stated in his very first teaching after his enlightenment, and he spoke of it as a path that led him to enlightenment. The Middle Way is the path of moderation, away from the extremes of self-indulgence and self-mortification. It is a path which is both physical and spiritual. It is not a static point but, rather, a dynamic path.

In our contemporary society, finding this middle way appears to be a collective challenge, affecting the majority of us. Self-indulgence is generally not regarded as a state out of balance but, rather, a sign of achievement and merit, as reflected by the overconsumption of the very rich today, who are seen as living a dream life in the eyes of many. As a counter force to this, there are ever more people experimenting with minimalist life-styles by reducing their consumption and number of possessions. Finding our own ideal mean state may take time, and may entail experiments of voluntary asceticism.

Wisdom in the enjoyment

According to Aristotle, pleasure and morality need to be connected. A person with 'practical wisdom' and moral virtue knows what is good for him and others. In contrast, in people who have been spoiled by pleasure or pain, the moral order becomes obscure, he says. Pleasure and pain are of vital importance, because 'the man who uses these well will be good, he who uses them badly bad'.[32] In our contemporary world, this implies that the pleasure of consumption cannot be detached from its ethical aspects, the impact of our actions. Addictive overconsumption leads to obscurity, and the loss of connection to the larger world beyond ourselves.

Excess enjoyment creates not only moral obscurity but also suffering. In the absence of self-control, pleasure is intertwined with pain: it is painful when pleasure is not available, in fact, all desire is accompanied by pain, says Aristotle. Suffering ends when we are free from desires.

What is freedom from desires like? Those who have attained self-mastery do not simply abstain from pleasure, but are glad to do so. There are no regrets, no pain involved. In contrast, self-restraint evokes suffering, as the person abstains from something they want and desire, so they are not yet in a state of self-mastery.

Self-control is the fruit of persistent practice and action; simply listening to teachings or philosophizing is not enough for it. Considering action is not a substitute for real action. The Indian poet Rabindranath Tagore wrote: 'You can't cross the sea merely by standing and staring at the water.'

A man with self-control can hold on to his vow, while one whose self-control is imperfect tends to deviate from his vow, the philosopher says. The latter is addicted to his desires, while the former is able, at his discretion, to resist the temptation of passion and lust. In this system, self-control and perseverance are among the good and desirable things, while lack of self-control is subordinate and reprehensible.

Most importantly, self-control and the cultivation of virtues lead ultimately to more, rather than less happiness, maintains Aristotle. His thoughts on pleasure belong to an ethical system related to the good life, which will be discussed in more detail in the next chapter.

Returning to one of our starting questions, whether the voluntary reduction of consumption (for example, for ecological reasons) reduces happiness, we can say that the ancient Greek philosophers argued that there is actually more happiness, rather than less, arising from a conscious, mindful relationship to desire, including self-control and the reduction of desires. Such a conscious attitude would also reduce our suffering and our moral obscurity. These ancient teachings are echoed in the contemporary approach of mindfulness.

Self-mastery does not need an ascetic self-denial but, rather, a golden mean or a Middle Way between self-indulgence and self-mortification, as argued by both Aristotle and the Buddha. To master the qualities for the path of the Middle Way we need a sustained and consistent practice. It is a path of getting ever more acquainted with the nature of our desires and longings, and both the suffering and the pleasure arising from them. An essential step is to become aware of ourselves in the context of the community and the larger world: our own desires and pleasures affect others as well, and may cause unnecessary suffering.

Our personal convictions about joy and pleasure

We all started our lives as hedonists. Our survival depended on it. We wanted to get what we needed, and as soon as possible. We cried when something hurt, to raise alarm and make it disappear. To begin with we lived in a symbiosis with our mother (biological mother or the main caregiver), not being able to differentiate ourselves from her, and, if she provided good care, we felt safe, powerful and almost omnipotent. We were able to steer the world according to our will, to provide us with as much joy as possible, and to make the pain, discomfort and displeasure disappear soon.

If someone has not received 'good enough' care during this early phase of life, they may well not be able to move on to the next levels of development (including self-transcendence and seeing oneself as part of the world, rather than the centre of it), and the state of deficiency within them may become perpetuated, such that they keep repeating this strategy, trying to fill the inner void. They may try to control the world to their liking, as if they were omnipotent.

As we become adults, with the development of our personality we usually outgrow this early, natural hedonism and the purpose of our lives will transform. Why, then, can the *radical hedonism* of our society affect many of us still so powerfully? The culture of overindulgence seems to resonate with something in us. Perhaps our early narcissistic life stage is reanimated. It may also be that the external seduction of pleasure meets our natural desire for joy and our deficit of joy in today's industrial society and our current life situation.

Either way, the theme of pleasure and joy belongs to us existentially, it preoccupies us and we must answer to it personally, and not just once but continuously.

Our desires are not given to us by fate. The basic assumption of economic models takes preferences and tastes for granted, not to be questioned. While this assumption respects individual freedom, it also hinders the reflection on our own freedom in forming these very tastes. Similarly, many of us tend to perceive our desires as natural and given, just as our eye colour. If we do so, we are more likely to either hand over control to our desires (overindulgence) or to suffer from unmet desires (suppression), or to live a mix of these strategies in distinct areas of our lives. For example, in our work life we may become bitter, due to self-denial day after day, hardly resembling our joyful and creative selves. In our after-work leisure time we may compensate for this with overindulgence in our consumption of food or media, as this feels necessary in order to cope with the former. Both of these strategies tend ultimately to generate suffering, and neither of them expresses our true nature.

Hedonism and the underlying personal drives and motives can be trained, learnt and unlearnt. The Greek philosophers, as well as modern science, warn us that our desires and pleasure-seeking habits are to a large extent learnt, and, as much as they can be learnt, they can be unlearnt as well. Mastering our desires and pleasures is not just an ethical undertaking (based on values: for example, we consume less as we want to reduce the negative impact of consumption) but actually also a way of gaining greater inner freedom, more balance and joy. *Sustainable hedonism* is a way of enjoying life that does not cost the Earth. It also reveals that ecologically responsible behaviour is not painful asceticism.

Sustainable hedonism can inspire us to make our ordinary experiences extraordinary. The key is our attention, our presence and refining our senses. A mindful presence can change even the most ordinary actions, like drinking a glass of water or washing our skin, into most delightful and fine acts, as if they had not happened before. We could enjoy them as if they were the 'first ever'. Our routine actions can turn into acts of delicate self-care. The profane can turn sacred.

We can also develop our ability to enjoy 'static pleasure', noticing and celebrating the very moment when finally our longing was fulfilled, our goal was met. We can take time to linger on this experience without moving on right away. We do not need to obey our restless mind, immediately wanting to jump to what comes next. Rituals and celebrations can serve us well. Simple rituals like ending our day with a friendly inner reflection can increase our sleep quality and mental well-being.

We could engage consciously with our pleasure-seeking self. How do we seek joy? What is the pleasure that our world, our community, our upbringing allows, prefers, and what does it forbid? We could spend time disentangling and exploring all these aspects. Which of these affect us the most, perhaps having an unwanted grip on us? Are these aligned to our current values and strivings? What could make our lives more joyful?

Are we open to changing our habits and our quest for pleasure? How do we respond to the collective call to reduce and adjust our use of resources? What helps us in our pro-social actions and what hinders us? Can we do more of what we find useful?

5

A *Flourishing Life*: Living Well and Doing Well

Happiness is the ultimate good, there is nothing more precious or desirable than this, according to Aristotle. Fame, wealth, enjoyment, knowledge, although one can strive for them, are all just means to make someone happy. In contrast, one seeks happiness not in order to get to something else through it, but because it is good in itself. However, the word for happiness used by Aristotle, '*eudaimonia*' covers something else than many other concepts of happiness.

In *eudaimonia* '*eu*' means good and '*daimōn*' is a supernatural being, a spirit. In the ancient world, daimon was the name of the 'movers' in the celestial spheres who moved the planets. There was a perfect order in the celestial spheres, and the world was orderly. This was called the '*cosmos*'. The philosopher held that humans' purpose was to achieve this perfection of the spheres within themselves. Thus, we may say that *eudaimonia* means that we become a good spirit, living in harmony with other beings of the *cosmos*. *Eudaimonia* is the central concept of Aristotle's ethics.

Today, the term *eudaimonia* is translated in various different ways: as happiness, flourishing, living well or well-being. The ancient concept of *flourishing life* has gained much recent attention, and it may offer a key to our collective pathway to a thriving life which does not cost the Earth.

According to Aristotle, happiness is 'good life and good action', and a 'happy man lives well and does well'.[1] In our contemporary language we could say that the good life is what we aim for, and it is largely the outcome of right action. *Flourishing life* clearly distinguishes itself from the current widespread interpretations of happiness as a feeling or as a sense of satisfaction (affective and hedonic interpretations). I would say that, according to Aristotle, happiness is not simply what we feel but, rather, what we do, how we live.

Happiness according to Aristotle: *flourishing life*

Does happiness depend on us, or is it just luck and a divine gift? If the gods can give so much, it would be reasonable to expect this supreme good to be their gift, argues Aristotle in his *Nicomachean Ethics*. It resonates with the expectations of many of us: we may expect God, the Universe or Fate to grant us happiness, and hope for a lucky turn of external circumstances such as a win on the lottery or meeting a perfect partner. We may have the (secret or not so secret) fantasy that our personal existence is unique and special, and our strivings will be acknowledged and rewarded in a 'fair' universe.

The philosopher, however, concludes that happiness cannot be merely the work of some divine providence, or even of chance: 'To entrust to chance what is greatest and most noble would be a very defective arrangement.'[2] 'Happiness seems, however, even if it is not god-sent but comes as a result of virtue and some process of learning or training, to be among the most godlike things.'[3]

Happiness is a lasting condition, since we would not say someone was happy if it were only for a day: 'For one swallow does not make a summer, nor does one day; and so too one day, or a short time, does not make a man blessed and happy.'[4] Therefore, the actions necessary to achieve happiness must also take place throughout life.

Happiness is a complete life. Circumstances are changeable: wealth can be destroyed, fame can be forgotten and health can turn into grave illness. If one were exposed to these changes, one would lie open to his own ever-changing feelings. A happy person, in contrast, is characterized by stability, he does not lose his mental balance. Small things do not affect him. Nor do great plagues necessarily affect him, but even if they do, he can become more and more a master of noble and great things. He is not stable because he is insensitive to or unaffected by bad luck, but because of his 'nobility and greatness of soul'. How can one become like this?

Happiness as conscious action

Happiness, according to Aristotle, is 'an activity of soul'.[5] An activity, not simply an emotional state. And since we can act to achieve it, he explains what to do:

- seek a golden mean in the pursuit of pleasures in order to achieve self-control;
- practise virtues with perseverance; and
- see your actions through the lens of friendship and community.

The meaning of the golden mean in pleasures was discussed in the previous chapter, as well as self-control. The topic of virtues needs more explanation.

According to Aristotle, a happy person lives a complete life because his actions are virtuous. Actions are not restricted to activities with tangible results, but include contemplation as well.

Aristotle distinguishes two main forms of virtues: *intellectual virtues* and *moral virtues*. *Intellectual virtue* is based on science and '*practical wisdom*'. So it is not merely intellectual, but it must be coupled with wisdom. What does this wisdom mean? According to Aristotle, those who possess *practical wisdom* are able to see what is good for themselves and for mankind in general. Today, this intellectual virtue can be interpreted as the ability to think critically and to have an integral vision of our world. The former implies being able to assess whether a piece of information is true and useful, and therefore being able to distance oneself from fake news, conspiracy theories, propaganda and populism. The latter implies being able to see major social trends and global phenomena, or, to use the terminology of radio, to receive the real signals amid the surrounding noise. In a world of increasing complexity and overwhelming information, both of these are essential skills for coping and thriving. In addition, *practical wisdom* brings insight into what could be a beneficial action for oneself and for others. It requires both self-awareness, insightful knowledge of oneself, and a connection and realistic assessment of the state of affairs of the world.

The *moral virtues* (or excellence of character) include courage, temperance, liberality (generosity), magnificence (with large donations as well as expenses), pride, good temper, wittiness, friendliness and truthfulness. From the point of view of our exploration, let us investigate the potential of a few of these.

Courage: According to Aristotle, courageous people perform courageous acts carefully, without being extremely fearful cowards or fearless rash persons. Today, fear (of the pandemic, the ecological and social challenges of our times) can make us frozen and inhibit our ability for action. At the other extreme, we may deny our fear and the risks that face us, and can be engaged in reckless action. Courage is the ability to act in the midst of the fear or threat, while not denying external reality or our own sense of fear. This helps us to seek adequate actions which are sustainable and do not harm us. Courage is a virtue which can be developed, thus it is not a one-off extraordinary action but, rather, a general attitude which keeps seeking an appropriate form of action in specific challenging situations.

Good temper: The good-tempered man is 'angry at the right things and with the right people, and, further, as he ought, when he ought, and as long as he ought.'[6] He is not led by passion and is not revengeful, but he is able to feel and express anger. Today, it implies the ability to regulate our negative emotions, not in the sense of not feeling or suppressing them, but to avoid automatic reactions to them. A good-tempered person can recognize and avoid hateful speech or action, be it in the form of the stigmatization of specific social groups, or in personal interaction, especially in online forums and social media, which tend to proliferate these actions. Anger about being treated unfairly or the state of affairs in climate politics and ecology can motivate political engagement or community action. However, anger needs to have the quality of temperance in order to be channelled into the right and useful actions.

Temperance is a mean with regard to pleasures, without the extreme of self-indulgence or the denial of bodily pleasures. Nowadays, self-indulgence and the inability to control our desires and impulses is actually encouraged (and valued) by consumer society, as well as by addictive social media. In parallel, many of us lost our instinctive ability to enjoy life, to feel the joy of our physical being and of our dealings. Our self-mastery, and regaining a greater control over our attention, time and money, can be beneficial for our own well-being, as well as crucial for a collective solution to the ecological crisis. Temperance, and the intellectual virtue of being well informed about the consequences of our life-styles and our mainstream economic and social systems can mutually reinforce each other and result an ethical action.

The philosopher holds that everyone should find their own way to a virtuous life. Aristotle does not think that there is a universal definition of the eternal 'good', the 'idea', thus he breaks with the Platonic tradition. Just as every craft has a different purpose, people in different occupations have different paths to happiness. We can also add that our path will also vary depending on our personality and abilities.

Virtuous life: pursuing intellectual and moral virtues

How to live a virtuous life? *Intellectual virtues* can be acquired through teaching.

A more difficult path leads to *moral virtues. Moral virtues* are based on 'perfected self-mastery'. These virtues are the result of habits, which are formed through persistent practice: repeated actions lead to 'perfected self-mastery'. An example of such action is noble-minded giving.

> 'I say that habit's but a long practice, friend,
> And this becomes men's nature in the end.'[7]

This is supported by our current knowledge of psychology and biology. Our brains are resilient and docile, far beyond compulsory education, and far beyond factual knowledge: we can learn joy, love, wisdom, a relationship to desires and impulses, inner freedom and all the important necessities of a good life.

What does persistent practice mean to us today, in our own lives? How much time do we dedicate for transforming our decade-old habits and convictions? Aristotle reminds us of the importance of perseverance and practice.

However, this perseverance does not mean rigidity and inflexibility. According to Aristotle, a man with correct self-control can be persuaded, as he is able to reconsider his position and does not cling to his convictions.

Interpreting these ideas, we could say that impulsivity, action driven by sudden ideas and influences, does not help achieve long-term goals. If a musician made his daily practice dependent on his mood, this would soon show in his performance. On the other hand, his passion and vision might change. There could be a transformation in his life which made him doubt that he should continue to live as a musician, as it was no longer aligned with his deepest desires and priorities in his current stage of life. That is, in addition to self-control, there is undoubtedly a need for internal flexibility, as well as a revision of goals and vows if need be.

Friendship: commitment along common values

No one wants to live without friends, no matter how abundant their lives are, says Aristotle. Influential and rich people need friends in particular, for what is great abundance worth if it cannot be shared with friends? It is exactly with them that it can be fully enjoyed. *Friendship* is one of the best things in life, and it cannot be replaced by any other kind of abundance, says the philosopher.

Aristotle uses the word '*philia*' to describe *friendship*, which is derived from the verb '*philein*', which is mostly translated as 'love', or 'affection'. In Greek thinking, however, *philein* does not primarily refer to an internal emotional state, but to an action that creates or maintains a cooperative relationship.[8] '*Philoi*', according to the Greeks, is a community of people created to serve some common purpose. Friendship here, then, is not based on instinctive sympathy or a sense of love, but can also be seen as a conscious action based on a shared value. In addition, friendship is based on commitment.

The philosopher uses the concept of *friendship* quite broadly to refer to various relationships: love, marriage, the parent–child relationship, citizen cooperation, the master–slave relationship and respect for gods or kings. The love understood as *philia* implies action and commitment and, as it is not primarily based on emotion, it is not exposed to the fluctuation of momentary feelings.

The friend is a mirror, helping us get to know ourselves: 'as then when we wish to see our own face, we do so by looking into the mirror, in the same way when we wish to know ourselves we can obtain that knowledge by looking at our friend. For the friend is, as we assert, a second self.'[9]

Human relationships can be based on utility, pleasure and moral goodness. The first two, according to the philosopher, are imperfect because they want to get something pleasant from the other. Therefore, they cannot be lasting, because if the other no longer offers utility or pleasure it will end. A 'perfect friendship' is lasting.

The 'perfect friend' is a great treasure. According to Aristotle, it is so rare because few people are fit and worthy of it. He holds that such a friendship requires our attention, our devotion, so we cannot have many of them at the same time.

There are also 'unequal' friendships between people with different wealth, power or situations. The essence of such an unequal relationship is loving, instead of expecting to be loved, as indicated by the delight of parents take in loving their children and their satisfaction in seeing them prospering. The children, in return, honour them. As said earlier, the Aristotle uses the term *friend* for a wide range of relationships, thus an 'unequal' friend could be now called an advocate, mentor, patron, backer, ally, associate or benefactor.

According to the ancient Greeks, a person acting for his happiness does so as part of a community, and not in isolation from it. Community is necessary: on the one hand, the relationship with others helps personal development, and on the other hand, community is the measure of this development. Aristotle is rather clear in the latter: for him, the public interest is more important than the well-being of the individual. At the beginning of the *Nicomachean Ethics* he says that 'even if the end is the same for a single man and for a state, that of the state seems at all events something greater and more complete whether to attain or to preserve'.[10] It is in strong contrast with our current dominant cultural norms in most Western countries, where priority and focus is given to individual interest.

The community is essential because the world, the city-state, is made up of these, says the philosopher. The exciting question is what this community is like, whether it supports *flourishing life* or less so, and, if yes, what makes it work well. According to Aristotle, the foundation is personal relationships, friendships, as these hold even states together.[11] Even today, we can say that larger social systems such as a city or a country can function well only if their members have good personal connections and belong to smaller communities which are based on positive norms. This could be one interpretation of social inclusion, a term used by social scientists and policy-makers.

Flourishing life: modern psychological approaches

How could modern psychological science support our aspiration for a *flourishing life*?

There are countless alternative approaches to *eudaimonia*: in today's happiness research it is defined either as a sense of the meaning and purpose in life, or as good psychic functioning, or as some combination of these two.[12]

Self-assessment: do I live a flourishing life*?*

Among the many indicators, I find the flourishing scale developed by Ed Diener and his collaborators particularly suitable for a personal assessment, as it includes not only the meaning of life but also the supportive relationships and the experience of competence. These are vital elements of 'being well' and 'doing well' and innate psychological needs according to the *self-determination theory*. By completing Table 5.1, the reader can assess their own life in terms of flourishing.

'Below are 8 statements with which you may agree or disagree. Using the 1–7 scale below, indicate your agreement with each item by indicating that response for each statement.'

The range of possible scores is from 8 (lowest) to 56 (highest possible). A high score represents a person with many psychological resources and strengths.

Table 5.1: Flourishing scale

Question	Score of the answer
	7 – Strongly agree
	6 – Agree
	5 – Slightly agree
	4 – Neither agree nor disagree
	3 – Slightly disagree
	2 – Disagree
	1 – Strongly disagree
I lead a purposeful and meaningful life	
My social relationships are supportive and rewarding	
I am engaged and interested in my daily activities	
I actively contribute to the happiness and well-being of others	
I am competent and capable in the activities that are important to me	
I am a good person and live a good life	
I am optimistic about my future	
People respect me	
Total score	

Source: Diener et al 2010.

The value of flourishing life

There is an extensive empirical literature comparing hedonic and eudaimonic motivations and actions. They seem to support the philosophical argument of Aristotle: pleasure-seeking life is inferior to eudaimonic life, a life based on the cultivation of virtues. Eudaimonic life was found to more likely bring a feeling of joy, satisfaction with life, a sense of meaning, as well as physical health, as compared to a hedonic life. People who live a *flourishing life* were found to be more giving, and more actively engaged in pro-social action.[13]

Why is it good to live a *flourishing life*? Where do these positive effects come from? One metaphysical reason may be that a human being's existential desire is to live a *flourishing life* (a life well lived). If a person is able to accomplish this, it will also have measurable positive effects on their mental and physical health during their life, and it will make them self-transcendent, caring for others and the Earth.

Another possible reason may be that we have a desire for stability in the flux of life, and that connection to the virtues, the meaning of life, can provide a more spacious perspective on all events of our lives, whether they be obstacles, troubles or ecstatic joys. If pleasure (or pleasant feelings) is not the ultimate measure, then the momentary lack of pleasure (or pleasant feelings) is not a personal failure, but only a temporary state.

The search for the meaning of life is possible in all life situations, confesses Viktor Frankl with his entire oeuvre and personal life. The Viennese psychiatrist and neurologist, founder of the third Vienna School of Psychotherapy, was held in Auschwitz while his wife, pregnant with their child, was killed in the Bergen-Belsen concentration camp. In his most famous book, *Man's Search for Meaning*, he writes that even in the concentration camp he had a choice, and even there it was possible to give meaning to life.[14] For example, he envisioned the future, when he would give a lecture on his experiences in the camp. He also imagined meeting his beloved wife again, which filled him with warmth in the harshest physical and mental coldness. According to Viktor Frankl, we have a choice, always and everywhere, and we can give meaning to our current experience, whatever that may be. It is our freedom.

Flourishing and 'conscious hedonism'

Studying all this, we may conclude that striving for a meaningful life is a superior life strategy. We could interpret it as a call to focus on values and meaningful life exclusively, paying utmost attention to our 'moral' selves and letting it rule our lives.

In my view, pleasure and flourishing do not exclude each other. We can experience the joy offered by a given moment without becoming addicted to our desires or harming others. The hedonism of Epicurus characterized by awareness and self-restraint, which we may also call 'conscious hedonism', is echoed in *mindfulness* today.

For the psychoanalyst Viktor Frankl, recalling the joyful moments of life in the death camp (which was also a widespread ancient hedonistic practice) was part of the recipe for survival. So often it is precisely those who can effectively undertake action for their own pleasure and for their joy who are able to relate to the core values of their lives and to their ability to take value-based action.

What does it imply in the current context of the ecological crisis? Can we consciously create a *flourishing life* while also enjoying it? This issue will be explored in the next section.

Living well and caring: a *flourishing life* and ecological justice

The current level of overconsumption and the climate emergency call for the reduction of our resource use.

There is a prevailing fear that the reduction of consumption would lead to a decline in living standards and happiness. Reduction of consumption may hurt if it is externally enforced or coerced, for example, in a scenario where a government is prompted to take radical measures. Loss normally hurts.[15] Recessions tend to have negative mental effects and can cause social scars, and these impacts of the COVID-19 pandemic are just unfolding. We are better off if we are able to choose an alternative pathway to tackle the crisis.[16] Tim Jackson, in his influential book, calls for *Prosperity without Growth*. This is the general aspiration of the degrowth movement and of a number of real-life initiatives.[17] They argue that the foundations of our society and economy need to transform and become more well-being centred. The discourse is thus not simply about reducing overall consumption (or production) but, rather, about realigning social goals, personal aspirations and habits.

Pro-environmental behaviour boosts well-being

The fear that the reduction of consumption would lower happiness is based on the assumption that there is a positive relationship between resource-intensive consumption and happiness. Empirical studies challenge this assumption and do not find such a link. Specific emission-intensive activities did not correlate with subjective well-being in Sweden.[18] Higher carbon footprints were associated with marginally lower levels of well-being in Australia.[19] According to a study of German data, the shift to more environmentally friendly consumption can increase well-being.[20] Many studies found positive correlations between personal well-being and pro-environmental behaviours (recycling, green purchasing and/or reducing consumption) among North American adults, British households, German adults, Swedish adults, Spanish adults, Mexican undergraduates and adults and Chinese adults from 14 cities.[21]

People engaging in solidarity economy, with sharing of books, tools, bikes, cars, rides and lodging were found to have a higher life satisfaction than those who never or rarely engaged in such sharing activities.[22] Alternatives to mainstream forms of work and consumption can enhance well-being. In sum, the downsizing of high-emission travelling, heating, cooling, food consumption (by eating less meat and more regional food) and voluntary simplicity are reconcilable with a happy and contented life.

There is a rather different fear as well, fused with frustration and anger. This fear is that too little is being done and too late. This may be felt by those suffering from rising sea levels, wild fires, stifling urban air, or those missing a more natural and balanced living. It is the concern of the Swedish activist Greta Thunberg, Extinction Rebellion, Fridays for Future, System Change Not Climate Change activists and similar groups and their supporters, and has sparked numerous mass demonstrations and actions of civil disobedience globally. These people are likely to suffer mentally from the *lack* of sufficient actions.

If the reduction of consumption is based on a voluntary choice, motivated by intrinsic values, it will most likely boost well-being. Those people who want to take action in order to protect the environment and the interest of future generations may actually feel good when they discover and perform these actions. For them, voluntary simplicity is an increase of quality of life and mental well-being.[23]

These contrasts between social groups call for a more differentiated approach to assessing the links between consumption and well-being: this relationship depends on personal values and attitudes. Overall generalizations mask crucial disparities, blur our understanding and, with it, the path to solutions.

Values are determinant

A series of experiments by Kirk Warren Brown and Tim Kasser show that people with intrinsic value orientation (focusing on personal growth, relationships and community involvement) are likely to both be more happy and behave in an ecologically responsible way.[24] In contrast, *materialism* was found to be associated with higher emissions and lower well-being. For these people, high consumption (and its high ecological price) was not a key to happiness. In their meta-analysis of 259 independent samples, Hurst, Dittmar, Bond and Kasser found that *materialism* was negatively associated with pro-environmental attitudes and behaviours like recycling, green purchasing and/or reducing consumption.[25]

A study of UK panel data found that a green self-image (one's own assessment of how environmentally friendly one's behaviour is) increases life satisfaction. However, this self-image was not consistently related to pro-environmental behaviour.[26] People may not know what such behaviour should be (ignorance). Or they could be reluctant to behave in this way, but still want to see themselves in a good light (cognitive bias). An extended empirical analysis confirmed the positive relationship between green self-image and life satisfaction in a pool of 35 European countries.[27] This well-being benefit was greater in societies with more unanimity with regard to pro-environmental attitudes. It highlights the importance of social norms: people like to do what is accepted and appreciated by the majority.

How could a transformation in values, attitudes and behaviour be initiated and supported? Education can play a key role, by promoting both sustainability and happiness.[28] There is evidence that materialism (giving priority to attaining possessions, image and status relative to other aims in life), which tends to hinder pro-social and pro-environmental behaviours, can be transformed as a result of interventions.[29] A further possibility is to inspire people by telling stories and teaching about a good life that is worth living. A conscious distance from the advertising of consumer culture may help inner reflection and setting priorities. We may shift our beliefs as to what makes a good life and what is the key to success.

Cultivating *flourishing life* in the 21st century

The normative philosophical framework of Aristotle could also provide inspiration, among many other teachings. The approach of a *flourishing life* suggests that acting for our own happiness not only does not exclude others but also can make us more able to care about others and promote the common good. The elements of conscious action, self-mastery, the practice of intellectual and moral virtues, nurturing friendships and relationships can provide a path to personal and collective thriving.

Table 5.2 summarizes my own interpretation of the teachings of Aristotle and its possible application to our current situation. I also show that *flourishing life* has numerous potential fruits. I do not aim for philosophical rigour or completeness but, rather, to offer an invitation to explore these ideas not only intellectually but also as experiences. Moral virtues are based on persistent practice, so the theory is only the first step, and serves primarily as a base to personal experience.

If we increasingly perceive our own happiness as a result of conscious action, rather than as the 'present of gods', a lucky combination of external circumstances, we develop our ability to act in alignment with our deepest needs and desires. We will feel, know and respect more what we deeply want. We will be more able to take action for these, rather than being steered in our actions by external expectations, commercial marketing and social media. We may get closer to what

Table 5.2: Cultivating a *flourishing life* nowadays and its fruits: potential impacts on personal well-being, social and ecological actions

Aspect of flourishing life	Features in the contemporary world	Fruits – possible outcomes
Regarding happiness as 'doing well', rather than as a momentary emotion, dependent on lucky events	Less exposure to external circumstances, good or bad; conscious actions for cultivating happiness as an inner attitude	More autonomy; greater mental stability; increased ability to act in alignment with one's deepest needs and desires; less socially or ecologically destructive behaviour, such as addictive, impulsive or conspicuous consumption
Cultivating intellectual virtue, including 'practical wisdom'	Ability to think critically and have an integral vision of our world; being informed of collective challenges (social, ecological) and potential solutions; ability to assess whether a piece of information is true and useful, to handle complexity; wisdom on what is good for oneself and for mankind	Self-care; conscious consumption; life-style adjustments; engagement in environmental action and alliances
Cultivating the moral virtue of courage	Ability to act in the midst of threat or fear	Active engagement for social and environmental justice, in the midst of major crisis
Cultivating the moral virtue of temperance	Self-mastery, a mean by regard to pleasures, avoiding the extreme of self-indulgence	Greater control of one's attention, time and money; autonomy and ability to distance oneself from consumerism
Cultivating the moral virtue of good temper	Angry at the right things and with the right people, but not led by passion and not revengeful; ability to regulate negative emotions, to avoid automatic reactions	Ability to cooperate and handle conflicts; avoidance of hateful speech or action; ability to motivate political engagement or community action

(Continued)

Table 5.2: Cultivating a *flourishing life* nowadays and its fruits: potential impacts on personal well-being, social and ecological actions (continued)

Aspect of flourishing life	Features in the contemporary world	Fruits – possible outcomes
Friendship and community	Value-based relationships with commitment; seeing oneself and one's action through the lens of others	Self-transcendence, moving beyond egoism; experiencing the benefits of giving and receiving social support, inspiration; solidarity, collaboration, cooperation, co-creation; more connection to nature; belonging to networks working for social transformation and ecological regeneration; applying ecological and social standards as measures for personal actions

really matters to us, rather than having supplementary strategies. As the next chapter shows, our aspirations as shown in value surveys are aligned to the core basic needs of *self-determination theory*: we aim for a life which is good for us. In becoming more eudaimonic, we are less likely to pursue radical, hedonistic actions, and thus our consumption, the use of our resources (time and money) is expected to shift.

A greater awareness of our pleasure-seeking habits, and a search for a desirable middle way is mentally beneficial in the long run. If we let go of excessive or addictive pleasure seeking it may initially hurt. Without our old habit, we may find ourselves in an unknown terrain, which could make us feel restless or insecure. If we take this step with an awareness of the expected benefits to our life, our temporary negative feelings will enter into a broader context, where other, positive feelings and thoughts are also present. We will have a capability to tolerate our mixed feelings, including negative ones. Gradually, we are likely to be rewarded by a sense of increasing freedom and competence, and probably our relationships will also benefit from this. Our transformation will increase our ability to meet our core psychological needs (of autonomy, belonging and competence), which have probably been unsatisfied thus far. Cultivating courage is likely to increase our sense of autonomy and competence.

Connection to nature is not a marked element of the original concept of *flourishing life*, and the abundance of nature was probably taken for granted at the time, but it has become an essential element of connectedness today. It is inherently linked to our ability to transcend ourselves, to connect to the larger world, to feel empathy and compassion. Aristotle might well say today that it is not possible to create an order in the *cosmos* around us and inside us by ignoring the Earth, its balance and health.

Intellectual virtues and practical wisdom provide greater awareness of the global phenomena in the world, including the multiple crisis phenomena, among them the ecological and climate crisis, and we will increasingly seek how to act in ways which are good for us and good for others.

Cultivating friendships, relationships and our own virtue of generosity would enlarge our perspective: the search for happiness will not be an isolated and competitive exercise but, rather, part of a larger collective.

These were my suggestions on how the original philosophy could be understood and applied to our contemporary context and challenges. These were guiding principles. The actual implementation can take many forms.

From conflict to unity: the individual and the world

Individual freedom is often interpreted and lived as a process which separates a person from others and the community, creating a conflict between self-interest and the public good. Such conflict may lead to a self-centred individual behaviour which is harmful to others, including overconsumption or environmentally damaging consumption habits. On the other hand, it may also be painful for the individual, due to the sense of isolation and the lack of meaningful belonging.

The notion of *flourishing life*, as well as modern psychological approaches, highlights that individual freedom and personal aspirations do not need to stand in conflict with the common good.

Our basic psychological needs encompass both freedom and close relationships ('autonomy' and 'belonging'), according to the *self-determination theory*. The actual need for freedom, autonomy, may vary from one individual to another, as well as the need for belonging. *Self-determination theory* holds that we all need both *autonomy* and *belonging*, as both of these are innate needs. On the one hand, we cannot live a *flourishing life* if we are not autonomous, even if we are in relationships or in a community, however supportive they may appear to be. This way, we are likely to be disconnected from our own values, needs and aspirations, and may have limited ability to experience our creativity and competence in this world. We may also lose our ability to exit from a harmful bond. On the other hand, we cannot live a good life if we do not belong, we are not loved, not accepted and do not love and live well with others, however elaborated our autonomy may be. This integration of our core needs for *autonomy* and *belonging* is one of the main challenges and chances of our age.

A sign of successful personal development is the integration of these two aspects: the more we become ourselves, embracing our innermost uniqueness and the essence of our existence, the more deeply we also connect with the world. According to Carl Gustav Jung, the fullness of personality is realized when one is connected with the conscious and unconscious aspects of their being as well as with the world. Our destiny is embedded in the destiny of the world, we preserve the common human past in the deeper layers of our souls (as collective consciousness and archetypes), just as we may even be able to sense the future in our dreams and intuitions. This unity between us and the world is also revealed by our archetypal dreams and random coincidences, synchronicities. This is what Jung calls '*unus mundus*', meaning 'one world' in Latin.

Therefore, becoming individual, one's own self is by no means egocentric. The self is infinitely more than the ego. The person during their development is not moving away from the world and others, but through their awareness they are able to connect with others and the world in a more integrated way. This process 'does not shut one out from the world, but gathers the world to oneself'.[30]

A flourishing life *is realized in the community*

A *flourishing life* is experienced by the individual but is realized in the community. And a suitable community can help with individual accomplishment. The two processes affect and reinforce each other.

We do not need to start building a world of a thriving life out of nothing, neither on an individual nor on a community level. On an individual level, we can connect to the experiences, abilities and inner forces that support this. This is discussed in detail in Chapters 7 and 8. On a collective level, existing innovative tools, as well as organizations, movements, initiatives, indigenous cultures and ancient traditions can augment the capacity of the individual.

The Andean concept of '*buen vivir*' builds upon aboriginal traditions and sees the good life as living in harmony with oneself, with others in the community and with nature. It breaks with the anthropocentric view of the world and demands legal rights for nature.[31] The African '*ubuntu*' expresses a sense of community. We can support and strengthen each other by sharing old and new stories of the good life, including those which come from our own experiences.

Islands can become networks. Islands of individuals can become communities. Isolated counter-cultural experiments can create a network of alliances, offering an alternative vision to the cultural mainstream.

There are communities that integrate economic, social, ecological and cultural aspects in their operations on a new level, living a life-style which is socially just, environmentally sustainable and brings mental well-being. Adopting a pioneering role, they monitor the challenges of the world and seek systemic answers to them. Examples could be the Global Ecovillage Network, the Transition Towns movement, the Wellbeing Economy Alliance, the Economics of the Common Good Movement, to name just a few.[32]

There are advanced new forms of organization and management tools that can resolve the long-standing conflict between 'me' and 'others', between individual interest and the interest of the community. We can advance from 'ego-system' to 'eco-system economics', using the terms of the thinker Otto Scharmer. There are consensual decision-making processes that can involve everyone while also remaining effective (for example, sociocracy, holacracy). There are organizations that allow their members to work together in a self-organized way and to act creatively and meaningfully for a common goal that matters for all.

Networks for sustainability

The Economy of the Common Good is a concept as well as a movement, prioritizing and quantifying the common good.[33] It aims to benefit not only the owners but also employees, suppliers, customers and the social environment. Core values include human dignity, solidarity, environmental sustainability, transparency and co-determination. The performance of companies/organizations is evaluated on the basis of the Common Good Balance Sheet. Customers gain in terms of transparency and can more consciously steer their consumption toward companies with ethical and sustainable standards. Companies can be supported by governments via tax reduction or preferential treatment at the procurement stage, as a way of acknowledging their positive external effects on society and the environment.

The Transition Network is a movement based on local action for global challenges and currently encompasses over 1,100 initiatives in 50 countries. It aims to promote the transformation of existing structures of economy, politics and society, as well as inner transition. Its aims are stated by the US Transition hub: 'We are reclaiming the economy, sparking entrepreneurship, reimagining work, reskilling ourselves and weaving webs of connection and support. We are engaging in courageous conversations; extraordinary change is unfolding.'[34] Totnes in the UK was the very first Transition Town, founded by permaculture educator Rob Hopkins and some others in 2006. Sustainable Frome in the UK and Ungersheim in France are other examples.

The Global Ecovillage Network typically includes newly established rural communities or revitalized old village communities, but there are also urban rejuvenation projects and permaculture design sites.[35] Some examples are Findhorn in Scotland, Sieben Linden in Germany, Tamera in Portugal, Damanhur in Italy, Aeroville in India, Ithaca in New York and Earthlands in Massachusetts, US, among approximately 10,000 communities. These are living laboratories of technological, social and cultural innovation, while honouring traditional knowledge. Sharing practices and education is the core of their activities. Ecovillages in richer Western nations aim for reducing their ecological footprint, which entails self-restraint in consumption. Living with nature and in a community tends to be so enriching that people do not experience any loss in their well-being or quality of life.[36] On the contrary, ecovillages in poorer countries (such as Africa) aim to ensure livelihoods and avoid hunger, which usually results in an increase of resource use. These poorer ecovillages are able to receive support within the network, for example, on how to reclaim land from the desert, produce clean energy for self-sufficiency, promote peace between rival ethnic groups or on other topics, depending on what is needed.

These three networks are just a few among the emerging initiatives that provide models for a sustainable life-style which goes together with a high quality of life and well-being.

Solidarity economy

The *solidarity economy* or *solidarity-based economy* is a comprehensive concept born in the 1990s that covers a myriad of different forms. It seeks economic development that prioritizes the welfare of people and the planet. It strives for ethical and values-based progress, guided by solidarity, equity, human rights, the rights of the Earth, self-determination, reciprocity and cooperation.[37] It is typically based on local initiatives. Citizens' engagement and responsibility is a key to the profound systemic transformation much needed for environmental sustainability, so (local) governments in some places actively support solidarity-based economic initiatives and seek alliances with these.

The transformation of agriculture and the food industry can take many forms. The COVID-19 pandemic highlighted the sensitivity of global supply chains, and the importance of alternatives which are more resilient. Community-supported farming and food cooperatives strive to establish a circular economy, to replace the anonymity of the supermarket with direct partnerships between local producers and consumers and to reduce packaging and food waste. The principle of solidarity entails fair prices for producers. Prices are lower for the consumers as well, thanks to self-organization, the lack of retail and marketing costs and low transport costs. Community gardens are on the rise, and they are not only about growing one's food, but also about a connection to nature and bonding with neighbours, both of which boost well-being. These initiatives share much of the philosophy of the 'zero waste' and the 'slow food' movements, all aiming for greater awareness in our consumption.

The *commoning* movement seeks novel ways of living and acting together.[38] It defines itself in contrast to profit-oriented market economy, top-down hierarchical power structures by emphasizing cooperation, autonomy, decentralisation, bottom-up structures with the sharing of power. It prioritizes neither public interest nor private interest but, rather, that of the group. *Commons* are products and resources of various kinds that are produced, maintained and used together. They can include natural resources such as the atmosphere, water reserves, lakes, the ocean, fields, seeds, urban spaces, as well as digital resources such as open source software, Wikipedia, research outcomes, intellectual or artistic products and so on. The rules depend on the specific type of resource and are self-determined by the group. A core element of commons is the community or group of people that create, maintain and use the commons. Commoning is as much about the people and their relationship as about the resources they share.

Elinor Ostrom, the Nobel Prize winner in Economics in 2009, describes in her fieldwork cases from Nepal, Indonesia, Nigeria and the US where local communities successfully maintain forests, pastures or fishing lakes together.[39] These communities have created rules that enable them to use these and care for them in a way that is both economically and ecologically sustainable. The historian Peter Linebaugh shows how the 1215 Magna Carta and its companion, the Charter of the Forest, protect the subsistence rights of people via the commons.[40] Commons have been practised by indigenous communities for centuries as well. Today, commoning can be an effective way of engaging local communities in climate action. It is a viable alternative to state or private ownership.

The *gift economy* is based on gift giving or sharing, without reciprocity or the expectation of compensation. Modern examples are blood or organ donation, or free shops (give-away shops) where all goods are free. Co-housing projects and other self-organized groups based on the gift principle are also on the rise.

Aristotle, happiness and the climate emergency

As presented in this chapter, Aristotelian happiness is a lasting state with a sense of completeness, beyond momentary joy. Its essence is value-based action accomplished in friendship and community.

Aristotle calls us to create order within ourselves, just as (according to his conviction) there is order in the outer world, the *cosmos*. This is helped by conscious action, the persistent practice of virtues. Happiness in his approach is a lasting state that is not endangered by changing circumstances, nor is it a matter of blind luck but, rather, the activity of the soul.

What is the order in today's *cosmos* that, for us, means harmony between the inner and outer worlds, between our soul and our actions, between the personal world and that of the community? What is the virtue we would like to see cultivated in our outside world as well as within us?

In a world of *flourishing life*, actions are organized according to value and virtue. And the ultimate reward of this is joy, a different kind of joy than that of short-term pleasure-seeking, as it is the joy of freedom and inner peace.

Research has shown that a person living with a 'good spirit' in the world of *eudaimonia* enjoys greater happiness which is more stable and lasting than does a person in the world of *hedonia* seeking pleasure. People with a *flourishing life* can connect with others better and enjoy nourishing relationships. In addition, their reward is better physical health.

Cultivating a *flourishing life* can be environmentally beneficial for several reasons (see Table 5.2). I argue that pursuing a more eudaimonic life makes us more collaborative, responsible and ecologically aware in general. A *flourishing life* can inspire voluntary simplicity, environmental and pro-social action, while at the same time also increasing mental well-being. Therefore, it can provide a normative philosophical strategy for a good life which is not harmful for others and for future generations.

Modern psychological approaches reveal the importance of social norms related to 'green consumption'. We are likely to do what is rewarded by the approval of others, although we may even fake it, fooling others and perhaps also ourselves. A core issue is that of values. Do we really want to act for the benefit of the planet and others or is it just an increasing social pressure? Or are we inherently selfish pleasure, power and money seekers? What drives us really? What are the values which determine our actions, perhaps even without our conscious awareness? Is there scope for shaping and modifying these values, especially if they are destructive and obstruct our good and sustainable life?

6

Values in an Era of Free Choice

Ancient and medieval cultures proclaimed general, universal values for those who belonged to them. In Judaism, God '*revealed*' the Ten Commandments and the laws to Moses. He and other prophets proclaimed God's will to the chosen people. In Christianity, God '*reveals*' himself, but in a broader way: it is not only through Jesus Christ, the prophets and the scriptures, but there are other, natural ways for understanding God such as the conscience of man or the contemplation of the beauty of nature. Muhammad, the later prophet, received direct revelations from the archangel Jibril in the cave on Mount Hira. The Buddha '*awoke*' to the truth when, after a long inner journey and meditation, his mind became clear and quiet. The teaching,' *dharma*', means the cosmic order and is constant by its nature. A common feature in Judaism, Christianity, Islam and Buddhism is that, according to their teaching, truth exists in absolute terms, independently of mankind, and is revealed to people through gradual recognition.

Nowadays, there is an increasing emphasis on subjective, internally lived values. 'Good' corresponds to what feels good.

It was only with 18th century liberalism that the idea became common that man himself knew what was good for him and that everyone also had the right to actualize it through liberty (within certain limits, foremost being that it does not restrict the rights of others). This is also the basis of universal suffrage. This classical liberalism, encompassing human rights and representative democracy (among other core values), is already a cornerstone of the Western social and political order, even if there are significant differences across countries in terms of the choice of values on which state involvement is based. In most countries there is no longer a state religion, and the (formal) restrictions for women, ethnic or other minority groups are gradually shrinking, although they have not completely disappeared. Thus, a door has opened to our personal freedom, offering a hitherto unknown choice in a large part of the world, in liberal democracies.

In these societies we are living at a time when we can put together the core values of our lives the same way that we fill our trollies in a self-service store. We seem to have unlimited freedom to draw from any philosopher, thinker, major religion or religious critic. The selection on offer can be confusing. We often do not know what we really want, or how to integrate our diverse values. As a result of this freedom of choice, there may be fewer people who can easily understand each other, with whom we feel that we are speaking the same language. It could be difficult to have a profound conversation about what is really important to us. We may become careful how we talk about these matters. We may lack a community to whom we belong, with whom we share our core values. And isolation hurts.

Today's freedom offers an opportunity to connect more consciously to the core values of our lives. The question is how much we take advantage of this historic opportunity. Friedrich Nietzsche, Fyodor Dostoevsky, Erich Fromm and others were quite pessimistic on this matter, arguing that most people do not want to live their freedom and tend to seek a solution in the apparent order and security of a dictatorship.[1] Based on this, the coming of fascism and Bolshevism was also predicted. Today, we still often elect authoritarian leaders, seeing them as strong and secure. Can we exercise our personal freedom today? What is the meaning of true freedom for us in our actions and aspirations?

Do our values enable and promote a *flourishing life* or, rather, hinder it? In order to answer these questions, we need to be aware of our own personal values, including those which are on the surface and those which we may not want to wear on our sleeve. The next section offers tools for a personal value inventory.

Personal value inventory

The simplistic capitalist belief is that competition is necessary, and the primary measure of success is the size of wealth and power. 'He is worth one million.' 'Do you want to know how much you are worth? Check your salary estimates calculator.' To what extent is this in line with the social consensus?

In the late 1970s the Israeli social psychologist, Shalom H. Schwartz, raised the question whether there are basic human values throughout all major cultures. He then dedicated most of his scholarly life to answering this question.[2] He originally identified ten distinct values, which he and his colleagues later differentiated further into 19 individual values.[3]

Schwartz calls 'value' all human goals and endeavours in the world, that is, he strives for a complete inventory. He lets the results themselves reveal which of these are widespread, and thus more 'important' than others. Value has no moral dimension by itself. Thus, in his terminology, the meaning of the term is much broader than in the philosophy of Aristotle, described in the previous chapter, which aimed to highlight the specific values necessary for a virtuous life (*eudaimonia*). While Aristotle makes revelations about the good life, 'value' in this social psychological approach is what people consider to be a value. So much for terminology. Now let us see the inventory!

What guides you? Test for identifying core personal values

The personal inventory offers a mirror. Which values guide your actions and your aspirations? Where are you heading, what is the current direction of your life?

There are 21 questions to be answered.[4] It is worth taking the time to reflect on them. One of the criticisms of Schwartz's study was precisely that there was too little time to respond, so there were many incomplete questionnaires. There is no urging of any interviewer now.

I will briefly describe some personal characteristics. Please read each description and rate how well each one describes you, using the following options.

1 Very much like me
2 Like me
3 Somewhat like me
4 A little like me
5 Not like me
6 Not like me at all

Personal characteristics:

A Thinking up new ideas[5] and being creative is important to me. I like to do things in my own original way.
B It is important to me to be rich. I want to have a lot of money and expensive[6] things.
C I think it is important that every person in the world should be treated equally. I believe everyone should have equal opportunities in life.

D It is important to me to show my abilities.[7] I want people to admire what I do.[8]

E It is important to me to live in secure surroundings.[9] I avoid anything that might endanger my safety.

F I like surprises and am always looking for new things to do. I think it is important to do lots of different things in life.[10]

G I believe that people should do what they are told.[11] I think people should follow rules[12] at all times, even when no one is watching.

H It is important to me to listen to people who are different[13] from me. Even when I disagree with them, I still want to understand them.

I It is important to me to be humble and modest. I try not to draw attention to myself.

J Having a good time is important to me. I like to 'spoil' myself.[14]

K It is important to me to make my own decisions about what I do. I like to be free and not depend on others.[15]

L It is very important to me to help the people around me. I want to care for their well-being.[16]

M Being very successful is important to me. I hope people will recognize my achievements.

N It is important to me that the government ensures[17] my safety against all threats. I want the state to be strong so it can defend its citizens.

O I look for adventures and like to take risks. I want to have an exciting life.[18]

P It is important to me always to behave properly. I want to avoid doing anything people would say is wrong.

Q It is important to me to have respect from others.[19] I want people to do what I say.

R It is important to me to be loyal to my friends. I want to devote[20] myself to people close to me.

S I strongly believe that people should care for nature.[21] Looking after the environment is important to me.

T Tradition is important to me. I try to follow the customs handed down by my religion or my family.

U I seek[22] every chance I can to have fun. It is important to me to do things that give me pleasure.

When you are done, you can review your answers.

Each question refers to a certain basic human value. For example, you can see to what extent conformity characterizes you from your answers to questions G and P. If you answered that this person is 'very much like

Table 6.1: Overview of basic values

Value	Question code		Your response
Conformity (restraint of actions likely to upset or harm others and violate social expectations or norms; self-discipline, politeness, honouring parents and elders)	G	P	-
Tradition (respect, commitment and acceptance of the customs and ideas that one's culture or religion provides; humble, devout)	I	T	-
Benevolence (preserving and enhancing the welfare of those with whom one is in frequent personal contact; helpful, honest, forgiving, responsible, loyal, true friendship, mature love)	L	R	-
Universalism (understanding, appreciation, tolerance and protection for the welfare of all people and for nature; broadminded, social justice, world at peace, world of beauty, unity with nature, wisdom)	C	H	S
Self-direction (independent thought and action; creativity, freedom, choosing own goals, curious, independent)	A	K	-
Stimulation (excitement, novelty and challenge in life; daring)	F	O	-
Hedonism (pleasure or sensuous gratification for oneself; enjoying life, self-indulgent)	J	U	-
Achievement (personal success through competence according to social standards; ambitious, successful, capable, influential)	D	M	-
Power (social status and prestige; authority, wealth)	B	Q	-
Security (safety, harmony, stability of society, of relationships and of self; social order, family security, national security)	E	N	-

Note: For more details on these specific values see Schwartz 2012.

me' or 'like me', then it indicates that you are strongly characterized by conformity. And if you answered 'Not like me' or 'Not like me at all' then conformity, it is unlikely to be your typical trait.

First, a data check may be useful. Is there an internal discrepancy in your answers concerning a particular value (you answered once that it is like you and other times that it is not like you)? What was the reason for this? An error? Misunderstanding? Ambivalence? If it was an error or a misunderstanding, you can now correct it (reading the explanatory notes may help to clarify certain phrases). If it is your inner ambivalence, simply observe this and be aware that this is the case for you right now. You can also redo the test, perhaps now focusing on values that you have acted on or thought about in the previous 24 hours.

What does your value inventory show? Which core values did you identify with the most? And which did you feel most distant from? Is there any surprising discovery in what you see about yourself? If yes, what is it? Do you spot a contradiction: that you identify with possibly conflicting values? These potential value conflicts will be discussed later.

What are the top three values most characteristic of you? And which three values are the least characteristic? Make a note of these.

How is this all around the Earth? How much do your values match those of others around the globe?

Universal values across cultures

In an age of liberty and diversity, it may come as a surprise that, according to Schwartz's research, there are universal values. Three core human values are held by the overall majority of people across 63 different countries in Asia, Africa, Latin America, the Middle East, Eastern Europe, Western Europe and Oceania.[23] These are:

- benevolence (mature love, true friendship) – preserving and enhancing the welfare of people with whom one is in frequent personal contact, with honesty, forgiving responsibility and loyalty;
- universalism (solidarity, unity with nature) – understanding, appreciation, tolerance and protection regarding the welfare of all people and of nature; and
- self-direction (autonomy) – independent thought and action: choosing, creating, exploring.

Mature love does not depend on a momentary feeling. It is not based on a romantic emotion or sensual desire, or not primarily, but it is a benevolent action that seeks the benefit of the other with commitment and responsibility. It is an intention and action. It could relate to a partner, spouse, family members, but also to close friends.

Self-direction refers to our own existence in the world. Benevolence focuses on the closest circle, our good intentions for our family or friends or close acquaintances, those with whom we are in frequent contact. Universalism extends this kindness to people and beings whom we do not know and to qualities that far exceed the level of our personal existence, such as world peace and respect for the Earth. We could view these as concentric circles.

Contrary to the prevalent recipe of success prescribed by the *homo economicus* worldview, it is not power or the search for pleasure which drives people primarily. Hedonism ranks only seventh out of ten identified core values, and power ranks last.

This is how we see ourselves: benevolence, universalism and self-direction are the most important values or human aspirations. Or this is how we want to show ourselves to others. I take these results with a pinch of salt. If our words mattered, we would be all be kind and loving, working for social justice, equality for all and world peace, and would live in harmony with nature. Wars, poverty, social and racial inequalities and ecological crisis would be fiction or history. Who would proclaim that love is not important to them? Or who would openly state that their acts of 'love' often hurt others? Who would say that their desire for equality and social justice has a selective tagged attached to it, restricting it to certain races and nations? In words and in general: yes, love is essential to us. In action and in specific situations: it depends. These may be blind spots, based on our conditioned habits, and we may not be aware how exactly our beliefs mismatch with our actions. We may not notice how our daily routines contribute to sustaining an unjust system or a repressive hierarchical relationship of any sort.

Nevertheless, this mirror shows the noble goals we are striving for. This is how we want to live, even if we do not (yet?) succeed. All in all, there is a universal image of a good life prevailing across different cultures, social arrangements and continents. I think that is a good reason for optimism.

We value what we need: self-determination theory and core values

Self-direction, benevolence and universalism are human aspirations aligned with fundamental psychic needs as described by the self-determination theory (SDT).[24] According to the SDT theory, there are three innate needs that are essential for a complete and fulfilled life.

There are individual and cultural variations in their extent, but these three needs prevail in all of us.

I would describe the three innate needs as follows.

1 *Autonomy*: We can decide for ourselves how we want to live and what we want to do, and we can preserve our internal freedom and decision making even if external conditions are restrictive.
2 *Competence*: We feel that we are able to be creative, to contribute to things that are useful to us, mobilizing our skills and abilities.[25]
3 *Relatedness* (love): We feel that we have special people around us who care about us, who love us and whom we can love and care about. In this way, we have a sense of belonging, that the world (an important part of the world from our perspective) accommodates us and we are able to find an (emotionally) safe and friendly home for ourselves.

Conditions that support these three core needs foster most volitional and high-quality motivation, with vitality, creativity, persistence and performance, and are vital for a *flourishing life* on both an individual and a collective level (Figure 6.1). The frustration of these needs conduces to ill-being, and severe or chronic restraint contributes to various forms of psychopathology and may also lead to an environmentally and socially destructive behaviour.

SDT has a growth-based perspective: people are not simply 'pushed' by physiological deficiencies (such as hunger, sexual desire) and

Figure 6.1: Basic psychological needs for a *flourishing life*

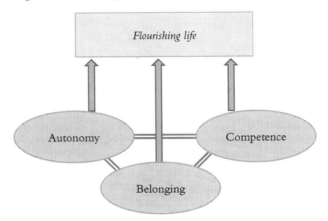

Source: Author's own.

otherwise passive, but they actively 'engage [in] activities that interest them, and move toward personal and interpersonal coherence'.[26]

All three values are essential

According to the theory, it is not enough to satisfy one or the other need for a thriving life: all three must be fulfilled, since all are innate and essential. We all need the experience of autonomy, of competence and that we can love and care and are loved and cared for (relatedness). If someone wishes to fulfil their need for relatedness, and joins a sect or an authoritarian organization, their need for autonomy will be curtailed, and probably their need for competence as well. If someone overly prioritizes their autonomy while neglecting (or harming) their relationships, their need for relatedness will not be fulfilled.

Note, however, that autonomy does not imply selfish individualism or ignorance of others and the collective. Empirical findings show over and over again that not only are autonomy and relatedness not contradictory but, rather, they tend to be highly correlated and co-occur in the best of social contexts and close relationships.[27] In this integrated vision of personal needs we need to find a strategy where these needs do not stand in conflict.

The basic needs of autonomy and competence appear to be reflected in the core value of self-direction. The basic need of relatedness seems to be expressed in the values of benevolence and universalism. We thus seem to value things which also reflect our core psychological needs.

What does it mean with respect to the pursuit of the three core values? As these values reflect the three core needs described earlier, which are all needed for a *flourishing life*, one could argue that all three values are necessary for a good life as well. In a successful life strategy where these values can be pursued, a mutually reinforcing relationship is likely to prevail between them. This is an assumption which could be tested in future research.

Thus, it is not optimal to only aspire to actualize each of these core values separately, or to focus on one or the other only. All of these values are essential for our flourishing. Therefore, the optimal strategy is to aim for coherence and integrity of the core values of autonomy, mature love and solidarity within ourselves. In this ideal state, these values mutually strengthen and reinforce each other. In addition, in healthy relationships and communities we can mutually contribute to the satisfaction of these needs in others, thereby creating positively reinforcing cycles where we all benefit.

Figure 6.2: Potential mutually reinforcing relationship of the three main values within a personality

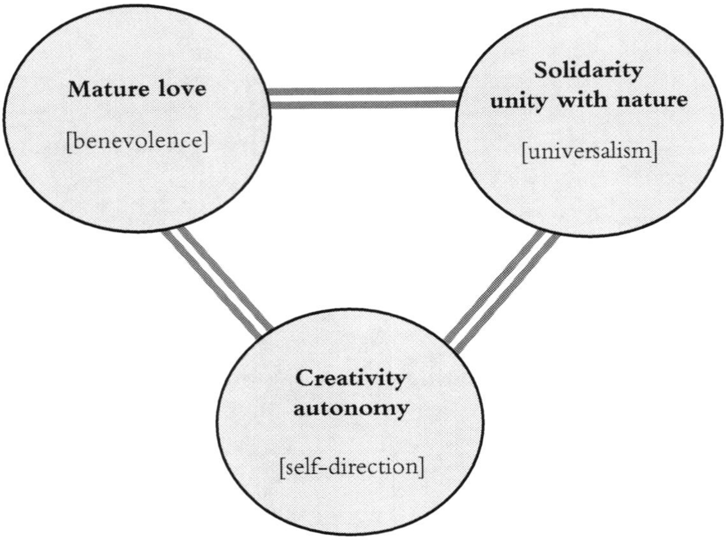

Source: Author's own.

The structure of values and aspirations

The complete value scheme has an inherent structure. Certain core human values are close to each other, while others are in conflict. These relationships can be observed on a two-dimensional map, where values are grouped alongside two major criteria:

- constancy versus change: certain values aim at preserving or strengthening existing structures or relations, as opposed to other values showing an openness to change, or even an appreciation of change;
- personal versus social: values with a personal focus enhance the individual, while values with a social focus support family, community or society.

Constancy could be anxiety based and focused on prevention of loss, while openness to change is likely to involve a growth perspective. Openness to change helps one to adapt to new situations and to cope at times of adversity. Therefore, I see change as more desirable for a thriving life than constancy.

Figure 6.3: Structure of core values

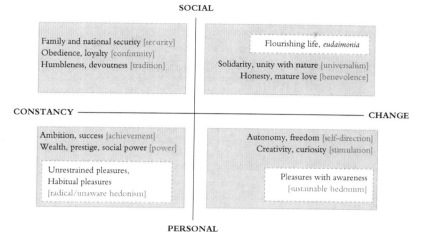

SOCIAL

Family and national security [security]
Obedience, loyalty [conformity]
Humbleness, devoutness [tradition]

Flourishing life, *eudaimonia*

Solidarity, unity with nature [universalism]
Honesty, mature love [benevolence]

CONSTANCY ———————————————— CHANGE

Ambition, success [achievement]
Wealth, prestige, social power [power]

Unrestrained pleasures,
Habitual pleasures
[radical/unaware hedonism]

Autonomy, freedom [self-direction]
Creativity, curiosity [stimulation]

Pleasures with awareness
[sustainable hedonism]

PERSONAL

Source: Adapted from Schwartz 2012, figure 2.

In contrast, I see no superiority of social focus over personal focus. Growth-oriented personal values, open to change, do not imply individualism and do not contradict pro-social values or attitudes. In my view, we can be autonomous, creative and curious, we can be conscious hedonists and at the same time love others, live in solidarity and feel unity with nature. A precondition for this is the integration of these personal and social values within the personality.

Certain values are closely related to each other:

- universalism and benevolence, the so-called '*self-transcendent*' values: they have a social focus, and their pursuit is also likely to entail flexibility, adaptability and openness to change;
- self-direction, stimulation: their essence is openness with an active search for potential change, and they have a personal focus;
- achievement, power: their aim is '*self-enhancement*', a strengthening of personal power and status, most likely within an existing structure or (larger) system, and could also be anxiety based;
- conformity, tradition and security focus on preserving what is already known and valued by the person, on preventing a potential loss, or on self-protection against threat, and are often based on anxiety.

Thus, the three most prevalent values – benevolence, universalism and self-direction – are not based on fear, self-defence or retreat but, rather, on growth and a trusting attitude toward the world.

I complemented the original concept of hedonism in the scheme of Schwartz, and differentiated its two main forms as discussed in previous chapters:

- 'radical hedonism' and 'unaware hedonism' are driven by habituation or addiction, and as such, imply the maintenance of existing consumption habits in a rather egoist, self-centred way;
- '*sustainable hedonism*' is a refined enjoyment of life with awareness, flexibility and an inner independence in the personal realm, as shown by the ancient Greek hedonist philosophers, especially Epicurus.

In addition, I added *flourishing life* to this map. It is 'social' as it is inherently embedded in a communal context of friends, intimate relations, close companions and the larger social and political community. It is 'open' as it is open to change, does not insist on maintaining existing views, habits or aspirations (but neither does it insist on their transformation by all means), therefore it has a flexible approach to the promotion of a good life.

Returning to the three most important personal values that you identified earlier: where are they in Figure 6.3? Side by side or opposed to each other? Some personal ambitions may be in conflict with social values. One may find it difficult to reconcile one's personal values with those of a relationship, group, community or society.

The conflict between self-enhancement and self-transcendence

There is a conflict between self-transcendence (benevolence and universalism) and self-enhancement (achievement and power), as shown by the opposites in Figure 6.3. Self-enhancement reflects a prevalent worldview of a strategy for success. An individual wants be prosperous, powerful and influential in order to ensure independence from others and freedom from physical or other deprivation. Striving for success is likely to involve competition with others for scarce resources and top positions. Paradoxically, however, the person remains tied to others, as external recognition and reward are the key measures of success. Well-being depends on whether one's efforts are rewarded by financial bonus, fame, honour, position or status. However, this makes one exposed and vulnerable.

Extreme aspiration for self-enhancement is vulnerable and volatile, as it does not have an optimal end point. As long as there is still a possibility to continue climbing upwards, as long as there are people who are more powerful, more wealthy, more respected, one may feel restless. Most likely, there will always be such people. For those who have based their career and life strategy on extreme self-enhancement, falling from grace may feel like complete annihilation.

An external or an internal measure of success

The motivation for self-enhancement (the values of achievement and power) is based on external standards, on achieving some external goal. In psychology this is called extrinsic motivation. The reward (or punishment) comes from outside, in monetary or other forms.

In contrast, the motivation for self-transcendence (the values of benevolence and universalism) is likely to be intrinsic. People follow these objectives because it feels right to them, and this is what they do 'naturally and spontaneously when they feel free to follow their inner interests'.[28] Monetary reward or external recognition may even impede such voluntary activities, as the psychic benefit of the activity may decline.[29] A prominent example of this is described by Richard Titmuss in the *Gift Relationship*, one of the most influential classic textbooks on social policy. Titmuss compared the blood donation systems in Britain and the US in the 1960s: in the former, the system is voluntary and free, and in the latter, it is partly market based and paid for. In the voluntary British system the quality of blood is better and the quantity is more. Why? In Britain, those who donate blood want to help. In contrast, the paid American system mobilizes those who really need the money, who may substance addicts who have an interest in lying about their actual health condition. In sum, a monetary reward can crowd out selfless help and thus damage social cooperation at the same time.

The search for wealth, popularity and appearances often makes people unhappy. The American psychologist Tim Kasser concludes that materialistic values undermine well-being, based on a decade's worth of empirical data.[30] He argues that people who centre their lives on materialistic pursuits are more likely to be dissatisfied with their lives, to have more negative emotions and to have less psychic adaptability. In addition, they engage less in ecologically friendly behaviours (using public transport, walking or cycling, buying second-hand, recycling, eating seasonal food and less meat, and so on).

There is also evidence that people giving priority to power and pleasure-seeking (as defined by Schwartz in his value scheme) tend to have more personal worries and to be more concerned about their health, safety, finances or social acceptance, especially as compared to people who prioritize self-transcendental values.[31]

People entering leadership positions may have to pay a special price for their status. The activity of their mirror neurons, responsible for empathy, tends to decrease: they may perceive the feelings of others less and may be less affected by them.[32] This could explain how some corporate leaders are able lay off thousands of employees without any regret.

Causes and cures of strenuous self-enhancement

Why, then, do so many people choose materialistic and reputation-related goals? Why would anyone want to live like this at all when it is bad for them?

The main reason seems to be existential uncertainty: those who are not able to find assurance in themselves look for it outside. Longitudinal research following the development of children into adulthood showed that people from restrictive families with little parental warmth and low socioeconomic status tend to be less autonomous and to have a strong preference for security.[33] Controlling, chaotic or neglectful parenting is likely to have a lasting impact, especially on adult attachment styles. Other studies show that those who have an attachment avoidance (who have not developed a secure attachment style, due to inadequate bonding by their mother or main caregiver) are less likely to choose self-transcendent values.[34] Those who feel urged to focus on their sense of safety and self-worth have less empathy and care for others and for universal values. They have to demonstrate tremendous achievement, to be exceptional in order to prove their right to exist. The world is not a safe place. They may be giants and dwarves at the same time: they can feel exceptional genius and at the same time feel like a useless nobody. Their strenuous efforts may actually make them truly exceptional and therefore influential and powerful. The 1939 short story by Jean-Paul Sartre, 'The Childhood of a Leader' (L'enfance d'un chef) describes how a child who questions his existence arrives at the conviction that he meant to be a leader.

People also tend to respond to external insecurity or (perceived) threats by pursuing external goals. Family poverty may be such a cause, but, under experimental conditions, general economic insecurity, relationship threats and, paradoxically, even the awareness of their own future death intensified people's extrinsic orientation: they wanted success and recognition rather than self-acceptance, affiliation or community feeling.[35] It may thus happen that anxiety about global challenges (including climate anxiety) may actually lead to people becoming more materialistic and externally oriented, which would further reduce their own ability to contribute to the solution. If this happens on a massive scale it may reduce humanity's collective chance for a necessary transformation.

Thus, simply put, in order to be able to be good to others, one has to feel safe in the world. The prerequisite for the pursuit of the goals of benevolence, universalism and self-direction (mature love, solidarity, love of nature, autonomy) which would make people ultimately happier, is to have a basic sense of emotional and physical security. And if this experience was not provided by early parental upbringing, or later by school education, the system of social institutions, then it is necessary to create it at a later stage in order to heal the early and prevailing wounds. These scientific results have major implications for how to find a path to overcoming the ecological crisis. We need to explore how professional counsellors, local communities and public institutions can create a safe environment and heal the traumas of insecurity, rejection, absence of parental warmth, restrictive parenting and negative discrimination in the school system or the workplace. This is a powerful argument for a well-functioning welfare system that offers a safety net and a chance for everyone to prosper. Social solidarity is therefore not a charity, but in the interests of the whole community.

This is a core theme in seeking a solution to the ecological crisis generated by capitalism and overconsumption; we need to look at how communities and public institutional systems can create a secure environment for all, including physical and emotional security.

Materialism is not an unfortunate fate, a fixed personal trait, but it can transform. Materialism was found to diminish as a result of interventions which encouraged intrinsic values, including personal growth, close interpersonal relationships and helping others, as has been shown by Kasser. The transformation process is more profound when people disengage from consumer culture and question its messages.[36]

In sum, acceptance, emotional security, love and kindness may be able to cure toxic attachment to power, success, external recognition, overconsumption or materialism. Creating an inner sense of security may help a person to feel at home in their own world and gradually turn toward choosing internal standards over external ones. Distancing oneself from consumer culture can support this process. This is how our world could actually move in the direction that we want to see, according to the value survey: both capable of mature love and solidarity, and a place for personal autonomy and creativity.

Fame, money, power and 'practical wisdom'

Further refining what has been said so far, it is worth distinguishing between success and power which serves self-enhancement and success and power in the service of others. In the latter case, success, money and fame are not the primary motivation of a person, and even if these happen to them, they will not be exposed to them, in fact, they will be able to remain free so that they can accept the possible transience of it all.

According to Aristotle, wealth and honour are essentially neutral, and their use will make them either an instrument or a barrier to a virtuous life. The philosopher also writes that money and power can specifically help to achieve certain goals, and that someone in their possession is better able to help others, those who do not possess similar fortunes. An advanced form of exercising power is when someone takes on a political or leadership role out of a sense of responsibility.

According to Aristotle, becoming a politician is an extremely important life path which offers opportunity for the service of the common good and the expression of a virtuous life. If a politician is endowed with 'practical wisdom', they are able to see public interest in the long run, as well as having a thorough understanding of the human soul, including their own.

The word 'politician' comes from the Greek 'polis', meaning to deal with the affairs of the city-state. A politician is therefore anyone involved in shaping public affairs who cares about the progress of the community. Such a person, such a politician, is vital at the local level or in connection with a specific relevant social issue. Political engagement can take the form of self-organization or it can be within existing institutions. In this sense, self-organized urban gardening, food cooperatives, food-sharing groups or repair cafes are also political activities, just as is participation in a citizens' council. Despite the fact that 99 members of the Irish Citizens' Assembly are chosen randomly, that is, they have no prior experience, they have proved to be able to able to make informed decisions that promote the public interest, for example with respect to climate change. Self-organized neighbourhood parliaments in India play a vital role in organizing basic local services and mobilizing citizens for joint action. Neighbourhood circles, citizens' councils and new social movements could be useful tools for engaging people, creating bottom-up politics, making breakthroughs in deadlocked issues.

What could a virtuous use of power look like in companies and organizations? A corporate leader who has not only intellectual knowledge but also practical wisdom (that is, they can align themselves to universal values and are able to see what is good for themselves and others) is fundamentally able to influence organizational culture. The wise leader is not afraid of autonomy, the initiatives and new ideas of employees, but explicitly encourages this. They may go further and break down traditional hierarchies.

In sum, if power and achievement are the end goals for someone, and express a desire for external recognition, then it is 'self-enhancement'. If power or achievement are not the end goals, then it is worth examining which core human value they serve, as it will characterize them. Power and success can also be tools for promoting the values of benevolence and universalism: as a responsible, wise leader, activist, politician.

Flourishing life *is preferred to hedonism*

Despite the heterogeneity of our actions and preferences in the world, we have a lot in common. It seems that as we move deeper in the direction of core human values, they become geographically universal and stable in historical time. Social psychological value research offers scientific evidence that there are globally shared core values. Further details may be revealed by studying culture, religion and tradition, including the constancy of these values, but that would go beyond the scope of this investigation.

The social psychological value research presented here indicates that the world of *eudaimonia* is coherent with the values of the majority globally, in contrast to the unrestrained pleasure-seeking of *hedonia*.

Pleasure-seeking is one of many potential human aspirations, but it is far from the most important (only seventh on the list of ten items). I made a suggestion for refining the original concept of hedonism into two different types: radical or unaware hedonism, and *sustainable hedonism*. While the former is likely to be destructive to personal and social well-being, the latter may promote it. Cultivating *sustainable hedonism* requires alternative norms, differing from those of mainstream consumerism and materialism.

Flourishing life is related to the three most favoured core values: autonomy (self-direction), mature love (benevolence) and solidarity and unity with nature (universalism). Mature love and solidarity are related to Aristotle's views on friendship, which include a broad range of relationships within the family and within the city-state. Autonomy can be seen as a vital element of the conscious active life described by the philosopher. A key difference is that autonomy can be virtuous, but is not necessarily so.

If this is so, then there is a contradiction between the dominant narrative of the egoist, competitive, pleasure-seeking *economic man* and the desired universal human aspirations and values shared across many countries and different cultures. Could this disparity be the reason for many of our crisis symptoms and dissatisfaction with the economic and political system? Is it possible that some of our institutional system is based on different presumptions and serves different objectives than what most of us want? It would be a good time to resolve this contradiction!

From values to action

What can we do to convert our values from mere aspirations to foundations for our personal and community lives? What can we do to reconcile our desires and our actions?

We can learn how to take conscious decisions instead of reacting automatically in challenging situations. The personal values on which we act are not static, not even for a single person for a single day. Psychic states, our actual level of consciousness and awareness, have an impact on the choice of action in a given moment, and have a lasting impact in the long run if persistently practised. There are proven tools for increasing our awareness, including mindfulness, experiential learning and the Theatre of the Soul, which will be presented in the next chapter.

There are a number of challenges and questions to which we may need to find our own answers. How can we achieve and integrate our three core values? Can we differentiate between autonomy and individualism or selfishness in ourselves? How can autonomous people create a collaborative, thriving community? How can we create and sustain a world where the fulfilment of one's true, inner freedom does not disintegrate but, rather, strengthens communities and global solidarity? How can we create and sustain communities which support individual autonomy and creativity?

Key to genuine transformation: invite and inspire

Now we seem to have clarity about which values support a thriving life. How can we efficiently transmit these values? One extreme, by coercion and control, seems to be a fast and efficient shortcut for many.

Group values, however positive they may be, hinder personal and collective thriving if the group tries to enforce them with coercion and punishment. Compliance with oppressive norms tends to be based on extrinsic motivation. People do what they are expected to do because of fear, anxiety or the hope of being rewarded for it. These so-called 'introjected values' are not assimilated and not integrated with other personal values.[37] Actions based on such values are not self-determined. To put it simply: values which are swallowed, but not digested, do not nourish life and liveliness.

I am not saying that all types of external control should be abolished. It is necessary to restrict the freedom of individuals if they harm others. We could discuss what we mean by 'harm' and where we draw the line. Do we allow destructive corporate behaviour? Do we let people continue to perform activities that damage the environment and the life chances of future generations? What kind of tools do we choose to limit or steer actions: regulation (forbidding or limiting certain actions, such as the trade in protected species, urban car use), financial incentives (taxes, subsidies), adjusting our infrastructure (for example, building better public transport to make it more attractive) or providing information (clear and reliable communication on longer-term problems and available solutions)? How do we protect the land rights of aboriginal peoples? Do we create rights of the Earth and fight crimes against them ('ecocide')? These are important questions, and need to be discussed. My focus here is different: how the transformation of values can be supported.

According to the self-determination theory, people tend to naturally internalize the values of their groups, especially if this gives them a sense of belonging and feelings of competence.[38] For a successful integration of group values, however, people first need to understand the rationale and meaning of these values and norms, and they need internal freedom, that is, the right to disagree without punishment, rejection or exclusion. They also need time for this. If, during this internal processing their sense of belonging to the group is not threatened and their sense of competence is not undermined, they are more likely to be able to integrate these values. They will be able to grow, and to develop an authentic behaviour based on intrinsic motivation and self-determination. As a result of this internal process, the values and value-based actions will be deeply personal, and not based on external expectations, rewards and punishments.

What does it mean in our current context of multiple social and ecological challenges? External group pressure tends to lead to partial outcomes. People may decide to comply, to act as if they were green, but actually they do little. It may be more about their image than real action: fake and without integrity. Shaming people for their behaviour (harmful consumption habits, low sensitivity to social issues) is unlikely to create inner change. As this threatens their sense of autonomy, competence and belonging, people are most likely to become anxious and defensive as a response. It is likely to trigger a stress reaction. They may freeze, choose to escape from the situation or start fighting, but their ability to deliberate in a refined intellectual and emotional way will become limited. This is not the mental state in which new values can be received or integrated. What could be a better strategy?

Personal change requires a state of openness and curiosity. It needs to be related to a sense of gain and growth. Who would want to just let go of things, past habits or convictions, unless feeling the call of something new? Who would want to become less self-centred, unless feeling that this makes sense in a new, larger context? Informing people about the rationale and meaning of pro-social, ecological values is essential and useful, but not enough. Further, respectful communication and friendliness can maintain their sense of belonging to the community or society, and they will not feel that their own freedom and sense of competence is threatened. These factors together will enhance the likelihood of a successful integration of new values. In sum, genuine inner value change does not happen just by external force or reward, but, rather, by a friendly invitation to a world that it is worth entering.

PART III

How Do We Get There?

7

The Laboratory of the *Flourishing Life*: Serious Change Can Be Playful

Anthropologist Jane Briggs travelled to the Arctic in the 1960s and asked the Inuit, who at that time still lived in igloos and kept their traditions, to receive her and help her survive. She lived among them for a year and a half, and learnt their language. She observed in detail how drama is used to educate and teach children.[1] When a child gets a tantrum, bites a parent, they are not scolded or punished but, rather, are shown in a playful way that involves the child what their action does to others (for example, the bite hurts the child's mother). They are not taught in words, especially not in angry words, but by playing out the situation, sometimes by dramatically magnifying it, how they can handle their own tempers and other people. The child and their parents tell and play stories together about life, relationships and conflict resolution. Briggs was impressed by the serenity and peace of the Inuit and saw herself, in comparison, as a fierce, excessive being, and learnt a lot from them.

Role playing is almost instinctive, and, just as children do it on their own without any encouragement, it was part of our human civilization even before the invention of writing: we told and played stories to each other.

Role playing was made into an art by Greek drama. In the tragedy, viewers were able to encounter the topics that occupied them as well, to experience the communal, collective nature of their own history, and thus to experience 'catharsis' – a state of stir, exaltation, relief and spiritual purification. The Greek word *catharsis* means purification.[2]

In the 16th–18th centuries the *commedia dell'arte* took theatre to the streets, to the people, using improvisational elements. But the scenes were performed by professional actors. The liberating spirit of the 20th century broke this barrier: more and more people recognized the healing, teaching and transforming power of drama, improvisation and role playing, and began to use it consciously, for example, in progressive education. These techniques could be a great help in our quest for a good life.

One can give recipes for a *flourishing life*, create supportive external conditions, but this will not happen without personal experience and transformation. What is the use of thinking about the 'good life' if we fail to realize it, live it and enjoy it?

We all strive for good in our own way. We want progress, growth. Still, we may stand in our own way and hinder our own progress. We often fail to do what is truly good for us. In economic terms, our 'true preferences' remain hidden. In addition, individual actions that seek to be good can be harmful to others. Thus, there are many reasons to curiously examine our personal values, convictions and life strategies: how could these better bring about a *flourishing life*?

This chapter aims to provide inspiration in the context of a thriving life, without trying to provide a comprehensive overview of experiential learning, mindfulness and psychodrama techniques and theories.[3]

Learning with our full being

Our ability to respond to the challenges of our age is still hindered by the intellectual tradition of seeing the mind as separate from and superior to the body. The Cartesian tradition, originating in the 17th century from René Descartes' philosophy, held that the only reliable source of knowledge is the mind ('cogito ergo sum'). This advocated rational thinking and inspired the scientific revolution of the Enlightenment, with the ambitious objective to comprehensively describe the world with scientific tools and mathematical models, and then take control of it all. The body and the external world were simply subjects to be rationally understood. This view has led to the devaluation of the body, with its sentiments and senses.

This view was challenged by the phenomenologist philosophy of the 20th century, by its leading thinker, Edmund Husserl (1859 –1938), and later by the French philosopher Maurice Merleau-Ponty (1908–61), who disputed the dualist body–mind division: 'rather than a mind *and* a body, man is a mind *with* a body, a being who can only get to the truth of things because its body is, as it were, embedded in those things'.[4] Merleau-Ponty held that perceptions play a fundamental role in understanding the world as well as engaging with the world.

The world of perception, or in other words the world which is revealed to us by our senses and in everyday life, seems at first sight to be the one we know best of all. [...] Yet this is a delusion. [...] the world of perception is, to a great extent, unknown territory as long as we remain in the practical or utilitarian attitude. I shall suggest that much time and effort, as well as culture, have been needed in order to lay this world bare and that one of the great achievements of modern art and philosophy (that is, the art and philosophy of the last fifty to seventy years) has been to allow us to rediscover the world in which we live, yet which we are always prone to forget.[5]

Thus, if we aim for a rediscovery of the world, our relationship to it cannot remain external, 'objectivist', rational and exclusively intellectual, but needs to become open, engaging and explorative, often with a sense of being unfinished or incomplete. It may feel riskier and more vulnerable, but it will reveal a great deal more of the world.

Our thoughts are intertwined with our emotions and our bodily sensations, all embedded in a larger living system around us, with which we interact. In my view, in order to build a caring, responsible, respectful relationship with others and the natural world, we need to start the rediscovery with ourselves. A key to this is to engage with our own body and our senses attentively, while not ignoring our mind.

Experiential action methods: a brief overview

Experiential action methods may include enactment, storytelling, role playing or improvisation, or a combination of these. They have long historical roots in our human culture and used to be vital means for learning. Role playing, storytelling and improvisation come more naturally to children, and less so to most adults. A potential reason could be our declining spontaneity and playfulness, due to social roles with a strict set of expectations which then become internalized.

There are a large range of methods,[6] including the following.

- *Psychodrama* uses *sociometry*, role theory, group dynamics and a range of dramatic techniques. It was developed by Jacob Levy Moreno from the 1920s, and directly or indirectly influenced many other methods (see more in depth discussion later in this chapter). Classical psychodrama may be used in its pure form, with its full set of tools and philosophical approach. Alternatively, specific psychodramatic techniques may be used and integrated with other methods in education, training or coaching.

- *Sociodrama* is Moreno's term for the application of psychodrama techniques to group, community or organizational situations. It may be applied for healing collective trauma or for inter-group conflict resolution.[7]
- *Playback Theatre* (Jonathan Fox and Jo Salas' method, with the first theatre in 1975) is improvisational theatre in which audience members volunteer stories from their lives and see them played back on the spot by the actors.
- *Theatre of the Oppressed* (developed by Augusto Boal in Brazil in the 1960s), *Forum Theatre, Social Presencing Theatre* are used for community development or to address collective themes.
- *Bibliodrama* is used for spiritual explorations, enacting biblical stories or religious texts.
- Systemic constellation work in a personal or organizational context works with the visible and latent structure of relationships.[8]
- *Drama therapy* makes use of role-play, theatre games, mime, puppetry and other improvisational techniques, in a wide variety of settings, including hospitals, schools, prisons, and businesses.
- *Adventure* or *wilderness therapy*, outdoor experiential therapy involves risk to boost self-esteem and cooperation games and common tasks to promote pro-social behaviour.

These methods aim to strengthen spontaneity, creativity, resilience, empathy and collective intelligence, and to catalyse individual and communal transformation.

Impact assessments are relatively scarce, especially in non-clinical settings, but some meta-analysis has demonstrated the impact and efficiency of these methods.[9] Some practitioners find that a positivist quantitative impact assessment is at odds with their methods. We seem to need more comprehensive research tools to see how these methods and interventions contribute to a *flourishing life* on both an individual and a collective level.

Weaknesses and limitations of these methods

Potential weaknesses of these approaches tend to relate to their improper application.

1 *The facilitator has limited skills or self-awareness.* The techniques may appear simple at first sight, but they are powerful, so they can have adverse

consequences if ineptly applied. In the popular encounter groups of the 1970s many self-nominated leaders applied confrontational techniques which often produced unfavourable outcomes, which resulted in scepticism toward active methods.[10] This highlights the vital importance of professional skills and ethical standards. Group dynamics and psychologically oriented work require complex skills as well as self-awareness on the part of the group leader. Training as a psychodrama director takes about five to seven years, and self-development is an integral part of the training. Facilitators applying experiential action techniques need to be equipped with sufficient knowledge of group dynamics, of the psyche and of themselves as persons. In sum, the applied technique and its complexity have to be aligned with the training and skills of the facilitator.

2   *The client and the method do not fit.* Not all methods are suited for all people. For *example*, the ability to participate in the imaginative process of role playing without losing touch with outer reality seems to be a minimal requirement for participation. Furthermore, participants must be able to: (i) experience surges of feelings without loss of impulse control, (ii) have some capacity to establish relationships, (iii) have some psychological mindedness.[11]

3   *The process lacks adequate warm-up.* A key factor for a successful action is the adequate warm-up of the group and the individual. In other words, people need to be ready and motivated for action and playful exploration, grounded in a sense of trust and safety. Otherwise, action can lead to stress and anxiety for participants and it will decrease their spontaneity and creativity, rather than increasing it.

4   *Insufficient group cohesion and absence of a constructive working climate.* Optimal group cohesion ensures that people are inclined to express and explore themselves, and to relate more deeply to others. The group is supportive and inclusive. Irvin Yalom also notes that 'Although cohesive groups show greater acceptance, intimacy and understanding, there is evidence that they also permit greater development and expression of hostility and conflict.'[12]

5   *The overwhelming choice of competing methods.* There are ever-increasing numbers of competing forms of action methods, which can make it difficult for a non-professional to make a good choice for themselves.

Not 'psycho' and not 'drama': the 'stage of happiness'

In recent years, I have supported people in their personal development, as well as teams and communities in their search for successful collaboration and co-creation. I call the method I use the Theatre of the Soul, which is based on classical psychodrama, complemented with mindfulness techniques. I coined the term Theatre of the Soul partly to create some distance from the not very inviting name 'psychodrama'.

In my view, psychodrama is a brilliant method, bound by its unfortunate name. Although the founder, Jacob Levy Moreno, derived the name from the Greek words soul (*psyche*) and action (*drama*), referring to the action of the soul and the theatrical genre, each of the words psycho and drama has connotations that can be alarming today. Who would want additional 'drama', especially if they already happen to have enough on their shoulders? 'Drama' may sound overreacting, exhibitionistic, narcissistic or fake. 'Psycho' may be also associated with mental illness, creating a stigma for many, or a state of helplessness. Who would want to reveal their vulnerability and weakness in a world where top performance tends to be an overall expectation both on good days and bad ones? Furthermore, journalists often consider 'psychodrama to be any psychologically-infused and somewhat dramatic situation', as noted by Adam Blatner, a prominent psychiatrist.[13] It is thus easier to come to a psychodrama session if it is personally recommended by someone close to us or if it has a different name, and then to see that psychodrama is very different from what these fears might suggest. What is psychodrama, then?

'Psychodrama has been defined as a way of practicing living without being punished for making mistakes.'[14]

Psychodrama is one of the accredited psychotherapeutic methods used in clinical settings, for example in Austria and Hungary, financed by public funds. Here, I focus on the non-clinical, non-psychotherapeutic

---

Box 7.1: What is psychodrama?

The psychodrama method is:

- an integrated approach to learning involving reflection, action, imagination and memory;
- a recognized approach to psychotherapy and counselling;
- effectively used in education and training, and academic mentoring at universities;[15]
- a sound basis for organizational development;
- a robust form of leadership training.

Source: Adapted from Australian and Aotearoa New Zealand Psychodrama Association.[16]

---

application and, in particular, on how it could support our quest for a *flourishing life*, a sustainable and joyful life both personally and collectively.

Psychodrama has focused on increasing the creativity and spontaneity of people from the very beginning, as reflected in the philosophy of its founder, Moreno. A book title summarizes this mission well: *The Art of Play: Helping Adults Reclaim Imagination and Spontaneity*.[17] Thus, it has been also a method for enhancing the subjective well-being of people, over and above tackling mental health issues.

The term of 'positive psychodrama' has been coined, integrating positive psychology and psychodrama.[18] While the effort to clearly elaborate how psychodrama can be applied for increasing well-being is most welcome, the term 'positive psychodrama' itself might be misleading, as if meaning the expectation of remaining 'on the bright side' and excluding 'negative' feelings or experiences altogether.

'Stage of happiness' ('*Bühne des Glücks*') was the term I used when, earlier, I briefly explored the potentials of psychodrama for promoting eudaimonic well-being.[19] However, it may be criticized and misinterpreted on the same grounds: can someone stand on this stage if they happen to be unhappy? The answer is: yes, of course. It is not about controlling or excluding any feelings or experiences but, rather, promoting well-being through a holistic and non-judgemental approach.

Moreno: the man who brought joy and laughter into psychiatry

Psychodrama was created by Jacob Levy Moreno in the 1920s and 1940s. Moreno was a psychiatrist and a social scientist, and a real explorer, full of curiosity and creativity. He realized that play, imagination and creativity are ancient human impulses, and are so powerful that we can even recreate our relationships, our lives. He learnt a lot from children. He also relied on his own experience: as a five-year old child, he and neighbouring children played God and the angels in the cellar of his home.[20] Moreno became God, sitting on a throne high up, and gradually became fully immersed in the role, so much so that he thought he could fly. He was reminded of reality when he broke his hand on the floor. Later, as an adult, he watched children inventing and enacting fairy tales in the Augarten of Vienna, and observed how naturally they took on a role and became part of a story which they co-created. Around 1922, he created the Theatre of Spontaneity ('*Stegreiftheater*') in his rented apartment in Vienna, where ordinary people acted out newspaper stories. He observed that the specific roles people played profoundly affected their behaviour, and also their lives outside the theatre. It was the beginning of group psychotherapy.

Moreno also organized self-help groups for Viennese prostitutes, and later worked in a refugee camp at Mitterndorf an der Fischa. After emigrating to the US in 1925 he elaborated his group-oriented methods and the study of the fabric of human relations, the attraction and repulsion within groups (*sociometry*). His method has since been further developed and refined by his wife, Zerka Moreno, his students and the achievements of modern psychology.

Zerka and the students were key to the survival of the method, as Moreno was a confrontational figure who had severe conflicts with colleagues, which led to his professional isolation and impeded the spread of the method. Moreover, his early writings are original and ground breaking, but are often conceptually unclear. As noted by Adam Blatner, Moreno's chief enemy was himself. The method and its theoretical background were elaborated and refined by Zerka Moreno and his students Grete Leutz, Max Clayton, Marcia Karp, Felix Kellermann and others.

What is the Theatre of the Soul?

Due to the negative overtones of the word 'psychodrama' to outsiders who have not yet experienced the method, I prefer to use the name Theatre of the Soul, which is merely a translation of the original term into today's language and cultural environment. The phrase 'Theatre of the Soul' retains the original message of psychodrama's founder, but peels off the alarming layer of meaning. What is behind the two keywords?

Theatre of the Soul is a kind of theatre where the stage belongs to all, where everyone is an artist. The stage no longer rises above us, but it is between us, on the same level with us.[21] In the Theatre of the Soul the duality between the actor and the spectator disappears: everyone becomes a participant. Nevertheless, the degree of participation can vary greatly, depending on the group process and individual motivation.

The soul is manifested through action and play. In the Theatre of the Soul, the body moves, and with it layers of consciousness that are inaccessible to the analytical, rational mind do as well. Experiences may also become available that come either from the pre-speech life stage or from the remote terrain of the unconscious. Intuitive wisdom becomes available.

The stage offers a 'surplus reality', with imagination and opportunity. We can travel forward in time as well as backwards. We can appear at any place of interest, be it a real place, a mythical place, a dream image or any imaginary world. Extraordinary encounters and conversations can happen with anyone we want. This includes our inner storyteller and our inner parts, whose company so much define our well-being, our feelings and our actions, often without our awareness.

In the Theatre of the Soul there are a number of different ways that the director can help someone to find an expressive form that feels true and right and to be able to meet with it. The essential precondition is the free, experimental space where one can linger in the state of 'I don't know yet' and can freely explore.

All forces come to life

In the Theatre of the Soul all forces come to life that are necessary for a *flourishing life* and connect us to our joyful, creative state of being. The world we long for can take shape. We will be able to relate to our deepest aspirations, clarify what is really important to us. In addition, we can gain insight into what hinders the actualization of this. Through curious, friendly attention and growing awareness, these destructive inner functions and parts can be transformed (Chapter 8).

The Theatre of the Soul is a theatre of reality where the experiences of the participants, including the inner and outer realms, are the 'script'. Everyone is an actor. No prior knowledge or extraordinary skills are needed. Paradoxically, the method really works when someone does not want to perform, to meet some perceived expectation, but is willing to show themselves authentically, as they are.

The nature of this work is quite unlike a sterile operating room where everything, even the patient's clothes, has to be left outside. People bring not only their own clothes here, but their whole world. A person cannot be interpreted without his or her peers. They affect each other and shape life in a continuous interaction. So we pay attention to the *protagonist's* (the main actor's) current environment and respect it: where he comes from, what his family and social environment are, what his culture and worldview are. An action and an inner functioning can be interpreted only in this context. The openness of the director is crucial here.

The role of the director

The director (sometimes also called producer) is a trained professional who creates a safe setting for free exploration. A good director has not only learnt the meticulous methodology but also developed their self-awareness over many years as a group member, and has thus developed the ability to connect with their own world and that of others in a refined and conscious way. And if they have made good use of the potentialities of the method for themselves, their creativity and love of life become tangible.

As director I work with hypotheses, possibilities, rather than a fixed solution toolkit or a rigidly formed world order. My openness is helped by the fact that I have lived in several countries, worked in multi-ethnic teams and got to know many different forms of communities. This openness is a general attitude, but it has to be activated in the present moment for good dramatic work by a so-called warm-up. I need to connect to my open, flexible and spontaneous self in order to invite others to do so as well.

Max Clayton, my respected mentor emphasized that

> it's not a method whereby the producer of the drama imposes their own ideas, or imposes their own solutions, but rather works with the warm-up of the protagonist so that the protagonist's own life force, the protagonist's own values are drawn out and enacted on the stage. No matter how shocking those actions may be, or how shocking those values may be, they are to be produced. We are to be confronted with the reality of the protagonist's world. We are not here to judge it. We are not to be repelled by it.[22]

The Theatre of the Soul seeks to reconcile two important and often conflicting desires: the desire for safety, for acceptance by others, and the desire for freedom and self-actualization by achieving one's full potential. Safety and freedom are the two pillars of the group work.

Theatre of the Soul for a *flourishing life*

The Theatre of the Soul can support both individuals and groups or communities in their pursuit of a *flourishing life*. Recent advances in positive psychology and self-determination theory provide a useful theoretical base for this, as do the toolbox of psychodrama and mindfulness. What does it mean in practice?

Current situation: An individual or a group can re-examine their current situation. It may be a dilemma, an unresolved situation, a lack of meaning, disconnection from one's core values, restlessness and ill-being, the need for clear goals and vision, or to know what the next steps could be.

Vision for a flourishing future: One can generate new perspectives for life, where one is 'feeling well and doing well'. This highlights the potential development of the person or the group.

- On an individual level, the person can explore their *flourishing self*. Going beyond the standard techniques of visualization and/ or writing about it, dramatic techniques allow the creation and experience of this *best possible future self* or *flourishing self*. The *aim* is to prepare them for future situations in which they function with a greater degree of flexibility, vitality and integrity.
- People do not simply write or speak about their *goals*, but they explore them through action. Supportive social forces as well as inner strength are also included, as well as external or inner hindrances, with the aim of resolving these conflicting forces.
- On a group level, the group may want to *enact their future vision of a flourishing life on a communal or on a global level*. This could include, for example, (i) a 'joint vision for a thriving group', (ii) 'flourishing life in our city/district/town/village/work laboratory/activist loft in 2050', (iii) 'An afternoon in Epicurus' garden – exploring sustainable hedonism'.
- The necessary *action* can be devised, based on the strengths of individual group members.
- Values can be made visible and explicit, motivating action as well as interaction between group members. For this, a group may create a play with the 'Witnessing of values', where each person shows a value of particular importance to them, for example, Humour, Beauty, Quiet Voice of the Smallest, and so on.

Celebration: The group can be a place for celebration and ritual as part of the dramatic play, marking a major discovery or a breakthrough in the process. Furthermore, the capacity to celebrate achievements or events of significance (be they individual or collective) may grow.

Strengths: We notice and appreciate all that is already there by identifying one's *character strengths* (using the terminology of positive psychology) or identifying one's *progressive roles* (using the psychodramatic term). In contrast to verbal counselling interventions, when people are asked to write or speak about these, in the Theatre of the Soul people can also enact them.

Needs: People's striving for (i) autonomy, (ii) competence and creativity and (iii) supportive, loving relationships are acknowledged, and the director as well as the group supports the satisfaction of these, both with positive experiences within the group and by finding the right life strategies for the outside world. Potential conflicts between these three core needs, and existing strategies and habits for meeting them, can be explored.

Mindfulness: Participants can enlarge their perceptions of themselves and the world. The Theatre of the Soul offers a potential pathway to greater mindfulness, as it is characterized by awareness of the present moment with flexibility and openness. Perceptions are refined. Spontaneity grows. The core concept of spontaneity is far from being 'mindless, instinctive or uninhibited impulsivity', but contains an element of self-control, as well as autonomy and freedom of external circumstances.[23] Mindfulness allows the rediscovery of the world in which we live.

'Friends and significant others': Personal concerns may be viewed in a larger perspective of relationships. What contributes to sustaining a difficult situation? And what supports a progressive transformation? Personal relationships as well as cultural and social forces may play a role, literally, on the stage. Similarly, the future vision of a *flourishing life* is not restricted to the person as an individual in isolation, but relationships (to humans or other beings) are also an inherent part of this future image. The dramatic action also help people to be aware of the perspective of others (empathy and awareness), as if seeing themselves and their actions in a mirror. Instead of being simply *responsive* to others, people may become more *responsible* for their own actions.

The invisible: The individual or the group can explore all those essential elements of their functioning which may not be visible, yet which affect their well-being greatly. The group can recognise patterns of interaction and interpersonal dynamics. They can investigate both formal and informal relationship networks.

Drama with mindfulness and awareness

Drama and mindfulness may be closer to each other than it may at first seem. Mindfulness techniques can be integrated with psychodrama.[24] In my own practice it is particularly useful in the warm-up phase, preparatory to an efficient action phase.

We learn to slow down, halt, notice all what we sense, feel and think, without judging or rejecting these. We adopt a friendly attitude, as if we were the best friend of ourselves, rather than critical judges.

We learn to perceive the world in new ways, beyond our everyday patterns. Through our changing perception we recreate our vision of the world, and that of our own history and our future. We recognize our role as co-creator of our own reality. We enhance our ability to create a *flourishing life* for ourselves. This creativity emerges naturally, not under pressure or control. Rather, we give time for ourselves to spend in the 'space in between', not yet knowing what is best.

The dramatic techniques can help us to be able to look at any situation from multiple perspectives. The spectrum of perception broadens, and, with it, the fixed identification with an emotion, a thought or a particular interpretation of a situation loses its grip on us.

Complexity may not be threatening and overwhelming any more. We may increasingly learn to witness and enjoy the diversity of the world and human relationships. We may learn that there are many ways to look at a situation and a problem, and that there is not necessarily a clear answer now. We may not be hesitant to say 'I don't know'.

After practising the techniques like *role reversal* many times, we develop the ability to instinctively do a *role reversal* with a person. After a while, we may be able to do this with imaginary, abstract or remote qualities such as Beauty, Future or Gaia. We will be also able to look at a situation from far afar, observing ourselves as well as all that surrounds us. We can take a bird's-eye view. Our vision will transcend the boundaries of the world previously visible to us, and can be enriched more by collective wisdom.

We may feel less that we need to fight strenuously for our values or aspirations but, rather, that we can support their manifestation with our vitality, our creativity and our ability to collaborate with others.

Transformative group experience

A key feature of the Theatre of the Soul is that it takes place in a group. The focus of a dramatic exploration can be on one member's personal theme as well as the functioning of the group as a whole, or on an important event in the outside world, depending on what concerns the group members at the moment.

A friendly, cooperative, non-judgemental group norm can override previous painful experiences such as shaming, excommunication, bullying, mobbing or relentless competition. A supportive group can represent a new kind of reference. This also changes the recipe for what is needed for coping, success, recognition of others, and in the world in general.

The world never appears in its entirety in our lives, but often through a few small groups like our families, colleagues or neighbours, and our experiences there determine what life strategy we develop.

It is therefore not unimportant what kind of groups they are. Who constitutes our world? And who are we becoming in this world?

If I were you: empathy rather than advice

We tend to spend a considerable amount of time imagining what other people may think or feel, and what they think of us and our relationship. Sometimes we wish that we knew more of the mystery of the other. If only we were able to read their minds! This may not actually be such a remote and esoteric idea as it may seem at first. I think that we tend to have more relational knowledge of and insights into people who are significant to us than we are aware of, and these can be accessed by action-based dramatic methods.

In the technique of *role reversal* we take the role of someone we know well, and embody that person's posture and voice and speak as if we were them. When we do this, a rich intuitive, emotional knowledge opens up. Our empathic abilities expand. We will gradually be able to recognize the feelings and views of the other, be they a supportive friend or an adversary in a conflict situation. We will also start seeing ourselves through their eyes. This helps us to understand relationship dynamics. Major relationship adjustments can originate this way, including resolution of a conflict, an ambivalent situation or 'unfinished business' with a deceased parent, to name just a few.

Abusive situations or past traumas are exceptions, as *role reversal* with the aggressor is normally not advisable, especially when enacting the threatening situation. The specific tools need to be aligned to the whole therapeutic process and the individual's needs. In general, the importance of careful attention to diverse personal needs holds for any intervention for all participants.

'I-and-you' instead of 'I-and-it'

Taking on roles and practising *role reversal* (lover with a lover, child with a parent, powerful with the powerless), we are increasingly able to change perspectives in all sorts of life situations. With this, we also leave behind our own separated individual view of the self, often judgemental, critical or rejective of oneself or of others. As the sense of separation fades, so we experience unity between polarities and opposites. Instead of an 'I-and-it' perspective, the 'I-and-you' and 'we' mindset arises, as expressed by the philosophy of Martin Buber.[25] Instead of an objectified world, we enter a relational world. We will be able to connect to the world with our whole being. I have a very personal experience related to this.

My father's imaginary diary

I longed for my father's attention time and again, more than he was able to give it. Then, one day I realized that we share this desire, that is, he longs for attention just as much as I do. It occurred to me that I would gift him with my attention and do it in a way that he never expected.

I wrote a diary, an imaginary diary. I wrote it in the first person singular, as if he was talking about himself. It began on the day of his birth and, as a diary, continued with entries for specific dates.

I included almost all the stories I had heard from him and I could recall. (It was actually not too many, as his way of telling his own life story was rather repetitive, focusing on a few highlights only, as is often the case.) I tried to write in the way he would talk about these, if he was able to talk about them. I role-reversed with him internally, aiming to become him, with all his features and concerns. I also added what I did not hear but I only sensed: feelings, moods, thought fragments. I used my imagination and intuition as well, including experiences that he could not have remembered or talked about. It began with the experience of birth, with an entry for that day: 'It hurt a lot. I am surrounded by strange noises. A familiar one is the heartbeat of my mother, but it is suddenly so far away.' Then it continued with maternal closeness, the siblings, the affection and the rivalry, then with the small joys and extreme fears of the Second World War, the goat called Rosy, who saved the family with her milk, the tons of bitter chocolate bars found in the vast stores of the brewery's cellar used as a bomb shelter, the experiences which created the deep desires, and life strategies for fulfilling them for a lifetime. Then came the skills and talents, the way they were discovered and refined, my father as a radio amateur. It continued with the 1956 revolution, the very first salary from the factory, his precious first Trabant automobile, his wedding, the births of his children, the wishes and hopes associated with them, the rare and precious travels in Western Europe, the breath-taking days of regime change, until the present time. This was a time travel witnessing a series of special moments, meticulously elaborate scenes but without the ambition to create a full movie.

The diary did not finish at the present moment. It continued into the future. On behalf of my father I described that he accepts his grey hair and declining strength. I depicted him visiting the Great Wall of

China, the thing he had been dreaming of for a lifetime. I added how he, a restless and hard-working person, is able to finally reach a state of calmness and joy, and to look back on his life with gratitude. I thus created a future, written in the present tense, hinting at the certainty of the occurrence. Finally, in order not to set boundaries, I closed the lines with a poetic infinity.

I felt some risk in this venture, as my father did not usually talk openly about his emotions. How would he take the joys, sorrows and frustrations attributed to him in my imaginary storytelling? I expected this to be the beginning of a dialogue, and that he would correct me, ask me to amend some stories and tell me many more. Then diary could be rewritten, made more complete. This would be a process of making it his own diary, his own biography, the way he would have written it himself if he happened to like to do such a thing. That is not what happened.

When he received the booklet he was taken by surprise and retreated into a secluded room. A few hours later he thanked me with tear-worn eyes, stirred, and when he finally found his words, asked me how come I knew all this. And when I told him to feel free to correct whatever he wanted, all he could say was that everything was as true as I had described, there was nothing to rewrite. Or perhaps, there was something, he added, 'the goat ... the goat was called Julie, not Rosy'.

The experience of community can be one of the keys to solving the global crisis

The process of promoting a *flourishing life* for ourselves personally and collectively cannot remain purely cognitive, as we tend to *think* about ourselves quite differently than how we actually *feel* or *act*. The incongruence often comes from instinctive urges and unconscious impulses. How can we become more acquainted with these? Somatic perceptions, feelings, intuitions can help, as well as art and playfulness, where we can step out of the world of our usual and habitual way of operating and can be surprised at ourselves. The Theatre of the Soul offers an opportunity for creating our *flourishing life*, on both a personal and a collective level.

Our personal concerns are often existential matters to others as well. We may realize that we are not alone with our problems. A supportive group may evoke the enlargement of our world: our awareness of the outside world may expand, as well as our personal freedom growing. Such group will give many people a new template for how to stay free and belong to others at the same time.

Role play is likely to increase empathy and has a sensitizing effect. During a dramatic play we take the role of strangers, often very different from us, and experience situations from their point of view, and this can multiply our insight and compassion. We can try out countless life situations. Gradually, we are able to understand what others may feel, even those from whom we have so far distanced ourselves. We may see what moves them, why they are the way they are. And perhaps we would do just that in their place.

Furthermore, we may increasingly comprehend how our actions affect others. With this, we are likely to recognize our responsibilities in our close circles and the wider world. This does not mean that we need to forget about our own needs. But it may well shift what we see as our essential needs, and, with it, also our strategies for satisfying them. Our ways of eating, travelling, working and, in general, seeking joy may transform. Our well-intentioned actions for supporting others may not take the form of occasional acts of charity any more, where 'I' is clearly divided from 'them', but, rather, a general attitude of compassion, originating from a sense of connectedness. Our approach to fairness and equity in society and the economy may also alter.

Experiencing a cooperative, friendly community and cultivating our own social skills can enhance the joy that our relationships give us. We may be able to gradually satisfy our existential longing for acceptance, respect and belonging, and with this experience our priorities may also shift. At the same time, we may become more motivated to consciously raise our capacity to be part of mutually enriching friendships and relationships.

We may no longer feel that we need to control people in order to trust them and to ensure the fulfilment of our desires. We may enter communities where we create the norms together, consider each other as partners and seek balance and harmony by being aware of our different needs and desires.

Material consumption may appear less appealing. Objects may no longer seem more trustworthy than people because one can control them – by buying and using them whenever and however one wants. We may realize that we are way more autonomous, competent and creative than we may have seen before. Our motivation to pursue what matters for us truly and what makes us feel right increases.

It may happen that those of us who had been striving to achieve a good life and security primarily by means of competition and achievement opt for a new life strategy. We may start seeing ourselves increasingly as part of a larger living system that is evolving and growing and striving for completeness. We may realize that this actually makes us stronger than struggling in isolation. Our priority may now be to learn how to live and navigate well in this relational world.

Over time, as our negative, self-defeating voices weaken and lose their power over us, we may feel less entitled to turn to others in a hurtful way, spreading the pain which is so natural to us. As the void which we may have felt heals, pleasure-seeking will be no more a short-term pain-killer, and our attitude to pleasure will be more liberated and conscious. A change of habits and life-styles will be possible, reducing the harm that we have caused – perhaps unaware – to other beings. This may affect our responsiveness to the ecological crisis: it is no longer an abstract subject or an inconvenient matter where someone wants to force us into something or make us feel guilty. If the boundaries of our world are moved way beyond the boundaries of the personal self, ever wider, and we feel connected to and care for other beings in the world, then the ethical considerations about their lives will no longer be external (and disturbingly moralizing), but will stem from within our being. We mean them well, and it comes naturally. We recognize our interdependence. Their thriving is our thriving as well. A successful life is no longer the success of the individual 'I', but the success of the communal 'we'.

The experience of community and personal potentials, supported by experiential learning methods like the Theatre of the Soul, allows us to gradually create new ways of operating individually and socially, and to tell and celebrate new stories of success. This is how we can create a new narrative about how to live well.

8

Inner Agents and Saboteurs of the Good Life: Role Theory

All the world's a stage,
And all the men and women merely players:
They have their exits, and their entrances;
And one man in his time plays many parts.

(William Shakespeare, *As You Like It*)

The scholarship of our inner roles: role theory

Jacob Levy Moreno developed his own role theory from 1923 on. In contrast to sociological role theory, which is a theoretical concept and primarily seeks to describe certain phenomena, for example gender roles, Moreno focused on practical application. He worked with refugees, prostitutes, schoolchildren, companies, church groups and politicians. He worked with psychiatric clients as well as ordinary people. In addition to *social roles*, he also explored '*psychodramatic roles*' (for example hero, explorer, movie star), where imagination is also gaining ground.

He did not stop here, as he looked at an individual through their relations. Therefore, he was intrigued by how one person's behaviour affects someone else or an entire group and, conversely, how they affect the person, that is, what interactions there are between different members (and their roles). He observed how the structure of a group can change and how its cohesion can be increased.[1] I learnt most about its practical application from my mentor, Max Clayton, and through my personal experiences.

Moreno's *role theory* bridges the individual and the community, psychology and sociology, as it examines intrapersonal (intrapsychic) phenomena as well as interpersonal (interpsychic) interactions. Moreno believed that dramatic tools can not only help individuals as such, but are also able reshape the overall culture. He envisioned a new culture: a world more creative, spontaneous, healing and connected.

Moreno, just like his Australian disciple Max Clayton, believed in the liberating and healing power of self-expression. Role playing, drama techniques, as well as dance, song, music, drawing and myriad of other forms of creativity are opportunities for one to create something new. Everyone can be an artist. Life is also an art, when one lives with freedom of self-expression.

Our roles: authentically

Many of us decide to fulfil our social roles as best we can, and we dedicate much energy and effort to meet the perceived standards. That is, we try to be 'good' scientists, farmers, teachers, businessmen, spouses, fathers or mothers, according to the norms ingrained in us, with the hope to gain approval, admiration and respect. This is a natural endeavour. We want to do our duties well. Furthermore, we can also decide, perhaps as a result of a crisis, an illness, a failure or a severe loss, to question and investigate our social roles, what we are doing and why we are doing it that way.

In addition, we can scrutinize a deeper layer as well. After all, in our lives we develop not only social roles but also psychic roles. These determine how we react to a situation, or what our inner voices and urges are at all. We are moved differently by the Rebel, Adventurer, Invalid, Defeatist or Sage living in us. Since several of our roles are active at any given moment, if they happen to be conflicting we may endure ambivalence and doubt. We would go and we would stay. We would do it and we would rather not.

Authentic life does not imply the elimination of all roles, as is sometimes proclaimed in new age literature. We are social beings and our psychic functioning has also its features, so we will continue to have a number of roles as long as we live. The key to authenticity is to be driven by those roles which are aligned to our momentary emotions and our values.

Authenticity is a rich repertoire of roles: in a given situation we are being present and act in alignment to that. Although the Injured Child or the Good Girl/Good Boy may appear in us, especially if it is a well-known, much practised behavioural pattern of ours, it does not take control, because we also perceive the presence of our other roles – for example, the Smart Adult, the Free Thinker, the Responsible Boss, the

Peacemaker or the Timeless Sage – and we choose a suitable one. It is also an internal freedom, the freedom to choose the right roles and functions.

The prerequisite for this is that we are able to look at our roles from the outside. We can recognize that none of them defines us exclusively. We are not just Business people or just Mothers. But we are not exclusively Rebels or Defeatists either. Several roles live in us. The key question is whether they help us in living well: are we able to consciously decide which role serves us in a particular situation, instead of having an automatic reaction? It is for our own good if we can gradually let go of our outdated and rigid roles that no longer support ourselves and our thriving.

After all, just as we once learnt our roles as an adaption to our environment, we may be able to learn new roles for the sake of our own development.

Our inner stage: role inventory

We can create a personal 'role inventory'. By naming and describing our roles, we venture on a creative process by which we also write the story of our lives. Two key questions arise.

1 What roles do we have?
2 How do we name them? Naming is as essential as detecting a role. It is a creative process, and is a key part of developing a playful and friendly attitude toward ourselves, including those parts of us which are difficult to accept and which we are likely to want to hide in order to avoid shame or appearing as a failure. I will show some examples later.

As a counsellor, I have found that most people are aware of only a fraction of their roles, so that it takes a while to create their inventory of roles, and external support is needed. The process, on the other hand, is an eye-opener and a potent experience in itself. While preparing our role inventory we may notice that, in addition to the obviously loud roles – typically, these are the prevailing voice and mood of the 'inner monologue' that automatically takes place within us, the way we speak to ourselves when we are on our own – there are also playful, humorous, aesthetic or artistic ones.

What roles could we have? In the following section I examine the roles according to how they help to meet or how they hinder basic needs. As discussed in Chapter 6, for a *flourishing life* we need to be able to meet all our three core psychological needs. According to the *self-determination theory* these are: (1) autonomy (*freedom*), (2) *competence*, (3) relatedness (*love, kindness*).[2] For a *flourishing life*, all three must be fulfilled, as all of them are basic human needs.

I propose a number of psychic roles as a starting point and inspiration. They are based on my perceptions and insights as a psychological counsellor and psychodrama group director. These roles neither aspire for a comprehensive description of the psyche nor pretend to be the manifestations of an ultimate truth of any sort. My aim is to inspire and invite all to a creative and playful inner exploration.

Progressive roles

The desire for freedom is aided by the Explorer, the Rebel and the Sage. What could these roles be like? I describe how I imagine them, but of course they can have other manifestations as well. The roles are not gender-specific, and the use of the gender pronoun in the text does not imply that a specific role is exclusively male or female.

The Explorer steps out of the ordinary boldly, curious to discover a new world. He is not afraid to take risks. He is helped by his rapid situational awareness and flexibility. He also relies on his intuition.

The Rebel has the ability to get out of situations where her opportunities are curbed, she is oppressed or weakened. She can help others to do this by inspiring or supporting them. She is able to form a clear judgement, to see through situations where injustice, unfairness or oppression occurs, and to take firm action against these.

The Sage is not harmed by the turbulence of the outside world, and through his persistent practice he already has the virtue of self-control, so that he can relate to matters of everyday life with clairvoyance. He is not blinded by his bad habits or cravings, or by all the glittering allure of the outside world. He views things, events and situations with a peaceful serenity of timeless wisdom. He is like a deep lake with clear water that is not stirred by the splash of a stone. Timeless, ageless, and his perspective extends beyond his personal life.

Our own inner Explorer, Rebel and Sage can help us to experience freedom. What this actually implies for a person in a particular situation, conflict or dilemma can be rather diverse. Moreover, we can also find other names for our own inner roles, if these feel more suited to us. We may also have other roles that help us.

The fulfilment of the longing for competence and creativity can be supported by the Artist and the Hero living within us.

The Artist is a dreamer and creator of new things. She knows her own diverse abilities and is able to use them, even in new ways, to

Table 8.1: Progressive roles related to basic psychic needs

Basic psychic need	Progressive roles supporting flourishing life
Autonomy	Explorer
	Rebel
	Sage
Competence, creativity	Artist
	Hero
Love, belonging	Friend
	Mother

combine different qualities and thus surprise herself and others. She loves and celebrates beauty in the world.

The Hero solves problems in unexpected ways, even on a social scale, showing the way to others. He is the one who can act even when others are clueless or paralysed. He excels in the virtue of courage.

Our longing for relatedness and love can be provided for by our role as a Friend or Mother. Here, the Mother expresses a universal quality, an archetype that can live in a man or in a childless woman as well, and is not limited to child bearing or rearing.

The Mother cherishes life and sustains vitality. She cares, nourishes, is sensitive to the needs of the other and reacts to them subtly. She is a gentle guard providing safety. She grieves and rejoices with her child, her friend.[3] She always sees herself connected, in the system of relationships and as part of the larger world. She sees the web of life as a unity of the biological and spiritual dimensions and thus says yes to it. She has a strong connection to Mother Earth.

The Friend perceives his life as intertwined with his important friendships, relationships and community. He is able to develop and foster his friendship with his 'best friend' and recognizes the depth and potential of this connection as well as its exceptional nature. He sees what he can give to others. He recognizes what he owes to others. He relates to others with openness, trust and cooperation. He seeks peer-to-peer relationships without the need for domination and subordination.

I suggest that almost everyone has some aspects of the Explorer, the Artist, the Friend or of other roles, although a *flourishing life* can be varied, as is the path to it. Since these are expressions of basic human needs – autonomy, desire for competence and connection – we can assume that most people with sufficient vitality will choose some strategy to fulfil them. These roles express a possible strategy, an attitude.

These roles are also in line with the most prevalent human values. As discussed in Chapter 6, across diverse cultures most people regard three values as the most important: 'self-direction' (independent thinking and action, creation, discovery), 'benevolence' (well-being of closer friends, relatives, helpfulness, friendship, love) and 'universalism' (understanding, respect, tolerance, world peace, equality, love of nature). The Explorer, the Artist and the Friend in us, as well as the other roles, therefore help to realize the values that are important to us.

Therefore we regard them as *progressive roles*.

Absent, underdeveloped, excessive and adequate roles

We can view the inner world of a person as a house, a house unique to them, and the roles as the inhabitants and guests of this house. Maybe the Explorer, the Artist, the Friend or some other role is just a rare guest there. But it could also be that they are already residents. They may even be the owners of the house. The nature of their presence or absence determines how they affect a person's life and, ultimately, their ability to live a *flourishing life*.

It may be that someone feels that he has nothing to do with an Artist. It is not his self-perception, and he does not think that anyone would see him as a creative, artistic person. His Artist self is alien or perhaps even repellent to him. In this case, the role is missing or underdeveloped. It is an invisible, rare and shy guest in this house.

In contrast, a role may become far too dominant: it appears and becomes vocal even when it should not. In this case, the person may not be able to react well to a situation. The obsessed Artist, for example, may be so preoccupied with his own activities that he neglects his partner or children. The Artist takes the lead when he needs the Mother or Friend role. His inner Artist is so loud and stubborn that he cannot activate other roles which are also essential to sustain a good life.

An 'adequate' role is present in a way that it is suitable in the particular situation or for our overall well-being. We are able to become assertive Rebels when we witness a social injustice and we are able to act efficiently and in proportion to our abilities and power. When a dear friend asks for our help we are able to become a Friend in a way that can give support and safety. When an opportunity presents itself, we are able to become an Artist who gives form to intuitive ideas or expression to our admiration of beauty in the world. 'Adequate' implies not too much and not too little, and the measure for this is completely personal and situational.

Following the example of the house, we wish its inhabitants not to be too loud, nor to oppress other residents or guests. We also want a guest who is dear to us to speak, to show us her precious qualities and to visit us more often. Ultimately, we want the visitors to the house to get along well with each other and be present in a way that inspires, helps and delights us.

Thus, after recognizing and naming the roles in the role inventory, we examine the quality of each role: whether they are absent, underdeveloped, excessive or adequate.

Saboteur roles

Our psychic roles and ego states can support us, but they can also prevent us from living a *flourishing life*. Each role (manifested as inner voice, urge or action) can be judged on whether it promotes development, well-being and balance or, rather, hampers or ruins them. While the former is a *progressive role*, the latter is a *saboteur role*.[4] When a *saboteur role* pops up, we are doing something that harms us, as if we were an enemy to ourselves. The presence of these roles is likely not only to reduce our personal well-being but to also limit our capacity to care about other beings and the Earth.

Saboteur roles are often a blind spot. We may have the illusion that for a successful personal (or organizational) development all we have to do is to clarify the values, the vision, the goals, the resources and the strategy. Certainly, it is useful to connect to these, perhaps with greater clarity than we normally do, but this is not enough. The experience of individual and collective hindrances and failures (including our ecological crisis, social injustice) calls for broadening our awareness.

But who would want to spend time dealing with their own destructive impulses? Those who are already aware of their saboteur parts may be afraid that they will grow and gain a stronger grip on their lives. As for those who are not aware of these saboteur parts, why would they want to be? After all, there may be a good reason why they have not wanted to get acquainted with them.

It may be a righteous life ideal which blocks a person from taking notice of anything that would contradict their self-image. This ideal is likely to be a perfection of some sort, related to success, achievement, love, selflessness, virtue or religious or spiritual aspirations of living without sin or attaining enlightenment. The person, identifying fully with this aspiration, would almost be destroyed by a failure. It would be a source of shame not to be fully aligned with this ambitious life task, so they eliminate anything from their consciousness that could contradict this ideal. This process could be unconscious, and is called repression in psychology. The avoidance of anything resembling 'failure' or 'negativity' may appear as a short cut to success but it is, rather, a detour, potentially leading to anxiety, guilt, rumination, physical illness, antisocial or self-destructive behaviour.

Others may think that they know the destructive impulses that live within them. They know the saboteur who prevents them from acting for their own long-term goals, or the one who weakens them with critical, humbling or hurtful thoughts. So why spend more time on this? Could not it make them feel worse? Yes, it could. And it could also bring a transformation, greater well-being and getting on better with others. It depends on how they relate to the saboteur. So the real question is how to relate to the saboteur inside us: the focus is on the 'how'.

Saboteur roles, be they giants or dwarfs, are in us, they affect us. We can choose to consciously relate to them. The virtue of self-discipline, cherished by Aristotle, could be also interpreted as the practice of handling our inner saboteurs, whatever desires and hostile voices they may represent. The pursuit of a *flourishing life* and happiness does not mean that we are focusing only on *progressive roles*. Awareness of inhibitory forces is also essential.

In the dimension of freedom, there may be a *saboteur role* for the Servant, the Overachiever and the Indulger.

The Overachiever strives to meet rules and expectations as much as possible. Her attention is fixed on the outside world, she hardly perceives herself in her own reality, and rejection or acceptance of the outside world is her only measure. She can be characterized by a lack of initiative, passivity regarding her own deepest desires and aspirations. But she can also be very proactive in matters related to performing well. She wants to do her business well by all means, the best she possibly can, and if something is not perfect she becomes frustrated, dissatisfied with herself and does not even realize what she has already achieved. She does not stop to celebrate. She keeps running, working, delivering, with a strong drive to prove. A burn-out may come as a complete surprise.

The Servant feels at home in hierarchical systems under the control of a strong leader, even if that leader is invidious or exploitative. The form of this control may change as he moves from the school desk to a company and then to another company, or joins a political movement, but he is always down and looking up, as it is only there that he sees real strength, not in himself. In an extreme case, he can reach the point of being ready to do anything on command, completely resigning his own conscience.

The Indulger strives for an easy life without effort. She seeks easy pleasures, and devours them. She cares little about tomorrow or others. She does not consider how her actions affect others. She is addicted to pleasures, she cannot get enough of them, and her greatest effort is to get as much of them as possible. The Sunk Indulger easily becomes addicted, and his addiction can take countless forms. At this extreme stage, the pain and harm caused to himself or others surpasses the fleeting pleasure of enjoying things.

In the dimension of competence and creativity, the Fool and the Court Clown may appear.

The Fool does not trust herself and her abilities. She thinks she is worthless in the eyes of others and everyone has given up on her. So she gives up on herself too.

The Court Clown masterfully entertains others and is also popular for his good humour and playfulness. He emerges jokingly from any situation which may be challenging to him. He does not dare to show or to act out his true self. He is outward-looking, fuelled by the acceptance of others, dependent on popularity, and is very vulnerable in this respect. He is easily distracted by a momentary impulse, a seductive opportunity.

The possible saboteurs of fulfilment of the basic need for love and relatedness are the Orphan and the Tyrant.

The Orphan feels alone, as if she was forgotten. She is filled with the pain of lack, so she either reaches out longingly or, sinking into herself, shuts herself off from the world. Her longing is so strong that almost nothing could fulfil it. She longs to be loved, to be accepted, to be recognized, but almost nothing, no experience, is enough to provide lasting contentment. Her existential reality is endless isolation and lack.

The Tyrant has decided that it is safest to be in charge. He controls people, situations, whatever he can. He wants to govern all this according to his firm vision. For him, this is the order. He has an extremely wide range of tools, including punishment, blackmail, threats, rewards and dividing people against each other. He severely punishes anyone who disobeys, as this is an existential threat to him. In the world, only the throne is a suitable place for him, so he will feel tormented if he cannot sit on it.

Both the Orphan and the Tyrant put themselves at the centre of the universe. Every relationship, every event is 'good' or 'bad' according to whether it is just 'good' or 'bad' for them, that is, whether it serves their desires, aspirations, or their own ideas about the order of the world. For them, the world is struggle where one has to fight to get what one wants. If they need something, they do everything to get it

Table 8.2: Progressive and saboteur roles related to basic psychic needs

Basic psychic need	Progressive roles (supporting flourishing life)	Saboteur roles (hindering flourishing life)
Autonomy	Explorer Rebel Sage	Servant Overachiever Indulger
Competence, creativity	Artist Hero	Fool Court Clown
Love, belonging	Friend Mother [Sage]	Orphan Tyrant

for themselves, the Orphan by overplaying his destitution, the Tyrant with control and unrestrained use of means. For the Orphan, it is a sign of success if she manages to gain some pity and, with it, tenderness and generosity. For the Tyrant, the sign of success is winning and gaining as much as possible. Success is a sign of merit, but only if he has won.

And just as everyone has universal *progressive roles*, so are *saboteur roles* just as likely to emerge. These *saboteur roles* sustain consumerism and resonate with the selfish moron of the *economic man*. It is our own inner Indulger, Fool and Orphan who, together with similar *saboteur roles* of others, create again and again the world that promises happiness but actually prevents it. Moreover, due to their destructiveness, they can even bring about their own annihilation.

Paradoxically, the roles that promote progress and prosperity, and the destructive roles that undermine it, are both present in parallel in our human existence. This is so both on a collective level and within a person. One may long for mature love and generosity (intrinsic values) and prioritize wealth and fame (extrinsic values). Mankind is both the creator and the destroyer of its world, often carrying the contradiction within itself and creates it in the outside world.

It is difficult to carry this contradiction within us, or even to admit it. What can we do to resolve this?

Resolving the inner paradox

The key to resolving the paradox is to turn to our inner world with openness, friendliness and curiosity. The aspiration is to witness ourselves in our wholeness.

1 It will be easier to start with our *progressive roles*, as this will make us aware of our strength and our ability to act well, and will increase our sense of competence and self-esteem, which is a good foundation for further exploration.
2 As part of this, we can explore whether there is a role that is missing or very small and is essential for us in living well.
3 Then it is worth taking stock of our *saboteur roles*, the impulses and actions holding us back from being able to live well.

Furthermore, it is important for us not to regard these inner roles as eternal and permanent, the curse or grace of destiny, but, rather, to view them as existing habits, ingrained patterns that may change. The methodology of role training and the experiences gained in the Theatre of the Soul can help in this. This is discussed in more detail in the following sections.

Case study 8.1: The studded road and the dancing broom

Malvin is a pretty, restrained woman in her forties with tidy hair and elegant clothes who meticulously wants to do everything right. This shows in her way of sitting and moving. I have a feeling that she is silently apologizing almost immediately after saying hello or after saying anything. The role of Servant seems to be overdeveloped: she is focused almost obsessively on the expectations of others, she constantly scans the outside world with her attention. She has no energy, time or money left for her own desires, because she is always taking care of others.

I ask Malvin in one of our group meetings to create a picture showing her relationship to the important goal she cherishes in her heart, whatever that may be. I do not know what it could be, and she does not name it either. I ask her to choose another group member as representative of her goal. As it is not our first group meeting she already knows the imaginary stage in the room, where fantasy and reality can be shown and created. She becomes active and places her desired goal as far away from herself as she can, at the far edge of the stage. She looks at the Goal with a sigh. I have the feeling that that sigh carries both desire and renunciation.

I ask if she can take a step towards it. She sighs louder, lowers her head and points in front of herself, "No. The road is scattered with push-pins." Her legs seem to be rooted to the ground. Standing next to her, I look at the 'studded path' and then ask, "What can be done here then?" She bends down and begins to pick up these (imaginary but very real) push-pins, one by one, slowly, with a rather gloomy look.

"You've started a big job. When do you think you will be done with that?" I ask her.

"Weeeeell ... in a long, very long time," she replies.

"Is this life enough for it?" I say aloud what occurs to me. "Do you perhaps have another idea for what could be done?" I inquire.

She reacts almost immediately: "I need a broom!"

"Create it! Choose this broom" – I point to the group, suggesting that she select a group member for the role – "and show how you sweep with it!"

Malvin finds her broom (selects a person) and takes action. She creates an image where the broom dances in front of her. There is no sign of any sweaty, arduous work. And she takes the steps with joy and liberation, moving forward with the dancing broom. She warms up, laughs. I leave time for this, as much as I feel she needs. This is how we end the scene. The picture looks fairy tale and rather expressive as it is.

At the next meeting Malvin tells the group that the image of the dancing broom came to life many times within her and that it meant a lot to her in difficult moments. Malvin discovers who is actually helping her: an Artist Malvin, a painter she knew and loved well in the past, but whom she undeservedly neglected for a long time. She remembers how much the joy of creation can give her! She takes a decision: she will give more space in her life to painting and to this Artist Malvin. So far, she has not paid much attention to it because of the push- pins have captured her full attention. It is time for something else! The broom was transformed this evening into a paintbrush, and Malvin became a creative person holding a brush. She embodied her Artist Malvin by taking on this role, experiencing fully her qualities and being. Artist Malvin is an inner part, a *progressive role*, which helps her development, so her attention to it and its development makes the whole personality of Malvin more integrated and better functioning.

Role training for authenticity: creative work with roles

Step 1: Strengthening progressive roles: *noticing the obvious*

Our everyday successes often seem natural. Our ordinary cognition, evolved for problem solving, routinely neglects the legion of things without problems. We may even not notice if something is actually working well in an area of our life or an episode of the day. If we turn our attention to this, we may realize that we are much more successful or healthier than we thought. By fine-tuning our perception, a grey weekday can turn coloured.

If we feel well and things go smoothly, do we attribute this only to lucky external conditions? Or do we also see what our part is in this? What exactly did we do? How did we do that? Do we know the *progressive roles* that live in us? Do we know how to 'summon' them in a given situation, as if rubbing the magic lamp evoked the genie in the fairy tale?

The range of *progressive roles* is endless, so everyone can find the most appropriate name for their own inner roles according to their faith, culture or worldview. It could be the previously mentioned Explorer, Artist, Sage, Friend or Mother. It could then be, for example, a Creative Activist, a Friendly Leader, a Man of Nature, a Tribal Wizard, a Playful Child or one of many other figures among ancient archetypes or those of artworks, a film hero or a figure in a novel. It may also be a transcendental or spiritual figure, compatible with the person's worldview.

In the Theatre of the Soul we enact the roles. We can experience the joy of such an encounter and the new impulse they bring. We can come into contact with our inner fire, our free being, embodied by the Explorer, to whom we owe a lot and whom we can count on for our courageous future steps. We can feel our inner peace, our own Sage. We can get together with the Friend who lives in us, who is able to cooperate with others, love others and experience the love of others, as well as the Mother, who sees herself as an integral part of the cosmos with benevolence and goodwill, which sustains her and which is sustained by her.

Staging our *progressive roles* can make us realize how much we already have, how we already doing well. We can recognize our inner wealth. We may be able to look at our lives with gratitude. This could inspire us to be even more aware of these *progressive roles* and to rely on them actively in trying situations.

Step 2: Seeing the invisible: missing roles

We may find that certain (features of) people inspire us, but that this feels far too remote from our current functioning and reality. We may feel that the *progressive roles* described earlier have nothing to do with us. They are absent or very rarely present in our lives. How could we see the invisible? How could anything sprout where perhaps there is not even a seed planted?

In a so-called role-training process there are a few key techniques which could help with this. A key prior step is to be aware of our *progressive roles* which seem to be adequate already in our lives. By refining our awareness we can notice that a desired and absent role may not be entirely missing. Perhaps it has already been present in certain phases of our lives.

A particularly powerful theatrical technique is an imaginary encounter with a respected person who inspires us or to whom we owe a lot. It could be a dear (childhood) teacher, a relative or a mentor, who is clearly supportive and appreciative of us.

I once led a play for a pastor in the Reformed Church called Anton, who invited three important helpers of his life to the stage: the Apostle Paul, Martin Luther and Jesus. They accompany him throughout his life, he said, and in difficult times he especially likes to remind himself of their presence. In the drama he could experience that they were standing by, encouraging him, and this revived him. When Anton did a *role reversal* with the Apostle Paul and witnessed himself through Paul's eyes, Paul (Anton as Paul) was able to express his acceptance and witness Anton's abilities. Then, taking his own role as Anton and receiving the message from Paul (played by another member of the group), the trust in himself increased.

The imaginary meeting with a person who is important to us can help us to look at ourselves with tenderness and acceptance. We become able to see the good in ourselves as well as the unfolding potentiality.

Having identified these underdeveloped *progressive roles*, we will be able to train them. The next step in a role-training process is enacting the role of a desirable but still small *progressive role*. Rather than intellectualizing, an experiential learning takes place. The person does not simply speak of, for example, wanting to be an Explorer, but they actually become one, experiencing this with their cognition, emotions and body. With an adequate warm-up in the process, a spirit of playfulness and the supportive presence of the group, they will enjoy this exploratory process. They can enact how it would be if they met significant persons in their lives as the Explorer, or encountered imaginary situations they long for or have a fear about. By this means, the role of Explorer can gradually be developed and strengthened. The ultimate test is real life: whether this role is able to support the person when needed.

Step 3: Befriending our saboteur roles

We can also be friendly with our *saboteur roles*. We can see such a role as a creative solution of our soul to cope with a difficult situation. If we look on the *saboteur role* with judgement or shame, we give up the possibility of change and healing. And if we deny its existence and expel it into the shadow of the unconscious, we give up the possibility of awareness. One way or another, we lock ourselves together with this destructive force.

However, as we gradually discover our *saboteur roles* and pay attention to their implicit message, the unfulfilled existential desire, they will transform. The pain is relieved and freedom of action grows. At the same time, it will also become easier to take responsibility for our sabotage actions in our relationships: we will be able to empathize with ourselves and others, and to recognize the consequences of our actions and take responsibility for them.

Saboteur roles are often clues to a vital need.

The Overachiever or the Servant could remind us of how important acceptance and security are to us. They can also show how important loyalty to our ancestors or companions is to us. We are able to provide a great deal to others and to contribute to sustaining the spoken and unspoken rules of the family, the tribe and the system.

We can look at to whom and how we want to be loyal, and identify the community where we can belong without self-denial, without making ourselves small and powerless. We can look at how and from whom we expect acceptance and how we can create the safety we long for.

The Indulger in us has a deep desire for joy, for happiness. He wants to live, and to live well. He knows some ways of ensuring this for himself, so he keeps repeating them. It is good to see his diligence, but he also needs help to achieve lasting joy and happiness. He is a reminder of what visceral, bodily beings we are, strongly tied to matter and the world of instincts. He reminds us that our body can be a place of pleasure if we live well in it and with it. He reminds us that without our body we cannot become spiritual, but also that without a soul the body is incapable of creating lasting happiness. He can teach us through the excesses of pleasure, and the suffering we experience. He can inspire us to seek joyful lives in new ways without harming ourselves or anyone else. He can inspire us to learn to live in a sustainable, healing, vital joy. He can inspire us not to give up: life can be joyful – for us too!

The Orphan or the Tyrant give a cue of our forceful life instinct, as they show that we strive to take care of ourselves, to ensure a place for ourselves in this world. They remind us of how important it is to feel valued, loved and seen as someone who has a place in this world, whose presence makes a difference. The Tyrant expresses the desire to succeed, as success and power also mean a place in the social hierarchy: access to goods, the attention of others, time and, last but not least, attractive partners. If the Tyrant is close to us and we know him well within ourselves, then we may already know how tiring it can be to always control others and be in charge. It is tiring and infinitely lonely.

With the experience of these roles, we can examine what success means to us. We can look at how we can take care of ourselves without becoming selfish or disconnected from others. We can develop our ability to relate to others: our empathy and our flexibility within a relationship. We can try to change our perspective, the way we look at the others and the world, by, for example, making a few imaginary *role reversals* with them.

Becoming aware of the whole repertoire of our roles, we look at ourselves, together with our inner contradictions. We recognize the generative and destructive modes of operation that characterize us. As the latter is often accompanied by shame and vulnerability, it takes courage to admit them, even to ourselves. Probably we will not be able to see and meet all of our *saboteur roles* at once. However, we can always take an important step at a given moment: we can recognize what is sabotaging us in a particular situation. We can meet that specific *saboteur role*. We may be able to acknowledge our imperfection and vulnerability. It could be a great relief.

Role training facilitates the in-depth work with inner roles. The technical name should not scare anyone – it is an activity full of life, play and art. It offers external help in the development of roles: with an external mirror and support, and by strengthening and multiplying individual capacity for action. Gradually, we learn to consciously pay attention to our urges and inner voices and to differentiate between them.

Our development may even require that in certain situations we do not listen to the inner voice, we do not react in the way we used to. This would help in that, in a critical situation, we are not dragged down by our destructive or outdated urges.

Case study 8.2: The larva and the butterfly

Chris is a middle-aged, athletic man with lively gestures. He joined the group because he was dissatisfied with his work at a reputable multinational company.

Chris felt that he wanted to be free, to live a life where he could be really his true self. A butterfly! But now he is just a larva, he says. I suggest him to show this larva as well as the butterfly. He willingly goes for it. First, he takes on the role of Larva. I support him with the fine details of the implementation so that he gets more and more attuned. Embodying the Larva, he is wobbly, loiters and is sluggish all over. "I'm like that when I work. I am about to fall asleep. I use 5 per cent of my brain capacity. I'm helpless. I'm numb. I look here, I look there, but I can't go anywhere. I can't do anything."

Then I ask Chris to look at the Larva (embodied truthfully by a selected group member) from the outside. He cries out in outrage: "At the age of eighty, I will feel that I have wasted my life. It was all in vain. Time has just passed. How can you be so helpless?" He sees a disgusting worm who is cursed to stay that way forever. He despises himself, as if he wants to destroy this part of himself that vegetates as a Larva.

I ask him to take on the role of Larva next and listen to his own words from there (voiced by a group member of his choice who is now playing Chris). Listening to this criticism, the Larva (Chris in the role of Larva) shrinks. His trouble gets worse: "I'm completely paralysed. I don't know what to do," he says quietly and sorrowfully.

In the role of the Butterfly he is able to discover his own body parts, his movements are becoming animated and slowly he flutters his (imaginary) wings. From this place, he is able to look at the Larva kindly, and encourages him.

Next, in the role of a Larva he listens to this encouragement. "Don't want too much of me at once!" he sighs. But then it slowly sinks in, the Larva starts moving and exploring. He discovers that he is able to punch a tiny hole and see the world through it. He finds this world inviting. The Larva then also discovers that if he does not keep staring at the ground but looks at the Butterfly, he gains strength from him. The Larva smiles, and his body also comes to life, he is able to move.

As a closure, I ask Chris to step out of the scene and look at it from the outside. The Butterfly and the Larva play their own parts and their interactions. (The selected group member replays it, faithful to the previously enacted version of Chris, without adding anything.)

Walking around the stage, Chris receives everything he sees, what he has experienced, and becomes aware of how it affects him now. Chris looks at the couple of the Butterfly and the Larva with satisfaction and pleasure. "It doesn't even seem that hard. If I keep my eye on the Butterfly, it will work." He straightens himself with relief. I ask him to repeat "it will work!" several times as he walks around, taking in the image on the stage. I ask several group members to stand behind him in a row, to walk around behind him and say these words together with him, with the exact tone and movements as Chris uses in front of them. Chris thus multiplies on stage. His auxiliaries strengthen him and the final, key phrase of the play. They form a moving circle. Chris speeds up and speaks louder and louder. Chris and all the others are being filled with elation and zest. The group members relate to this action as if it were their own and repeat it with pleasure. This finale is thus a joint celebration.

Case study 8.3: The transformation of squeezing perfectionism

Barbara was fed up with the pressure of the multinational business world; she found the organizational culture soulless and could not identify with her company's goals. She felt like she was just a cog in the machine and doing it all just for the money. She had been feeling this for a long time, but she could not move on. It was then that she contacted me. She came for a few individual sessions first, then joined a group. After a few weeks she began to feel better, to know what she actually wanted. She also applied for a new job at a non-profit foundation in a refreshing green location, which, to her greatest surprise, she got. She was overjoyed about that. A new era is approaching finally!

At the beginning of a group meeting she reported that, strangely, things were getting worse in her current workplace. She was feeling the squeeze intensify, and it was insufferable. She was incapable of doing anything. She did not understand what this is all about, as she had already moved on both mentally and practically. An encouraging future was awaiting her and all she had to do was to wait out the period of notice. Why couldn't she be lighter, more at ease? What was it all about? She did not want to become decrepit, right now, at the very end!

I spotted two main themes: the 'encouraging future' and the 'squeeze'. I asked her to show this Encouraging Future, and then the Squeeze. For this, first three group members were selected who would help her display to them. She selected them.

During the Enactment, Barbara realizes that her Squeeze is holding her way too strongly and overwhelming her with her messages 'work harder, it is not enough yet', and she cannot even see the Future. After experiencing it for a while, she becomes angry with the Squeeze and pushes it to the side, wanting to make it disappear. I ask her what this Squeeze could be and what was the use of carrying it so long and so far. Barbara immediately replies: "She made me succeed. I was diligent, persistent. I could achieve a lot. Actually, I thank her a lot."

"Is there something of these that you may still need? Here, in the Theatre of the Soul, there may be a magic transformation where a function which has served external goals so far can become your aid in pursuing your own goals," I tell her.

Barbara replies that she still needs Persistence, and would want to take it to her new job.

I ask her to create this new scene, with herself, Persistence and the Future. Persistence now stands behind her back, with her hand on Barbara's shoulder blade. She experiences this support behind her, and is able to look at the Future openly.

Conclusion: the use of inner exploration

Role theory offers a novel and innovative approach to exploring values, motivations and human behaviour vital to overcoming our current collective challenge of reducing consumption and resource use while at the same time sustaining or increasing our well-being. Discovering our *progressive roles*, our character strengths, can increase our sense of competence and strengthen our autonomy and ability to function well in relationships. When we meet our basic psychological needs (of competence, autonomy and belonging), our well-being is likely to rise and, with it, our ability to engage in responsible action that benefits others and nature.

An inner work with our *saboteur roles*, in contrast, can be expected to reduce our harmful behaviour towards ourselves, others and nature. We are less likely to seek happiness and pleasure in places where we do not get it, or not in a lasting way. As a consequence, not only is our well-being expected to rise, but we may well adjust our priorities, our consumptions habits, and will be more likely to engage in more caring behaviour in general.

The Theatre of the Soul is an experimental laboratory where one can discover one's own *flourishing life* with one's whole being. It can be useful for anyone who wants to understand the 'not obvious' behind their behaviour, decision or relational situations. This can be useful for students of economics in understanding their methodological choices, their professional world. Business leaders, decision makers, may discover that they have more room for manoeuvre than they thought so far, and perhaps it does not require as much effort and struggle. Conscious people who care about the fate of the world may be able to connect to the basic values of their lives, and at the same time this may not block their joy and playfulness.

We can move away from both potential extremes: we do not need to feel that all the burdens of the world rest on our shoulders and we can never do enough, nor that we are insignificant and our deeds do not matter in the gigantic economic order because all the rules are given and solid. We discover in ourselves our free and creative selves, and also our generous, caring and loving self as well.

Conclusions: *Flourishing Life* in the World

Happiness science: implications beyond happiness

The recently blooming empirical science of happiness is relevant not only to those who seek happiness. It became popular by providing an alternative to sickness-based approaches to mental health, by focusing on the drivers of well-being rather than on the drivers of ill-being (the typical concern of psychology and psychiatry). These two sets of drivers were shown to partly differ from each other. We need different interventions to cure mental illness and to promote well-being. Happiness science gave us a set of tools to improve our well-being, which is very much aligned to our current cultural ideal of pursuing happiness and seeing ourselves as masters of our lives. Aiming for maximizing happiness (and happiness only) may have its downside, however, as argued in Chapter 3.

What has the science of happiness brought us beyond happiness? It has refined our notions of happiness by differentiating between moods, feelings, hedonic and cognitive assessments, myriad forms of well-being. Thus, its results can support us not only in our aspirations for a joyful life but also to live a life which is meaningful, complete and authentic. It can inspire and refine our reflection on the nature of the good life, on both the individual and collective level. What is the good life we really want? And what is the good life we actually seek through our actions? Perhaps these two differ at the moment.

Happiness economics played a major role in challenging the mainstream consensus on the priority of material indicators of progress, such as GDP, and provoked a discussion on potential alternatives (Chapter 2). This search for alternatives is ever more intense, due to the urgent climate change and ecological crisis that challenge the aspiration for unlimited growth on a finite planet.

The economics of happiness examines how the external conditions, institutional frameworks, affect life satisfaction or happiness. (Positive) psychology focuses primarily on the internal factors, the attitude, that individuals can influence, including their response to external circumstances. There are more and more approaches that emphasize the links between the two and that aim for a unified approach (critical psychology and so on), but each discipline ventures more and more to the terrain of the other. Pursuing a good life is, in fact, a complex interplay of external circumstances and internal responses. Ever more people venture beyond the realm of their personal lives, question existing collective norms and rules and seek corrective actions at the level of (self-organizing) communities and movements.

In my view, researching happiness and subjective well-being is important, but not enough to guide us. A responsible reaction to the dire challenges of our economy, society and ecology requires an additional aspect. And this aspect is that of values and ethics.

Value-based economics and our values in the economy

Our values determine how we act, what kind of world we create together. As shown in Chapter 1, in the case of economists their values influence their choices: (i) the methodology chosen by researchers (how much they take for granted the neoclassical economic methodology and its image of the human), (ii) the decisions made by businessmen, for example in the reorganization of a company. There is a widespread belief that economics is a 'positive' science, value free, that can prevent professionals from becoming aware of hidden value choices. It can also hinder self-examination. What is the 'black box' of the economist's soul like?

In economics education it would be essential to integrate personal reflection as well as dialogue with each other. What drives us as individuals? What are we striving for at the community level? How does our individual behaviour affect others?

An intellectual reflection and cognitive comprehension is a good starting point, but it will remain limited and ignore much relevant information about oneself. The discovery of emotions, physical sensations and a more comprehensive awareness of oneself and that of others and of the outer world is also essential to understand motivations, choices and behaviours. In addition to pure understanding, it may reveal 'true preferences' concealed thus far, and therefore increase the ability to act more in alignment with these. Experiential methods can be particularly useful in promoting this exploration. Our norms, habits and perceptions can be scrutinized and made more apparent to us.

This inner reflection can also contribute to a greater understanding of how we create and sustain our collective norms and institutions, and in what ways we want to create alternative norms and institutions.

Chasm between our aspirations and collective norms

Based on the empirical evidence of value research, I argue that we live in a divided world: our most important values stand in contrast to the prevailing norms of consumer society, as is suggested by consistent and clear empirical evidence.

There seems to be a universal value consensus, shared by the majority of people across countries and continents, as shown by social psychological value research (see Chapter 6). In particular, we want to live autonomously, kindly, honestly, with friendship and compassion with our own closest relations; we want our loved ones to thrive; and in the world at large we wish for tolerance, protection of all people and nature, world peace, equality and love of nature. All in all, we value personal freedom and compassion. Other aspirations such as power, success, wealth or hedonist pleasure-seeking are way less important priorities, as suggested by these results.

In parallel, our prevailing common myth of the good life is based on materialistic ideals of wealth, power and influence, intertwined with the positive image of consumption.

This causes countless internal and external conflicts, suffering and destruction. Now climate change, the accelerating sixth mass extinction resulting from human activity and the failure to keep global warming under control are ever more alarming signs of this destruction. Yet, many people seem to take these rules of the game for granted, as if they were laws of nature, such as gravity. It may be due to social norms, not being adequately informed, or lack of initiative for action. People may prefer to just do what most others do, making 'normal' life and work arrangements, with common habits and consumption patterns complying to the social norm, even if these are in many ways not optimal for them. They may not know what else they could do; or they may feel helpless and small in contrast to the established institutions and order. There may be also systemic reasons which hinder people from opting for alternatives: current laws and public infrastructure may work against their ideals and a desirable transformation. Some may opt for creating personal islands, aiming for well-being in their own families and leisure time, while accepting different norms in their work and consumption.

There may be personal psychological reasons for the chasm as well: some of our inner drives may actually resonate well with the dominant materialistic value system of capitalism. These inner forces may remain latent, invisible to us (they were certainly concealed to the surveying scientists). If this is so, many of us may actually live with this inner chasm, having values and aspirations for love, harmony, respect for oneself and others, and yet and at the same time having urges which oppose these. We may want to love and respect others and nature, but our skills to put this into effect may be limited. We may be short of empathy, the ability to love in such a way that others actually feel loved and supported by us; thus, through our actions we may end up sustaining division and harm. We may long for a thriving life and we may sabotage it as well. It may be these inner forces that also sustain individualism, selfishness and overconsumption.

What could a world be that is free from this rift? How could we take our core values and aspirations earnestly and create an economic and social system that fits our inner compass better? What is the alternative narrative that emerges from current psychological, social science research and ancient Greek philosophy?

More virtuous and better hedonist

A *flourishing life* offers an alternative, where our value-seeking, moral selves and our instinctive, pleasure-seeking selves may be integrated. It also offers a pathway to a life that is both sustainable and happy. We will be able to actively contribute to the collective effort to create a more ecologically sustainable world in a way which does not reduce our well-being.

It is not simply a matter of becoming a 'better person' morally, or striving harder for perfection. It may well be that such an endeavour would, rather, paralyse our joyful, playful and spontaneous selves, as we would have to deny or fight against many aspects within ourselves, and this is often combined with much guilt and anxiety. Instead, we need to cultivate the skills to act upon our values efficiently and, at the same time, to become better hedonists as well.

We can learn to become better hedonists by savouring all that our life already offers to us with our full awareness. I call this *sustainable hedonism* (Chapter 4) and show where it is placed our map of values (Figure 6.3). We may expand our ability to act in virtuous ways, which promotes our own well-being as well as the well-being of others (Chapter 5). And we can do both at the same time.

A 'thriving life that does not cost the Earth'

What could this life be on a personal level? Based on the arguments described earlier in this book, people living such thriving lives not only expect happiness from the good turn of external circumstances but also recognize the crucial role of their own beliefs and actions. They regard happiness not just as an emotion but as the result of conscious action. For this, they are ready to cultivate their own virtues and excellence with persistent and committed action. They explore how their talents, abilities and aspirations can turn into excellence and virtue, so that they can live an autonomous and creative life for their own good and for the benefit of the community. Their actions are aligned to their innermost values.

They are able to look at their own lives from a perspective that exceeds their individual interests and desires, to see it as a part of a larger whole, interconnected with the well-being of many others. They are aware that their actions and consumption habits affect others, and with this awareness they seek ethical solutions. They wish to advance a collaborative and fair world: a thriving life for all.

People living thriving lives see themselves as part of nature, living in unity with it. In this way they recognize that it sustains them and that they have a responsibility for sustaining it. They respect and admire the Earth, its landscapes and beings. They recognize the natural cycle of life in the whole world with all its resources. They also consider consumer goods as part of such a cycle, as part of a circular economy. They question their privileges to consume more than the capacity of the planet can handle. They question that they are given 'rights' by the prevailing economic order that override those of the next generation or of people born in poorer countries or circumstances. They are therefore ready to resign some of the pleasurable goods and experiences which are offered by consumer society.

On a communal and social level, the vision of a *thriving life that does not cost the Earth* encompasses ecological and social criteria. It implies that there are natural limits to economic growth. The living world carries a value in itself, a value beyond the perspective of economics and humans. The economy is only a part of human culture and the Earth, and its activities have natural limitations: it cannot destroy or threaten their existence or their future. In public policy, goals need to be separated from means, where money and growth (GDP, corporate profit) are just means. The goal of public policy is to provide a minimal social safety net for all, as well as the opportunity of a *flourishing life* for all.

Intellectual understanding can help a lot in this, supported by the scientific results presented earlier. I believe that the process cannot stop here, as many of our positive and saboteur inner forces are not fully accessible to our thinking self. Neither may we be aware of how our beliefs, habits and responses determine (and limit) our actions and lives, and our ability to live a good life.

There are limits to our rationality and our cognition. To expand our abilities, it is necessary to connect with our intuitive, instinctive, bodily being as well. We need to refine our perception of the world, including ourselves and others, and to learn a new way of using our senses. Arts, experiential learning methods and mindfulness techniques can aid it, including the Theatre of the Soul and its elaborate methodology presented in Chapters 7 and 8.

Reassessing our needs

A thriving life also implies that we are free to enjoy life but not addicted to its pleasures. We turn to our desires, needs and habits with curiosity, not taking their existence or the way of satisfying them as self-evident. This awareness and exploration enlarges our inner freedom (from 'must have's'), and also our outer freedom in the world (from 'must do's'). Our autonomy grows.

There seems to be a strong case for the reassessment of our needs. On a material level, we may need to challenge our existing distinction between 'necessary' and 'optional' things in our lives. A reconsideration of what is 'necessary' and a transition to *voluntary simplicity* is not only environmentally responsible, but may remove the pressure from us to earn the money to finance all this.

Rather than restricting our notion of needs to material needs *only*, we need also to be aware of our psychological needs. As I argued in the earlier chapters, the three core needs defined by self-determination theory (SDT) could be a good guide in this. SDT argues that we all long for a life with *autonomy*, *competence* and *belonging*; these are universal core human needs, albeit with some individual diversity in their extent. As shown in Chapter 6, these needs overlap with our main universal values as found in social psychological surveys. We strive for things that are good for us.

As individuals we benefit greatly if we live in alignment with our inner needs (and values): autonomously, creatively and with compassion, instead of simply complying to external norms about 'success and good life', mostly based on appearance, fame and wealth. Attending all of these three core needs is not only a good tool for self-care, but may also liberate us from following more redundant strategies like overconsumption or impulsive pleasure-seeking (*radical hedonism*). Fulfilling these needs may gradually heal our inner 'saboteur' forces, which are dysfunctional or harmful to ourselves or to others. A life based on autonomous action, the ability to convert one's competences and skills to creative manifestation, as well as the experience of being accepted, respected, loved and cared for, as well as the experience that we are able to accept, respect, love others and care for them is a good life. It not only meets our core needs but is likely to lead to actions which are socially and environmentally also caring and responsible. As was said earlier of the happy life, this too may need a conscious and persistent practice on our part.

The challenge is: how can we promote the three core psychological needs of *autonomy*, *competence* and *belonging*, while also achieving the behavioural and systemic transformation necessary for tackling the climate catastrophe? It is a major challenge: how to appreciate the inner processes of healing, transformation and their tempo while confronted with the urgency of the required changes.

The basis for transformation: sense of safety

A sense of safety is a necessary prerequisite for personal change. Research shows that people tend to respond to external insecurity or (perceived) threats by seeking external success and recognition, even if this involves giving up their inner goals. Thus, for someone to be able to live in a self-transcendent and autonomous way, which would then also make them happier, it is necessary to have a basic sense of security in the world.

Therefore, if we are looking for a way out of the ecological crisis generated by capitalism, the dead end of selfishness, we must also look at how families, communities and the system of state institutions can create a safe environment. The inner sense of safety can best be established by a caring early family environment. It is also in our common interest that this safety is given to as many people as possible, or that the painful lack of safety can be mended later. This can be helped by support for mothers and parents – even before the birth of the child – and a school system that ensures the emotional safety and well-being of children. Concerning external conditions, this is a strong argument for a well-functioning welfare system that offers a safety net and a chance for everyone to thrive. It encompasses financial security at the time of unexpected, challenging life events, but it also means creating *basic capabilities* for everyone, so that each person has the opportunity for a *flourishing life*. These public policy measures can foster the desired social transformation needed for a sustainable future. Caring is therefore not merely a charity but serves the interest of the whole community.

Creating and restoring a sense of safety is an element of individual or group psychotherapy and counselling. In the Theatre of the Soul we can also create 'safe space', which has proven to have beneficial effects.[1]

Physical and emotional safety, as well as acceptance and affection, may gradually cure toxic attachment to power, success and external recognition. This is how our world will actually be aligned to our innate aspirations (according to the value survey presented in Chapter 6): 'self-transcendent', capable of mature love and selflessness, as well as true inner freedom.

Cultivating freedom beyond individualism: autonomy

Contrary to some popular beliefs, autonomy is not equal to selfish individualism, the attitude of 'I do whatever I want, no matter what'. Autonomy is the ability to make clear decisions which are aligned to innate values and desires, and at the same time autonomy is compatible with having mutually supportive relationships.

A free person recognizes that they have a choice in where they want to belong to. Recognizing the innate needs both for autonomy and for belonging, they seek to reconcile these two. They are able to take an active, conscious part in the development of common norms and the operation of the community. In this way, their role will be 'political', that is, communal, as the interests of others also appear in their considerations, beyond their own interests. And the manifestation of this kind of political activism may be surprising, as it can be playful and joyful, in addition to being responsible and committed.

They are ready to question existing habits, unspoken or implicit social consensus, and will be active participants in the development of new habits and norms. With moving, they stir. With rebelling, they construct.

Existing utopia

This thriving life is a utopia that already lives within us and among us. There are islands of communities, companies, movements and people that already live a thriving life that does not cost the Earth. We already have the needed repertoire of tools for such a life.

We have a large set of practical tools and interventions. Examples could be targeted ecosystem restoration, uplifting nature's carbon cycle by supporting 'sinks', as well as transforming energy production, transportation, construction and food production, just to name a few.[2]

On a global level, the ethical foundations of a more just, sustainable and peaceful global society were elaborated in the Earth Charter in 2000, as a result of a decade-long global consultation. 'It articulates a mindset of global interdependence and shared responsibility.'[3] Its four pillars include (1) respect and care for the community of life, (2) ecological integrity, (3) social and economic justice and (4) democracy, nonviolence and peace. It has also become a movement across 89 countries.

The UN Sustainable Development Goals (SDGs) represent the major contemporary global policy effort for both tackling climate change and ending poverty and other deprivation. Comprehensive, ambitious targets were adopted by 193 countries in 2015, envisioning the kind of world we want by 2030. Measurable indicators are defined. A global vision and action on this scale is unprecedented.

We can clearly see the global, planetary nature of these concerns, moving beyond typical country-specific targets. They include spill-over indicators: air pollution, groundwater pollution, tax evasion, arms trade, species extinction and overfishing. These are indicators that are difficult to measure and may not yet be measured. This is clearly a pioneering character of the SDGs, although the analytical work is far from being complete.

It is a major progressive step, although there appear to be some unresolved issues in my view. The potential conflicts between the specific goals and their interconnections are not addressed. The objective of economic growth is also included, measured with the GDP per capita indicator that is challenged by many (as mentioned in Chapter 2), and it is not clear how its conflict with other goals is to be resolved. One might conclude that the international political community has not yet embraced a whole systems-thinking approach to economic development, social and ecological issues.

The future envisaged by the SDGs was not simply the result of some bureaucratic negotiations in airless offices, but included a worldwide consultation process on an unprecedented scale. Some five million people in 83 countries were approached and asked what kind of world they wanted to live in. The aim was to arrive at a globally shared vision of a good life. The UN also emphasizes that achieving these targets requires everyone: not only governments, but also the work of non-profits, communities and individuals. On the UN website, *The Lazy Person's Guide to Saving the World* is published, with a list of activities which can be done as a 'sofa superstar', as a 'household hero', as a 'neighbourhood nice guy', or as an 'exceptional employee' at work.[4] The list full of detailed practical actions is a suggestion that anyone can modify and amend.

The 2015 encyclical letter '*Laudato si*' of Pope Francis '*On care for our common home*' is a landmark Catholic document on current environmental and social issues. The title itself is a reference to Saint Francis of Assisi's canticle: 'Praise be to you, my Lord, through our Sister, Mother Earth, who sustains and governs us, and who produces various fruit with coloured flowers and herbs'. The Buddhist approach to happiness is popularized by the books and teachings of the 14th Dalai Lama. Both Christianity and Buddhism have inspired a range of alternative economic approaches as well.

There are ever more companies and institutions that integrate ethical standards or aim at maximizing the common good, rather than financial profit only. There are firms that implement the 'circular economy' model and/or operate based on employees' self-determination, solidarity and ecological awareness. There are ever more businesses, residential communities and other organizations that are able to multiply their resources by questioning outdated norms and approaches to success. They may build on new values (shared by their members) such as solidarity, self-determination, integral thinking, systems design and ecological mindset and seek an appropriate organizational form for this. These initiatives may actively shape the legal system, too.

In addition to private and state ownership, 'commons' are becoming more prevalent, ranging from open source programs in information technology, to 'creative commons' licenses in the arts and community-owned producer or residential communities (Chapter 5). Here, the individual interest and benefit are inseparable from the common interest and the benefit of the community.

In addition to the external, technological toolbox, there are also tools that can help to resolve the internal contradictions within the human soul that hinder the realization of a *flourishing life*. Many of these were discussed in Chapters 7 and 8.

In sum, there are countless revolutionary economic, social, ecological and communal solutions that show a way out of the current crisis, as well as new solutions at the system level, where the specific aspects are integrated. Only a fraction of these have been mentioned here. The necessary personal and systemic transformation can build upon the experience of many people and communities, and can be reinforced by acting together.

By critically revisiting our own personal convictions about 'success' and a good life, not only are we likely to enhance our own well-being, but we can contribute to the solution of the ecological and social crisis. These aspirations are not in conflict with each other. And we are not alone with these aspirations.

Notes

Introduction

1 O'Neill et al 2018; Raworth 2017.
2 O'Neill et al 2018, p 88.
3 Ryan and Deci 2019; Deci and Ryan 2000.
4 Polanyi 2001.
5 'Community, identity, stability' is the World State's motto in the novel *Brave New World* by Aldous Huxley. 'Serve the People' originates from the title of a speech by Mao Zedong, delivered on 8 September 1944, and is currently the unofficial motto of China. 'Peace, rain, prosperity': the national motto of Lesotho. 'Be fast, bold, open and build social value': core values of Facebook. 'Respect resource limits, create resilience, freely share ideas and power': values of the Transition Towns movement.
6 Heede 2019, table C1.

Chapter 1

1 For example: Ferber and Nelson 1993; Hollis and Nell 2006; Leibenstein 1976 to name just a few.
2 Source: Harsányi 1997, p 133. Harsányi uses the terms 'real preferences', 'true preferences' or 'informed preferences' interchangeably to describe what a person would really want if they had all the necessary information.
3 Ariely 2010; Thaler 2016.
4 Kahneman and Tversky 1979; Kahneman et al 1991.
5 For example: Corning 2005; Sahlins 2017.
6 Persky, one of the defenders argues: 'Despite these warnings, I suspect that the majority of economists remain confident of the survival of their favorite species. In fact, many see Economic Man as virtually the only civilized species in all of social science' (1995, pp 221-2).
7 Just to name a few critiques: Dawson 2014; Eisenstein 2011; Felber 2019; Oswald and Stern 2019; Raworth 2017.
8 Carter and Irons 1991; Frank et al 1993; Marwell and Ames 1981.
9 Cipriani et al 2009; Rubinstein 2006.
10 Frey and Meier 2003.
11 Oswald and Stern 2019.
12 van Dalen 2019.
13 For example: Cipriani et al 2009; Frank et al 1993.

[14] Source: Robbins 1932. Milton Friedman (Nobel Prize-winning American economist) called the former a 'positive' science, distinguishing it from 'normative' science.

[15] Myrdal 1972.

[16] Boulding 1969, p 3.

[17] Atkinson 2009; Boulding 1969.

[18] Rethinking Economics, and The New Weather Institute 2017.

[19] van Dalen 2019.

[20] Drucker 1939.

[21] Churchill 1939

[22] Bentham 2000, p 1.

[23] Stigler and Becker 1977.

[24] Increasing freedom contributed to a higher subjective well-being in post-communist Hungary (Lelkes 2006b).

Chapter 2

[1] Keynes 1963, pp 362–3.

[2] Easterlin 1974; 1995.

[3] Di Tella and MacCulloch 2008; Helliwell 2003; Helliwell, Layard et al 2013; Oishi and Kesebir 2015; Sarracino 2010.

[4] While in 1980, in the US, the top 1 per cent earned an average of 27 times more than the bottom half of the total population, by 2014 this ratio had increased to 81 (Piketty et al 2018, p 557).

[5] Source: Kubiszewski et al 2013, figure 6, p 65. Their estimates included 17 countries, containing 53 per cent of the global population and 59 per cent of the global GDP, and encompassed the period 1950–2003.

[6] A few examples of the extensive literature: Kubiszewski et al 2013; Mazzucato 2018; Stiglitz et al 2010; Stiglitz et al 2019.

[7] European Commission 2009.

[8] Diener et al 2018.

[9] Clark et al 2018.

[10] Kasser 2002.

[11] Dittmar et al 2014.

[12] Lessenich 2016; Brand and Wissen 2017.

[13] FAO 2016.

[14] OECD 2017 and OECD 2020. Overweight or obese population (indicator). doi: 10.1787/86583552-en. Access date: 22 October 2020.

[15] These forms of existential fears are described in detail by Irvin D. Yalom (1980).

[16] Veblen 1899.

[17] Capra and Luisi 2014.

[18] Kartha et al 2020.

[19] Graham and Pettinato 2002.

[20] Frank 1999; Layard 2005.

[21] Stutzer 2004.

[22] The term 'hedonic treadmill' was first used by Brickman et al (1978), although the idea of rising (material) aspirations dates back much earlier.

[23] Cantillon et al 2019; Hills et al 2002.

[24] In the most recent catalogue of mental illnesses, the *Diagnostic and Statistical Manual of Mental Disorders* (DSM-5) only 'gaming' was included as a form of addiction, and

not the other types of behaviours mentioned here. Internet addiction was heavily discussed, but ultimately not included. As the *Manual* is continuously being revised by mental health experts, it may change in the future. The objective of the *Manual* is clearly medical and psychiatric, and not psychological or social psychological.

[25] Kuss and Griffiths 2017.

[26] We are social, and Hootsuite 2020.

[27] Survey by Digital Awareness UK and the Headmasters' and Headmistresses' Conference. Blog post: 'Research: teenage use of mobile devices during the night' https://www.hmc.org.uk/blog/research-teenage-use-mobile-devices-night/. Access date: 22 October 2020.

[28] The survey reached a total of 1,000 parents and their children nationwide (paired interviews of 500 parents and 500 children between the ages of 12 and 18) (Robb 2019).

[29] Brown et al 2016.

[30] We are social, and Hootsuite 2020.

[31] Global Web Index survey, https://blog.globalwebindex.com/trends/2019-in-review-social-media/. Access date: 22 October 2020.

Chapter 3

[1] Grinde 2012.

[2] Kabat-Zinn 1990; Kabat-Zinn 2003.

[3] Davidson and Begley 2013. This is the foundation of psychotherapy and positive psychology as well.

[4] This approach leads back to the notion of 'cardinal utility', that is, the early view that individual preferences are measurable. For a theoretical and methodological discussion on this, see Ferrer-i-Carbonell and Frijters 2004; Frey and Stutzer 2002; Kahneman and Krueger 2006; Ng 1997.

[5] See for example: Elster 1983; Frank 1985; Frank 1997.

[6] There is empirical evidence that expert judgements on the 'good life' tend to overlap with the subjective assessment of the 'good life' by people in case of *basic needs*. This has been tested on survey data with 30,000 individuals from 21 countries, using measures of labour market situation, health, housing conditions and social relations (Lelkes 2006a).

[7] Critical community psychology is an 'emerging approach committed to promoting individual and social well-being through the adoption of an ecological, justice-oriented and value-based perspective'. Kagan et al 2020; Natale et al 2016.

[8] Lyubomirsky, Sheldon and Schkade 2005.

[9] Clark et al 2017, p 136.

[10] See a review of the subject of pleasure by Biswas-Diener et al 2015.

[11] Originally, Cantril (1965) explicitly asked the individuals to reveal what the 'best' and the 'worst' meant for them, and only then requested the assessment of their current situation by actually pointing to the specific point on the 'ladder'.

[12] Kahneman and Krueger 2006; Sandvik et al 1993.

[13] Krueger and Schkade 2008.

[14] Schneider 2011.

[15] Danner et al 2001.

[16] The conclusion is based on the results of 30 studies by Veenhoven (2008). This was confirmed by Diener and Chan (2011) in their review article in a meta-analysis of meta-analyses, that is, summing up hundreds of studies.

17 Grant, Wardle and Steptoe 2009.
18 Goudie et al 2014.
19 Boehm and Kubzansky 2012; Brummett et al 2005; Ostir et al 2001.
20 See the literature review of De Neve et al 2013.
21 Ifcher and Zarghamee 2011.
22 Guven 2012.
23 Aknin, Dunn and Norton 2012.
24 Christakis and Fowler 2009.
25 Huxley 1932, p 180.
26 Huxley 1932, p 38.
27 Huxley 1932, p 181.
28 Lelkes 2013.
29 Bradburn 1969.
30 Davidson 1992; Davidson and Begley 2013.
31 Hoebel et al 1999.
32 For example: Diener and Iran-Nejad 1986; Diener and Emmons 1985.
33 See the research and the literature review presented by Hershfield et al (2013).
34 Schwartz et al 2002.
35 Dolan 2020.
36 Lyubomirsky et al 2005; Martin et al 2002; Oishi, Diener and Lucas 2007; and the literature review of De Neve et al 2013.
37 See the literature review of Oishi et al (2007).
38 Pressman and Cohen (2005) mention potentially harmful effects on immune, cardiovascular and pulmonary function.
39 Grant and Schwartz 2011.
40 Diener et al 1991.
41 Layard 2013.

Chapter 4

1   Source: https://www.overshootday.org/. Access date: 22 October 2020.
2   Source: 2016 edition of the National Footprint Accounts, with a briefing note, on https://www.footprintnetwork.org/2016/03/08/national-footprint-accounts-2016-carbon-makes-60-worlds-ecological-footprint/. Free Public Data Set of the National Footprint and Biocapacity Accounts 2019: https://www.footprintnetwork.org/licenses/public-data-package-free/. Access date: 23 September 2020.
3   Kartha et al 2020.
4   Kartha et al 2020, table 5.
5   Source: Global Footprint Network data, https://data.footprintnetwork.org/#/. Access date: 22 October 2020.
6   Personal Footprint Calculator: https://www.footprintcalculator.org/. Access date: 22 October 2020.
7   The advocates of '*strong sustainability*' do not consider decoupling economic activity from environmental impact feasible in absolute terms and call for reductions in material and resource consumption (Jackson 2009).
8   Fromm 1997, p 13.
9   O'Keefe 2002.
10 Athenaeus 1854.
11 Diogenes Laertius 1925, 2.75.

[12] Diogenes Laertius 1925, 2.77.

[13] Diogenes Laertius 1925, 2.66.

[14] Diogenes Laertius 1925, 2.69.

[15] Diogenes Laertius 1925, 2.74–5.

[16] Epicurus' own writings did not survive, only a recollection of his thoughts based on writers who lived over 200 years after him, including the Roman poet Lucretius and the Roman politician Cicero.

[17] Philosophical literature calls his ethics '*egoistic hedonism*'. It is hedonistic, because pleasure is the ultimate good in his opinion. It is egoistic, because it is about the pleasure of the individual.

[18] O'Keefe 2010, p 120.

[19] Epicurus 1994.

[20] We do not know for sure from the existing writings how Epicurus sustained himself and the Garden. Some suspect a rich legacy, others say they may have lived on donations.

[21] Philodemus of Gadara, from a work whose title is uncertain, preserved in Herculaneum Papyrus 1005, column W, lines 10–14. In: Epicurus 1994.

[22] See for example the longitudinal study examining the relations of childhood environmental factors with adult values (Kasser et al 2002).

[23] Brown et al 2016.

[24] Aristotle 1999, p 16, Book I/10.

[25] Max-Neef 1991; Doyal and Gough 1991.

[26] Guillen-Royo 2016; Rauschmayer, Omann and Frühmann 2011; World Commission on Environment and Development 1987. The latter is popularly known as the Brundtland Report.

[27] Rawls 1971; Sen 1985; 1992.

[28] Sen 1985; Sugden 1993.

[29] Nussbaum 2001; Nussbaum and Sen 1993.

[30] Nussbaum 2000.

[31] Shambala 1991.

[32] Aristotle 1999, p 24, Book II/3.

Chapter 5

[1] 'the happy man lives well and does well; for we have practically defined happiness as a sort of good life and good action' (Aristotle 1999, p 12).

[2] Aristotle 1999, p 14.

[3] Aristotle 1999, p 14.

[4] Aristotle 1999, p 11.

[5] Aristotle 1999, p 18.

[6] Aristotle 1999, p 65.

[7] Aristotle 1999, p 121.

[8] Simon 2007, p 180.

[9] Aristotle 1915, section 15 I2i3 a.

[10] Aristotle 1999, p 4.

[11] Aristotle 1999, p 127.

[12] See, for example, Ryff and Singer 2008; Delle Fave et al 2012; Michaelson et al 2009; OECD 2013.

[13] Baumeister et al 2013; Fredrickson et al 2013; Huta and Ryan 2010; Lelkes 2017; Steger, Kashdan and Oishi 2008.

[14] Frankl 2006.
[15] Kahneman et al 1991.
[16] Büchs and Koch 2017; Jackson 2009.
[17] Schumacher 1989; Liegey and Nelson 2020.
[18] For example, Andersson et al 2014.
[19] Ambrey and Daniels 2017.
[20] Welsch and Kühling 2011.
[21] See the review of Kasser 2017.
[22] Kasser 2017.
[23] Kasser 2017.
[24] Brown and Kasser 2005, and a later follow-up study: Brown et al 2016.
[25] Hurst et al 2013.
[26] Binder and Blankenberg 2017.
[27] Welsch and Kühling 2018.
[28] O'Brien 2016; Sterling et al 2018.
[29] See the publications of Tim Kasser with a series of his own experiments as well as an extensive review of other studies: Kasser 2018; 2002.
[30] He calls this process 'individuation': Jung 1989, p 476.
[31] Acosta 2017.
[32] Dawson 2012; Felber 2012.
[33] Economy of the Common Good: https://www.ecogood.org/. Access date: 22 October 2020.
[34] Transition US: https://transitionus.org/what-is-transition/. Access date: 22 October 2020.
[35] GEN: https://ecovillage.org/. Access date: 22 October 2020.
[36] Grinde et al 2018.
[37] Source: Intercontinental Network for the Promotion of Social Solidarity Economy. http://www.ripess.org/what-is-sse/what-is-social-solidarity-economy/?lang=en. Access date: 10 January 2020.
[38] Bauwens, Kostakis and Pazaitis 2019; 'Was sind Commons?' The Commons Institute. https://commons-institut.org/was-sind-commons. Access date: 22 October 2020.
[39] Ostrom 1990.
[40] Linebaugh 2009.

Chapter 6

[1] Dostoevsky 1912; Fromm 1941.
[2] Schwartz 2012; Schwartz et al 2012. Various major questionnaires operationalized his value theory: the Schwartz Value Survey, the Portrait Values Questionnaire (created primarily for children from 11–14) and the short version in the European Social Survey core questionnaire.
[3] Schwartz et al 2012.
[4] Human values scale in the European Social Survey, Round 9, 2018/2019, core questionnaire (European Social Survey 2020). The questions were proposed and elaborated by S. Schwartz.
[5] Having new ideas, with an emphasis on the creative side of having them through generating them myself.
[6] 'Expensive': in the sense of costing a lot rather than their being 'luxury' items.

7 The idea is to show whatever abilities you have, with no assumption that you actually have great abilities. It is important to you to be perceived as being able.

8 You want your actions to be admired, not your person.

9 In the sense of the surroundings actually being secure, and not that you feel secure.

10 Important for yourself (your life) is the focus.

11 The idea here is that when someone else tells you what to do in actual interpersonal interaction (implying also that the person has some authority), you should do it.

12 'Rules' in the sense of 'rules and regulations'.

13 'Different' in almost any way. The key idea is that you see difference/diversity positively and as something worth learning about.

14 'Spoil myself': 'treat myself' is another idiom. Strongly negative 'self-indulgence' is not intended.

15 In the sense of not to *have to* depend on people.

16 'Care for': here in the sense of actively promote their well-being.

17 'Ensures' in the sense of 'guarantees'.

18 'Exciting' more in the sense of 'exhilarating' than 'dangerous'.

19 Get/have this respect, not deserve respect.

20 'Devote': is intended to convey deep concern for these people and readiness to invest your time, resources and energy in their welfare.

21 'Care for': look after, basically synonymous with 'looking after' in the second sentence.

22 'Seeks': active pursuit rather than 'taking every chance'.

23 Schwartz and Bardi 2001. The data included representative and near-representative samples from 13 nations, replicated with school teachers in 56 nations and college students in 54 nations.

24 Deci and Ryan 2000; Ryan et al 2008; Ryan and Deci 2019.

25 Self-determination theory calls this basic need 'competence', which means that the person feels competent, feels that he has the opportunity to show this. While I also feel that a sense of competence is essential, I think of this also as a means to the ability to create, to generate something which is of value to the person.

26 Deci and Ryan 2000, p 230.

27 Ryan and Deci 2019, p 141.

28 Deci and Ryan 2000, p 234.

29 Titmuss 1970. A wide range of psychological evidence on this subject is reviewed by Deci and Ryan 2000.

30 Kasser 2002.

31 Schwartz, Sigav and Boehnke 2000. Relations of individuals' value priorities to their worries were investigated in seven samples from four cultural groups ($N = 1,441$).

32 Hogeveen, Inzlicht and Obhi 2014.

33 Kasser, Koestner and Lekes 2002; Sheldon and Kasser 2008.

34 Mikulincer et al 2003; Otway and Carnelley 2013.

35 Sheldon and Kasser 2008.

36 Kasser 2018.

37 The underlying psychological process, 'introjection', is actually a defence mechanism which aims to reduce anxiety.

38 Deci and Ryan 2000; Ryan and Deci 2019.

Chapter 7

1 Briggs 1998.

[2] Aristotle first used the word '*catharsis*' in his *Poetics* (c 335 BC).

[3] For a presentation of the underlying concepts and theories, several foundational books are available, including among many others, for example: Karp 1998; Blatner 2000; von Ameln et al 2000; Gershoni 2003; Clayton and Carter 2004; Holmes et al 2005; Gerstmann and Kramer 2009. For a recent systematic review paper discussing the main techniques currently used, see Cruz et al 2018.

[4] Merleau-Ponty 2004, p 56.

[5] Merleau-Ponty 2004, p 39. Note that he does not deny the value of science, but questions that science (or a scientist) can penetrate 'to the heart of things, to the object as it is in itself' or is 'capable of absolute and complete knowledge'.

[6] The edited volume Blatner (2019) includes specific chapters on Forum Theatre by Mecca Antonia Burns, sociodrama by Ron Wiener, bibliodrama by Patrick T. Barone, souldrama by Connie Miller, as well as science communication by Justine Jones, to name just a few.

[7] Kellermann 1998; 2007.

[8] See, for example, an application to organizational context by Riepl (2016).

[9] Testoni et al (2016) found causal relationship between spontaneity and the occurrence of depression and low well-being.

a) Drama therapy: a systematic review of drama therapy intervention studies between 2007 to 2017 found 24 articles (Feniger-Schaal and Orkibi 2020).

b) Psychodrama: a meta-analysis of 25 experimentally designed studies (Kipper and Ritchie 2003) finds 'an overall effect size that points to a large size improvement effect similar to or better than that commonly reported for group psychotherapy in general. The techniques of role reversal and doubling emerged as the most effective interventions.' Wieser (2007) reviewed 52 studies, including 8 randomized control-trials, 14 controlled studies and 30 naturalistic studies. Orkibi and Feniger-Schaal (2019), in their meta-analyis of 31 peer-reviewed articles on psychodrama interventions published in English between 1 January 2007 and 31 December 2017, concluded that 'psychodrama intervention research in the last decade suggests there are promising results in all methodologies, and highlights the need to enhance methodological as well as reporting quality and to theorize and examine modality-specific mechanisms that lead to therapeutic change'. See also the volume with 50 different studies on empirical research in psychodrama: Stadler, Wieser and Kirk 2016.

Some practitioners find that a *positivist quantitative impact assessment* is at odds with their method. Blatner (2000) notes: 'Many forms of therapy are not readily amenable to more current requirements of research, while a few other approaches are more amenable – especially those that can be described in a manual. (The problem with such approaches is that they address some common denominators in most psychiatric problems, such as sloppy and self-defeating thought patterns. It is not surprising that tightening up thinking would be shown to be statistically effective in most problems, but that doesn't mean it gets to the roots of the problem!)' Kirk (2016) welcomes an alternative, constructivist scientific approach which enables capturing meaning and the essence of human experience.

[10] Blatner 2000.

[11] Kellermann 1992.

[12] Yalom 1985.

[13] Blog post: 'Action Explorations: a new category'. https://blatner.com/adam/blog/?p=782. Access date: 22 October 2020.

[14] Karp 1998, p 3.

[15] See, for example, Postlethwaite 2019.
[16] https://psychodrama.org.nz/about/ Access date: 22 October 2020.
[17] Blatner and Blatner 1997.
[18] Orkibi 2019; Goldberg 2009.
[19] Lelkes 2018.
[20] The story is told by Grete Leutz (1974), a close collaborator of Jacob L. Moreno, in her reference work.
[21] Moreno worked with an elevated stage, and with spectators, as well as a balcony, as is visible in his theatre in Beacon, New York. The balcony was used for the concretization of the transcendental. Most modern psychodramatists use an ordinary room with a designated area declared to be the stage, surrounded by the seats of the participants in a semi-circle arrangement.
[22] Clayton and Carter 2004, p 231.
[23] Orkibi 2019, p 12.
[24] For example: Mayrhofer 2020.
[25] Buber and Kaufmann 1970.

Chapter 8

[1] Moreno's role theory was further developed by Blatner, Clayton and others, including Aszalós 2017; Blatner 2000; Clayton 1992; 1994; Leutz 1974; Zánkay 2015. It was applied in many areas, including organizational development (Riepl 2016).
[2] SDT uses the term 'relatedness'. With 'love' I am referring to the quality of the desired connection, that is, supportive, benevolent and kind.
[3] According to Aristotle, this is found in mothers most of all (Aristotle 1999, p 150).
[4] Saboteur roles is my own terminology, and psychodramatic role theory does not use such a term. Instead, for example, Max Clayton's approach speaks of 'coping' roles or 'fragmenting' roles. The 'saboteur' role I use thus refers to a role that is either 'coping' or 'fragmenting', that is, either suboptimal or explicitly destructive.

Conclusions:

[1] Krüger 2020.
[2] Strassburg et al 2020; Hawken 2017.
[3] 'What is the Earth Charter?' https://earthcharter.org/about-us/. Access date: 22 October 2020.
[4] United Nations 2018.

References

Acosta, A. (2017) *Rethinking the World from the Perspective of Buen Vivir*. Leipzig: Konzeptwerk Neue Ökonomie.

Aknin, L.B., E.W. Dunn and M.I. Norton (2012) 'Happiness runs in a circular motion: evidence for a positive feedback loop between prosocial spending and happiness'. *Journal of Happiness Studies* 13: 347–55.

Ambrey, C.L. and P. Daniels (2017) 'Happiness and footprints: assessing the relationship between individual well-being and carbon footprints'. *Environment, Development and Sustainability* 19(3): 895–920.

Ameln, F., R. Gerstmann, J. Kramer (2009) *Psychodrama*. Berlin: Springer.

Andersson, D., J. Nässén, J. Larsson and J. Holmberg (2014) 'Greenhouse gas emissions and subjective well-being: an analysis of Swedish households'. *Ecological Economics* 102: 75–82.

Ariely, D. (2010) *Predictably Irrational: The Hidden Forces That Shape Our Decisions*. Rev. ed. New York, NY: Harper Perennial.

Aristotle (1915) *Magna Moralia*. Oxford: Clarendon Press.

Aristotle (1999) *Nicomachean Ethics*. Translated by W.D. Ross. Kitchener: Batoche Books.

Aszalós, P. (2017) 'Intervenciós célok protagonista játékokban. Szerepelméleti megközelítés'. *Pszichodráma* (autumn): 28–35.

Athenaeus (1854) 'Deipnosophistae Book 12'. Translated by CD Yonge. The Cyreneics Resource. The Lucian of Samosata Project. http://lucianofsamosata.info. Access date: 20 October 2020.

Atkinson, A.B. (2009) 'Economics as a moral science'. *Economica* 76(1): 791–804.

Baumeister, R.F., K.D. Vohs, J.L. Aaker and E.N. Garbinsky (2013) 'Some key differences between a happy life and a meaningful life'. *The Journal of Positive Psychology* 8(6): 505–16.

Bauwens, M., V. Kostakis and A. Pazaitis (2019) *Peer to Peer: The Commons Manifesto*. London: University of Westminster Press.

Bentham, J. (2000) *An Introduction to the Principles of Morals and Legislation*. First edition: 1789. Kitchener: Batoche Books.

Binder, M. and A. Blankenberg (2017) 'Green lifestyles and subjective well-being: more about self-image than actual behavior?' *Journal of Economic Behavior & Organization* 137(May): 304–23.

Biswas-Diener, R., P.A. Linley, H. Dovey, J. Maltby, R. Hurling, J. Wilkinson and N. Lyubchik (2015) 'Pleasure: an initial exploration'. *Journal of Happiness Studies* 16(2): 313–32.

Blatner, A. (2000) *Foundations of Psychodrama: History, Theory, and Practice.* 4th ed. New York, NY: Springer.

Blatner, A. (2019) *Action Explorations: Using Psychocramatic Methods in Non-Therapeutic Settings.* Boston: Parallax Productions.

Blatner, A. and A. Blatner (1997) *The Art of Play: Helping Adults Reclaim Imagination and Spontaneity.* Rev. ed. New York, NY: Brunner/Mazel.

Boehm, J.K. and L.D. Kubzansky (2012) 'The heart's content: the association between positive psychological well-being and cardiovascular health'. *Psychological Bulletin* 138(4): 655–91.

Boulding, K.E. (1969) 'Economics as a moral science'. *The American Economic Review* 59(1): 1–12.

Brand, U. and M. Wissen (2017) *Imperiale Lebensweise: Zur Ausbeutung von Mensch und Natur im globalen Kapitalismus.* Munich: Oekom Verlag.

Brickman, P., D. Coates and R. Janoff-Bulman (1978) 'Lottery winners and accident victims: is happiness relative?' *Journal of Personality and Social Psychology* 36(8): 917–27.

Briggs, J.L. (1998). *Inuit Morality Play: The Emotional Education of a Three-Year-Old.* New Haven; London: Yale University Press.

Brown, K.W. and T. Kasser (2005) 'Are psychological and ecological well-being compatible? The role of values, mindfulness, and lifestyle'. *Social Indicators Research* 74(2): 349–68.

Brown, K.W., T. Kasser, R.M. Ryan and J. Konow (2016) 'Materialism, spending, and affect: an event-sampling study of marketplace behavior and its affective costs'. *Journal of Happiness Studies* 17(6): 2277–92.

Brummett, B.H., S.H. Boyle, I.C. Siegler, R.B. Williams, D.B. Mark and J.C. Barefoot (2005) 'Ratings of positive and depressive emotion as predictors of mortality in coronary patients'. *International Journal of Cardiology* 100: 213–16.

Buber, M. and W.A. Kaufmann (1970) *I and Thou.* New York, NY: Simon & Schuster.

Büchs, M. and M. Koch (2017) *Postgrowth and Wellbeing.* New York, NY: Palgrave Macmillan.

Cantillon, B., T. Goedemé and J. Hills (eds) (2019) *Decent Incomes for All: Improving Policies in Europe.* New York, NY: Oxford University Press.

Cantril, H. (1965) *The Pattern of Human Concerns*. New Brunswick, NJ: Rutgers University Press.

Capra, F. and P.L. Luisi (2014) *The Systems View of Life: A Unifying Vision*. Cambridge: Cambridge University Press.

Carter, J.R. and M.D. Irons (1991) 'Are economists different, and if so, why?' *Journal of Economic Perspectives* 5(2): 171–7.

Christakis, N. and James Fowler (2009) *Connected: The Amazing Power of Social Networks and How They Shape Our Lives*. New York, NY: Little, Brown and Company.

Churchill, Winston (1939) 'Review of "The End of Economic Man"'. *Times Literary Supplement*, 27 May, 306.

Cipriani, G.P., D. Lubian and A. Zago (2009) 'Natural born economists?' *Journal of Economic Psychology* 30(3): 455–68.

Clark, A.E., S. Fleche and P.R.G. Layard (2018) *The Origins of Happiness: The Science of Well-Being over the Life Course*. Princeton, NJ: Princeton University Press.

Clark, A.E., S. Fleche, R. Layard, N. Powdthavee and G. Ward (2017) 'The key determinants of happiness and misery', pp 122–43 in *World Happiness Report 2017*, edited by J.F. Helliwell, R. Layard and J. Sachs. New York, NY: Sustainable Development Solutions Network.

Clayton, G.M. (1992) *Enhancing Life and Relationships. A Role Training Manual*. Victoria, Australia: ICA Press.

Clayton, G.M. (1994) 'Role theory and its application in clinical practice', pp 121–44 in *Psychodrama since Moreno: Innovations in Theory and Practice*, edited by P. Holmes, M. Karp and M. Watson. London; New York, NY: Brunner-Routledge.

Clayton, G.M. and P.D. Carter (2004) *The Living Spirit of the Psychodramatic Method*. Auckland: Resource Books.

Corning, P.A. (2005) *Holistic Darwinism: Synergy, Cybernetics, and the Bioeconomics of Evolution*. Chicago: University of Chicago Press.

Cruz, A., C.M.D. Sales, P. Alves and G. Moita (2018) 'The core techniques of Morenian psychodrama: a systematic review of literature'. *Frontiers in Psychology* 9: 1263.

van Dalen, Hendrik P. (2019) 'Values of economists matter in the art and science of economics'. *Kyklos* 72(3): 472–99.

Danner, D.D., D.A. Snowdon and W.V. Friesen (2001) 'Positive emotions in early life and longevity: findings from the nun study'. *Journal of Personality and Social Psychology* 80(5): 804–13.

Davidson, R.J. (1992) 'Anterior cerebral asymmetry and the nature of emotion'. *Brain and Cognition* 20(1): 125–51.

Davidson, R.J. and S. Begley (2013) *The Emotional Life of Your Brain: How Its Unique Patterns Affect the Way You Think, Feel, and Live – and How You Can Change Them*. New York, NY: Plume.

Dawson, J. (2012) *From Islands to Networks: An Exploration of the History and a Glimpse into the Future of the Ecovillage Movement*. Totnes: Berghahn Books.

Dawson, J. (2014) 'How do we redesign a new economic theory framed by ecological systems?' *The Guardian*. 7 February.

De Neve, J.E., E. Diener, L. Tay and C. Xuereb (2013) 'The objective benefits of subjective well-being', pp 54–79 in *World Happiness Report 2013* Vol. 2, edited by J.F. Helliwell, R. Layard and J. Sachs. New York, NY: UN Sustainable Network Development Solutions Network.

Deci, E.L. and R.M. Ryan (2000) 'The "what" and "why" of goal pursuits: human needs and the self-determination of behavior'. *Psychological Inquiry* 11: 227–68.

Delle Fave, A., I. Brdar, T. Freire, D. Vella-Brodrick and M.P. Wissing (2012) 'The eudaimonic and hedonic components of happiness: qualitative and quantitative findings'. *Social Indicators Research* 100(2): 185–207.

Di Tella, R. and R.J. MacCulloch (2008) 'Gross national happiness as an answer to the Easterlin paradox?' *Journal of Development Economics* 86(1): 22–42.

Diener, E. and M.Y. Chan (2011) 'Happy people live longer: subjective well-being contributes to health and longevity'. *Applied Psychology: Health and Well-Being* 3(1): 1–43.

Diener, E. and R.A. Emmons (1985) 'The independence of positive and negative affect'. *Journal of Personality and Social Psychology* 47: 1105–17.

Diener, E. and A. Iran-Nejad (1986) 'The relationship in experience between various types of affect'. *Journal of Personality and Social Psychology* 50: 1031–38.

Diener, E., S. Oishi and L. Tay (2018) 'Advances in subjective well-being research'. *Nature Human Behaviour* 2(4): 253–60.

Diener, E., C.R. Colvin, W.G. Pavot and A. Allman (1991) 'The psychic costs of intense positive affect'. *Journal of Personality and Social Psychology* 61(3): 492–503.

Diener, E., D. Wirtz, W. Tov, C. Kim-Prieto, D. Choi, S. Oishi and R. Biswas-Diener (2010) 'New well-being measures: short scales to assess flourishing and positive and negative feelings'. *Social Indicators Research* 97(2): 143–56.

Diogenes Laertius (1972) Translated by R.D. Hicks. (First published 1925). *Lives of Eminent Philosophers: Book II*. Cambridge, MA: Harvard University Press.

Dittmar, H., R. Bond, M. Hurst and T. Kasser (2014) 'The relationship between materialism and personal well-being: a meta-analysis'. *Journal of Personality and Social Psychology* 107(5): 879–924.

Dolan, P. (2020) *Happy Ever After: A Radical New Approach to Living Well*. London: Penguin Books.

Dostoevsky, F. (1912) *The Brothers Karamazov*. Translated by Constance Garnett. New York, NY: The Lowell Press.

Doyal, L. and I. Gough (1991) *A Theory of Human Need*. London: Macmillan Education UK.

Drucker, P.F. (1939) *The End of Economic Man: The Origins of Totalitarianism*. New York, NY: The J. Day Company.

Easterlin, R.A. (1974) 'Does economic growth improve the human lot? Some empirical evidence', pp 89–124 in *Nations and Households in Economic Growth. Essays in Honor of Moses Abramovitz*, edited by P.A.D. and M.W. Reder. New York, NY: Academic Press.

Easterlin, R.A. (1995) 'Will raising the incomes of all increase the happiness of all?' *Journal of Economic Behavior and Organization* 27: 35–47.

Eisenstein, C. (2011) *Sacred Economics: Money, Gift, and Society in the Age of Transition*. Berkeley, CA: North Atlantic Books.

Elster, J. (1983) *Sour Grapes: Studies in the Subversion of Rationality*. Cambridge: Cambridge University Press.

Epicurus (1994) *The Epicurus Reader: Selected Writings and Testimonia*. Translated by Brad Inwood and Lloyd P. Gerson. Indianapolis, IND: Hackett.

European Commission (2009) 'Beyond GDP – Measuring Progress in a Changing World. Communication from the Commission to the Council and the European Parliament – COM(2009) 433 Final'.

European Social Survey (2020) *ESS-9 2018 Documentation Report*. 2.0. Bergen: European Social Survey Data Archive, NSD – Norwegian Centre for Research Data for ESS ERIC.

FAO (2016) *How Much Food Is Lost or Wasted?* Food and Agriculture Organization of the United Nations. http://www.fao.org/3/a-C0088e.pdf. Access date: 22 October 2020.

Felber, C. (2012) *Change Everything: Creating an Economy for the Common Good*. London: Zed Books Ltd.

Felber, C. (2019) *This Is Not Economy: Aufruf zur Revolution der Wirtschaftswissenschaft*. Vienna: Zsolnay Verlag.

Feniger-Schaal, R. and H. Orkibi (2020) 'Integrative systematic review of drama therapy intervention research'. *Psychology of Aesthetics, Creativity, and the Arts* 14(1): 68–80. doi: 10.1037/aca0000257.

Ferber, M.A. and J.A. Nelson (eds) (1993) *Beyond Economic Man: Feminist Theory and Economics.* Chicago, ILL: University of Chicago Press.

Ferrer-i-Carbonell, A. and P. Frijters (2004) 'How important is methodology for the estimates of the determinants of happiness?' *The Economic Journal* 114(July): 641–59.

Frank, R.H. (1985) *Choosing the Right Pond: Human Behavior and the Quest for Status.* Oxford: Oxford University Press.

Frank, R.H. (1997) 'The frame of reference as a public good'. *The Economic Journal* 107(November): 1832–47.

Frank, R.H. (1999) *Luxury Fever: Why Money Fails to Satisfy in an Era of Excess.* New York, NY: Free Press.

Frank, R.H., T. Gilovich and D.T. Regan (1993) 'Does studying economics inhibit cooperation?' *The Journal of Economic Perspectives* 7(2): 159–71.

Frankl, V.E. (2006) *Man's Search for Meaning.* Mini book ed. Boston, MA: Beacon Press.

Fredrickson, B.L., K.M. Grewen, K.A. Coffey, S.B. Algoe, A.M. Firestine, J.M.G. Arevalo, J. Ma and S.W. Cole (2013) 'A functional genomic perspective on human well-being'. *Proceedings of the National Academy of Sciences* 110(33): 13684–89.

Frey, B.S. and S. Meier (2003) 'Are political economists selfish and indoctrinated? Evidence from a natural experiment'. *Economic Inquiry* 41(3): 448–62.

Frey, B.S. and A. Stutzer (2002) 'What can economists learn from happiness research?' *Journal of Economic Literature* 40(2): 402–35.

Fromm, E. (1941) *Escape from Freedom.* New York, NY: Farrar & Rinehart.

Fromm, E. (1997) *To Have or To Be?* London: Abacus.

Gershoni, J. (ed) (2003) *Psychodrama in the 21st Century: Clinical and Educational Applications.* New York, NY: Springer.

Goldberg, M.C. (2009) 'Positive psychodrama and the early works of J.L. Moreno'. *Group* 33(4): 359–72.

Goudie, R.J.B., S. Mukherjee, J.E. de Neve, A.J. Oswald and S. Wu (2014) 'Happiness as a driver of risk-avoiding behaviour: theory and an empirical study of seatbelt wearing and automobile accidents'. *Economica* 81: 674–97.

Grant, A.M. and B. Schwartz (2011) 'Too much of a good thing: the challenge and opportunity of the inverted U'. *Perspectives on Psychological Science* 6(1): 61–76.

Grant, N., J. Wardle and A. Steptoe (2009) 'The relationship between life satisfaction and health behavior: a cross-cultural analysis of young adults'. *International Journal of Behavioral Medicine* 16: 259–68.

Grinde, B. (2012) *The Biology of Happiness*. Dordrecht; New York, NY: Springer.

Grinde, B., R.B. Nes, I.F. MacDonald and D.S. Wilson (2018) 'Quality of life in intentional communities'. *Social Indicators Research* 137(2): 625–40.

Guillen-Royo, M. (2016) *Sustainability and Wellbeing: Human Scale Development in Practice*. Abingdon, Oxon; New York, NY: Routledge, Taylor & Francis Group.

Guven, C. (2012) 'Reversing the question: does happiness affect consumption and savings behavior?' *Journal of Economic Psychology* 33(4): 701–17.

Harsanyi, J.C. (1997) 'Utilities, preferences, and substantive goods'. *Social Choice and Welfare* 14(1): 129–45.

Hawken, P. (ed) (2017) *Drawdown: The Most Comprehensive Plan Ever Proposed to Reverse Global Warming*. New York, NY: Penguin Books.

Heede, R. (2019) *Carbon Majors: Updating Activity Data, Adding Entities, and Calculating Emissions: A Training Manual*. Snowmass, CO: Climate Accountability Institute.

Helliwell, J.F. (2003) 'How's life? Combining individual and national variables to explain subjective well-being'. *Economic Modelling* 20: 331–60.

Helliwell, J.F., R. Layard and J. Sachs (2013) *World Happiness Report 2013*. New York, NY: UN Sustainable Network Development Solutions Network.

Hershfield, H.E, S. Scheibe, T.L. Sims and L.L. Carstensen (2013) 'When feeling bad can be good: mixed emotions benefit physical health across adulthood'. *Social Psychological and Personality Science* 4(1): 54–61.

Hills, J., J. Le Grand and D. Piachaud (2002) *Understanding Social Exclusion*. Oxford: Oxford University Press.

Hoebel, B.G., P. Rada, G.P. Mark and E. Pothos (1999) 'Neural systems for reinforcement and inhibition of behavior: relevance to eating, addiction, and depression', pp 558–72 in *Well-Being: The Foundations of Hedonic Psychology*, edited by D. Kahneman, E. Diener and N. Schwartz. New York, NY: Russell Sage Foundation.

Hogeveen, J., M. Inzlicht and S.S. Obhi (2014) 'Power changes how the brain responds to others'. *Journal of Experimental Psychology* 143(2): 755–62.

Hollis, M. and E.J. Nell (2006) *Rational Economic Man: A Philosophical Critique of Neo-Classical Economics*. London: Cambridge University Press.

Holmes, P., M. Karp and M. Watson (2005) *Psychodrama Since Moreno: Innovations in Theory and Practice*. London: Routledge.

Hurst, M., H. Dittmar, R. Bond and T. Kasser (2013) 'The relationship between materialistic values and environmental attitudes and behaviors: a meta-analysis'. *Journal of Environmental Psychology* 36: 257–69.

Huta, V. and R.M. Ryan (2010) 'Pursuing pleasure or virtue: the differential and overlapping well-being benefits of hedonic and eudaimonic motives'. *Journal of Happiness Studies* 11(6): 735–62.

Huxley, A. (1932) *Brave New World*. London: Chatto & Windus.

Ifcher, J. and H. Zarghamee (2011) 'Happiness and time preference: the effect of positive affect in a random-assignment experiment'. *American Economic Review* 101(7): 3109–29.

Jackson, T. (2009) *Prosperity without Growth: Foundations for the Economy of Tomorrow*. 1st ed. London; New York, NY: Routledge.

Jung, C.G. (1989) *Memories, Dreams, Reflections*. Rev. ed. Edited by A. Jaffe. New York, NY: Vintage Books.

Kabat-Zinn, J. (1990) *Full Catastrophe Living: Using the Wisdom of Your Body and Mind to Face Stress, Pain, and Illness*. New York, NY: Random House.

Kabat-Zinn, J. (2003) 'Mindfulness-based interventions in context: past, present, and future'. *Clinical Psychology: Science and Practice* 10(2): 144–56.

Kagan, C., M. Burton, P. Duckett, R. Lawthom and A. Siddiquee (2020) *Critical Community Psychology: Critical Action and Social Change*. 1st ed. Abingdon: Routledge.

Kahneman, D. and A.B. Krueger (2006) 'Developments in the measurement of subjective well-being'. *The Journal of Economic Perspectives* 20(1): 3–24.

Kahneman, D. and A. Tversky (1979) 'Prospect theory: an analysis of decision under risk'. *Econometrica* 47(2): 263–92.

Kahneman, D., J.L. Knetsch and R.H. Thaler (1991) 'Anomalies – the endowment effect, loss aversion, and status quo bias'. *Journal of Economic Perspectives* 5(1): 193–206.

Karp, M. (1998) 'An introduction to psychodrama', pp 3–13 in *The Handbook of Psychodrama*, edited by M. Karp, P. Holmes and K.B. Tauvon. London; New York, NY: Routledge.

Kartha, S., E. Kemp-Benedict, E. Ghosh, A. Nazareth and T. Gore (2020) *The Carbon Inequality Era: An Assessment of the Global Distribution of Consumption Emissions among Individuals from 1990 to 2015 and Beyond*. Oxford: Oxfam and Stockholm Environment Institute.

Kasser, T. (2002) *The High Price of Materialism*. Cambridge, MA: MIT Press.

Kasser, T. (2017) 'Living both well and sustainably: a review of the literature, with some reflections on future research, interventions and policy'. *Philosophical Transactions of the Royal Society A: Mathematical, Physical and Engineering Sciences* 375(2095): 20160369.

Kasser, T. (2018) 'Materialism and living well', in *Handbook of Well-Being*, edited by E. Diener, S. Oishi and L. Tay. Salt Lake City, UT: DEF Publishers. DOI:nobascholar.com.

Kasser, T., R. Koestner and N. Lekes (2002) 'Early family experiences and adult values: a 26-year prospective longitudinal study'. *Personality and Social Psychology Bulletin* 28(6): 826–35.

Kellermann, P.F. (1992) *Focus on Psychodrama: The Therapeutic Aspects of Psychodrama*. London; Philadelphia, PA: Jessica Kingsley Publishers.

Kellermann, P.F. (1998) 'Sociodrama'. *Group Analysis* 31(2): 179–95.

Kellermann, P.F. (2007) *Sociodrama and Collective Trauma*. London; Philadelphia: Jessica Kingsley Publishers.

Keynes, J. Maynard. 1963. *Economic Possibilities for Our Grandchildren: Essays in Persuasion*. New York, NY: W.W. Norton & Co.

Kipper, D.A. and T.D. Ritchie (2003) 'The effectiveness of psychodramatic techniques: a meta-analysis'. *Group Dynamics: Theory, Research, and Practice* 7(1): 13–25.

Kirk, K. (2016) 'Grasping the tail of a comet: researching and writing about psychodrama in the 21st century'. *Zeitschrift für Psychodrama und Soziometrie* 15(S1): 323–26.

Krueger, A.B. and D.A. Schkade (2008) 'The reliability of subjective well-being measures'. *Journal of Public Economics* 92(8–9): 1833–45.

Krüger, R.T. (2020) *Störungsspezifische Psychodramatherapie: Theorie und Praxis*. Göttingen: Vandenhoeck & Ruprecht.

Kubiszewski, I., R. Costanza, C. Franco, P. Lawn, J.T., T. Jackson and C. Aylmer (2013) 'Beyond GDP: measuring and achieving Global Genuine Progress'. *Ecological Economics* 93: 57–68.

Kuss, D. and M. Griffiths (2017) 'Social networking sites and addiction: ten lessons learned'. *International Journal of Environmental Research and Public Health* 14(3): 311.

Layard, R. (2005) *Happiness: Lessons from a New Science*. London: Penguin Books.

Layard, R. (2013) 'Mental health: the new frontier for the welfare state'. *IZA Journal of Labor Policy* 2(2): 2–16.

Leibenstein, H. (1976) *Beyond Economic Man: A New Foundation for Microeconomics*. Cambridge, MA: Harvard University Press.

Lelkes, O. (2006a) 'Knowing what is good for you. Empirical analysis of personal preferences and the "objective good"'. *Journal of Socio-Economics* 35(2: Special Issue: The Socio-Economics of Happiness): 285–307.

Lelkes, O. (2006b) 'Tasting freedom: happiness, religion and economic transition'. *Journal of Economic Behavior and Organization* 59(2): 173–94.

Lelkes, O. (2013) 'Minimising misery: a new strategy for public policies instead of minimising happiness?' *Social Indicators Research* 114(1): 121–37.

Lelkes, O. (2017) 'From radical hedonism to purposeful life'. Presented at the 15th Conference of the International Society for Quality-of-life Studies (ISQOLS), 27 September, Innsbruck.

Lelkes, O. (2018) 'Eudaimonie statt Hedonismus: das Glück als aktive und kreative Lebensaufgabe: Psychodrama als Bühne des Glücks'. *Zeitschrift für Psychodrama und Soziometrie* 17(1): 101–7.

Lessenich, S. (2016) *Neben uns die Sintflut: die Externalisierungsgesellschaft und ihr Preis*. Munich: Hanser Berlin, im Carl Hanser Verlag.

Leutz, G.A. (1974) *Psychodrama: Theorie und Praxis*. Berlin; Heidelberg; New York, NY: Springer.

Liegey, V. and A. Nelson (2020) *Exploring Degrowth: A Critical Guide*. London: Pluto Press.

Linebaugh, P. (2009) *The Magna Carta Manifesto: Liberties and Commons for All*. Berkeley, CA: University of California Press.

Lyubomirsky, S., L. King and E. Diener (2005) 'The benefits of frequent positive affect: does happiness lead to success?' *Psychological Bulletin* 131(6): 803–55.

Lyubomirsky, S., K.M. Sheldon and D. Schkade (2005) 'Pursuing happiness: the architecture of sustainable change'. *Review of General Psychology* 9(2): 111–31.

Martin, Leslie R., H.S. Friedman, J.S. Tucker, C. Tomlinson-Keasey, M.H. Criqui and J.E. Schwartz (2002) 'A life course perspective on childhood cheerfulness and its relation to mortality risk'. *Personality and Social Psychology Bulletin* 28(9): 1155–65.

Marwell, G. and R.E. Ames (1981) 'Economists free ride, does anyone else?' *Journal of Public Economics* 15(3): 295–310.

Max-Neef, M. (1991) *Human-Scale Development: Conception, Application and Further Reflections*. London: Apex.

Mayrhofer, D. (2020) 'Achtsamkeitsbasierte Interventionen und Selbstmitgefühl im Psychodrama: Wege der Integration'. *Zeitschrift für Psychodrama und Soziometrie* 19(1): 109–20.

Mazzucato, M. (2018) *The Value of Everything: Making and Taking in the Global Economy*. 1st US ed. New York, NY: Perseus Books.

Merleau-Ponty, M. (2004) *The World of Perception*. (First published in French as *Causeries* in 1948). London; New York, NY: Routledge.

Michaelson, J., S. Abdallah, N. Steuer, S. Thompson, N. Marks, J. Aked, C. Cordon and R. Potts (2009) *National Accounts of Well-Being: Bringing Real Wealth onto the Balance Sheet*. London: New Economics Foundation.

Mikulincer, M., O. Gillath, Y. Sapir-Lavid, E. Yaakobi, K. Arias, L. Tal-Aloni and G. Bor (2003) 'Attachment theory and concern for others' welfare: evidence that activation of the sense of secure base promotes endorsement of self-transcendence values'. *Basic and Applied Social Psychology* 25(4): 299–312.

Moreno, Z.T., L.D. Blomkvist and T. Rützel (2000) *Psychodrama, Surplus Reality and the Art of Healing*. London; Philadelphia, PA: Routledge.

Myrdal, G. (1972) 'How scientific are the social sciences?' *Journal of Social Issues* 28(4): 151–70.

Natale, A., S. Di Martino, F. Procentese and C. Arcidiacono (2016) 'De-growth and critical community psychology: contributions towards individual and social well-being'. *Futures* 78–79: 47–56.

Ng, Y. (1997) 'A case for happiness, cardinalism, and interpersonal comparability'. *The Economic Journal* 107(November): 1848–58.

Nussbaum, M.C. (2000) *Women and Human Development: The Capabilities Approach*. 1st ed. Cambridge: Cambridge University Press.

Nussbaum, M.C. (2001) 'Adaptive preferences and women's options'. *Economics and Philosophy* 17: 67–88.

Nussbaum, M.C. and A.K. Sen (1993) *The Quality of Life*. Oxford: Oxford University Press.

O'Brien, C. (2016) *Education for Sustainable Happiness and Well-Being*. New York, NY: Routledge.

Organisation for Economic Co-operation and Development (OECD) (2013) *OECD Guidelines on Measuring Subjective Well-Being*. Paris: OECD Publishing.

OECD (2017) *Obesity Update 2017*. Paris: OECD.

Oishi, S. and S. Kesebir (2015) 'Income inequality explains why economic growth does not always translate to an increase in happiness'. *Psychological Science* 26(10): 1630–38.

Oishi, S., E. Diener and R.E. Lucas (2007) 'The optimum level of well-being: can people be too happy?' *Perspectives on Psychological Science* 2(4): 346–60.

O'Keefe, T. (2002) 'The Cyrenaics on pleasure, happiness, and future-concern'. *Phronesis* 47(4): 395–416.

O'Keefe, T. (2010) *Epicureanism*. Berkeley, CA: University of California Press.

O'Neill, D.W., A.L. Fanning, W.F. Lamb and J.K. Steinberger (2018) 'A good life for all within planetary boundaries'. *Nature Sustainability* 1(2): 88–95.

Orkibi, H. (2019) 'Positive psychodrama: a framework for practice and research'. *The Arts in Psychotherapy* 66: 101603.

Orkibi, H. and R. Feniger-Schaal (2019) 'Integrative systematic review of psychodrama psychotherapy research: trends and methodological implications'. *PLOS ONE* 14(2):e0212575.

Ostir, G.V., K.S. Markides, M.K. Peek and J.S. Goodwin (2001) 'The association between emotional well-being and the incidence of stroke in older adults'. *Psychosomatic Medicine* 63(2): 210–15.

Ostrom, E. (1990) *Governing the Commons: The Evolution of Institutions for Collective Action*. Cambridge: Cambridge University Press.

Oswald, A.J. and N. Stern (2019) *Why Does the Economics of Climate Change Matter so Much, and Why Has the Engagement of Economists Been so Weak?* Royal Economic Society Newsletter, October.

Otway, L.J. and K.B. Carnelley (2013) 'Exploring the associations between adult attachment security and self-actualization and self-transcendence'. *Self and Identity* 12(2): 217–30.

Persky, J. (1995) 'Retrospectives: the ethology of homo economicus'. *Journal of Economic Perspectives* 9(2): 221–31.

Piketty, T., E. Saez and G. Zucman (2018) 'Distributional national accounts: methods and estimates for the United States'. *The Quarterly Journal of Economics* 133(2): 553–609.

Polanyi, K. (2001) *The Great Transformation: The Political and Economic Origins of Our Time*. 2nd ed. Boston, MA: Beacon Press.

Postlethwaite, J. (2019) 'From rational to relational: reflections on embracing a psychodramatic approach in academic mentoring'. *AANZPA Journal* 28(December): 47–60.

Pressman, S.D. and S. Cohen (2005) 'Does positive affect influence health?' *Psychological Bulletin* 131(6): 925–71.

Rauschmayer, F., I. Omann and J. Frühmann (eds) (2011) *Sustainable Development: Capabilities, Needs, and Well-Being*. London; New York, NY: Routledge.

Rawls, J. (1971) *A Theory of Justice*. Cambridge, MA: Harvard University Press.

Raworth, K. (2017) *Doughnut Economics: Seven Ways to Think like a 21st-Century Economist*. London: Random House Business Books.

Rethinking Economics, and The New Weather Institute (2017) *33 Theses for an Economics Reformation*. London. https://www.newweather.org/wp-content/uploads/2017/12/33-Theses-for-an-Economics-Reformation.pdf. Access date: 22 October 2020.

Riepl, R. (2016) 'Gruppen in Bewegung setzen. Das Wechselspiel zwischen Managementthema und Teamdynamik in der organisationsinternen Aufstellungsarbeit', pp 197–215 in *Organisationsaufstellungen: Grundlagen, Settings, Anwendungsfelder*, edited by G. Weber and C. Rosselet. Heidelberg: Carl-Auer-Systeme Verlag.

Robb, M.B. (2019) *The New Normal: Parents, Teens, Screens, and Sleep in the United States*. San Francisco, CA: Common Sense Media.

Robbins, L. (1932) *An Essay on the Nature and Significance of Economic Science*. London: Macmillan.

Rubinstein, A. (2006) 'A sceptic's comment on the study of economics'. *The Economic Journal* 116(510): C1–9.

Ryan, R.M. and E.L. Deci (2019) 'Brick by brick: the origins, development, and future of self-determination theory', pp 111–56 in *Advances in Motivation Science*, edited by A.J. Elliot. Vol. 6. Cambridge, MA: Elsevier.

Ryan, R.M., V. Huta and E.L. Deci (2008) 'Living well: a self-determination theory perspective on eudaimonia'. *Journal of Happiness Studies* 9(1): 139–70.

Ryff, C.D. and B.H. Singer (2008) 'Know thyself and become what you are: a eudaimonic approach to psychological well-being'. *Journal of Happiness Studies* 9(1): 13–39.

Sahlins, M. (2017) *Stone Age Economics*. London; New York, NY: Routledge Classics.

Sandvik, E., E. Diener and L. Seidlitz (1993) 'Subjective well-being – the convergence and stability of self-report and non-self-report measures'. *Journal of Personality* 61(3): 317–42.

Sarracino, F. (2010) 'Social capital and subjective well-being trends: comparing 11 Western European countries'. *Journal of Socio-Economics* 39(4): 482–517.

Scharmer, C.O. (2009) *Theory U: Leading from the Future as It Emerges*. San Francisco, CA: Berrett-Koehler.

Schneider, K. (2011) 'Toward a humanistic positive psychology: why can't we just get along?' *Existential Analysis* 22(1), 32–38.

Schumacher, E.F. (1989) *Small Is Beautiful: Economics as If People Mattered*. New York, NY: HarperPerennial.

Schwartz, B., A. Ward, J. Monterosso, S. Lyubomirsky, K. White and D.R. Lehman (2002) 'Maximizing versus satisficing: happiness is a matter of choice'. *Journal of Personality and Social Psychology* 83(5): 1178–97.

Schwartz, S.H. (2012) 'An overview of the Schwartz theory of basic values'. *Online Readings in Psychology and Culture* 2(1). https://doi.org/10.9707/2307-0919.1116.

Schwartz, S.H. and A. Bardi (2001) 'Value hierarchies across cultures: taking a similarities perspective'. *Journal of Cross-Cultural Psychology* 32(3): 268–90.

Schwartz, S.H., L. Sigav and K. Boehnke (2000) 'Worries and values'. *Journal of Personality* 68(2): 309–46.

Schwartz, S.H., J. Cieciuch, M. Vecchione, E. Davidov, R. Fischer, C. Beierlein, A. Ramos, M. Verkasalo, J. Lönnqvist, K. Demirutku, O. Dirilen-Gumus and M. Konty (2012) 'Refining the theory of basic individual values'. *Journal of Personality and Social Psychology* 103(4): 663–88.

Sen, A.K. (1985) *Commodities and Capabilities*. Amsterdam: North-Holland.

Sen, A.K. (1992) *Inequality Reexamined*. Oxford: Clarendon Press.

Shambhala (1991) *The Shambhala Dictionary of Buddhism and Zen*. 1st ed. Boston, MA; New York, NY: Shambhala.

Sheldon, K.M. and T. Kasser (2008) 'Psychological threat and extrinsic goal striving'. *Motivation and Emotion* 32(1): 37–45.

Simon, A. (2007) 'Barátság és önmegértés Arisztotelésznél', pp 178–203 in *Töredékes hagyomány: Steiger Kornélnak*, edited by G. Betegh, I. Bodnár, P. Lautner and G. Geréby. Budapest: Akadémiai K.

Simon, H.A. (1956) 'Rational choice and the structure of the environment.' *Psychological Review* 63(2): 129–38.

Stadler, C., M. Wieser and K. Kirk (eds) (2016) *Psychodrama. Empirical Research and Science 2*. Wiesbaden: Springer Fachmedien Wiesbaden.

Steger, M.F., T.B. Kashdan and S. Oishi (2008) 'Being good by doing good: daily eudaimonic activity and well-being'. *Journal of Research in Personality* 42(1): 22–42.

Sterling, S., J. Dawson and P. Warwick (2018) 'Transforming sustainability education at the creative edge of the mainstream: a case study of Schumacher College'. *Journal of Transformative Education* 16(4): 323–43.

Stigler, G.J. and G.S. Becker (1977) 'De gustibus non est disputandum'. *American Economic Review* 67(2): 76–90.

Stiglitz, J.E., J. Fitoussi and M. Durand (eds) (2019) *For Good Measure: An Agenda for Moving beyond GDP*. New York, NY: The New Press.

Stiglitz, J.E., A. Sen and J. Fitoussi (2010) *Mismeasuring Our Lives: Why GDP Doesn't Add Up*. New York, NY: New Press.

Strassburg, B.B.N., A. Iribarrem, H.L. Beyer, C.L. Cordeiro, R. Crouzeilles, C.C. Jakovac, A.B. Junqueira, E. Lacerda, A.E. Latawiec, A. Balmford, T.M. Brooks, S.H.M. Butchart, R.L. Chazdon, K. Erb, P. Brancalion, G. Buchanan, D. Cooper, S. Díaz, P.F. Donald, V. Kapos, D. Leclère, L. Miles, M. Obersteiner, C. Plutzar, C.A. de M. Scaramuzza, F.R. Scarano and P. Visconti (2020) 'Global priority areas for ecosystem restoration'. *Nature* 586: 724–48.

Stutzer, A. (2004) 'The role of income aspirations in individual happiness'. *Journal of Economic Behavior and Organization* 54(1): 89–109.

Sugden, R. (1993) 'Welfare, resources, and capabilities – a review of Inequality Reexamined by Amartya Sen'. *Journal of Economic Literature* 31(4): 1947.

Testoni, I., M. Wieser, A. Armenti, L. Ronconi, M.S. Guglielmin, P. Cottone and A. Zamperini (2016) 'Spontaneity as predictive factor for well-being', pp 11–23 in *Psychodrama: Empirical Research and Science*, edited by C. Stadler, M. Wieser and K. Kirk. Wiesbaden: Springer.

Thaler, R.H. (2016) *Misbehaving: The Making of Behavioural Economics*. New York, NY; London: W.W. Norton & Company.

Titmuss, R.M. (1970) *The Gift Relationship: From Human Blood to Social Policy*. London: Allen & Unwin.

United Nations (2018) *The Lazy Person's Guide to Saving the World*. https://www.un.org/sustainabledevelopment/takeaction/. Access date: 22 October 2020.

Veblen, T. (1899) *The Theory of the Leisure Class: An Economic Study of Institutions*. New York, NY; London: Macmillan Co.; Macmillan.

Veenhoven, R. (2008) 'Healthy happiness: effects of happiness on physical health and the consequences for preventive health care'. *Journal of Happiness Studies* 9(3): 449–69.

We are social and Hootsuite (2020) *Digital 2020 Global Overview Report*. https://wearesocial.com/digital-2020. Access date: 22 October 2020.

Welsch, H. and J. Kühling (2011) 'Are pro-environmental consumption choices utility-maximizing? Evidence from subjective well-being data'. *Ecological Economics* 72: 75–87.

Welsch, H. and J. Kühling (2018) 'How green self image is related to subjective well-being: pro-environmental values as a social norm'. *Ecological Economics* 149: 105–19.

Wieser, M. (2007) 'Studies on treatment effects of psychodrama therapy', pp 271–92 in *Psychodrama: Advances in theory and practice*, edited by C. Baim, J. Burmeiste and M. Maciel. London: Routledge.

World Commission on Environment and Development (ed) (1987) *Our Common Future*. Oxford; New York, NY: Oxford University Press.

Yalom, I.D. (1980) *Existential Psychotherapy*. New York, NY: Basic Books.

Yalom, I.D. (1985) *The Theory and Practice of Group Psychotherapy*. 3rd ed. New York, NY: Basic Books.

Zánkay, A. (2015) 'A szerepelmélet alkalmazása a dramatikus munkában'. *Pszichodráma* (Winter): 6–19.

Index